SPIRITUALITY FOR MISSION

SPIRITUALITY FOR MISSION

Historical, Theological, and Cultural Factors for a Present-Day Missionary Spirituality

MICHAEL COLLINS REILLY, S.J.

Maryknoll, New York 10545
1978

The Catholic Foreign Mission Society of America (Maryknoll) recruits and trains people for overseas missionary service. Through Orbis Books Maryknoll aims to foster the international dialogue which is essential to mission. The books published, however, reflect the opinions of their authors and are not meant to represent the official position of the Society.

Library of Congress Cataloging in Publication Data

Reilly, Michael Collins.
Spirituality for mission.

Reprint of the ed. published by the Loyola School of Theology, Ateneo de Manila University, Manila, Philippines, which was issued as no. 12 of the Logos series, and also in series: Ateneo University publications.
Bibliography: p.
Includes indexes.
1. Missions. 2. Spirituality. I. Title. II. Series: Logos (Manila) ; no. 12.
BV2061.R424 1978 266'.001 78-878
ISBN 0-88344-464-X

Imprimi potest: Benigno A. Mayo, S.J. Provincial, Philippine Province.
Nihil obstat: Philip J. Calderone, S.J., *Censor deputatus.*
Imprimatur: Jaime Cardinal L. Sin, D.D., Archbishop of Manila, September 15, 1975.

This edition was typeset in the Philippines and printed in the United States of America

Orbis Books, Maryknoll, New York 10545

ACKNOWLEDGEMENTS

Were it not for the following, this book would not have been possible: my brothers in the Society of Jesus in both North America and the Far East whose example, encouragement, and questioning rest at the roots of any contemporary missionary spirituality; my director at Union Theological Seminary, New York City, Dr. Johannes C. Hoekendijk, whose example was also of no small inspiration to me and to whom I owe much in the way of insight from non-Catholic Christianity; my aunt, Margaret L. Collins, who, without ever knowing it, helped much to make this book an actuality.

CONTENTS

I

INTRODUCTION

Kenneth Scott Latourette, the great historian of Christian missions, has compared the expansion of Christianity to the ebb and flow of the tides. Like the tides, Christianity has moved forward in waves; and, like the tides, each major wave has been followed by a recession, although the recessions have never brought the movement back to its point of departure. The Christian religion advanced initially after the death of Christ until the year 500; it surged ahead again after the dark ages between 950 and 1350; the discovery of the New World was the occasion for the next major advance between 1500 and 1750; and, finally, Christianity achieved its greatest advance during the "great century" of the missions, 1815 to 1914. The Christian faith declined during the following periods: 500 to 950; 1350 to 1500; and 1750 to 1815. Writing in 1940, Latourette was optimistic about the future prospects of Christianity, although he was unsure whether the period following 1914 would prove to be a period of recession or advance.[1]

From our viewpoint in the 1970's, we can see many factors which might give us optimism about the condition of Christianity today. It has become a world-wide and less a Western religion; the ecumenical movement has made advances; Roman Catholicism is experiencing a renewal; and, another of Latourette's favorite themes, the personality of Jesus Christ continues to capture the imagination of men. In recent years, two of the more popular plays and films have centered on the personality of Jesus, *Jesus Christ Superstar* and *Godspell*. And yet we can wonder, as Latourette wondered in 1940, whether the closing decades of this century will represent an advance or a recession in the ebb and flow of Christianity. The world itself has changed politically, economically, and socially from the world of the nineteenth century, the "great century" of the Christian missions. But more important than this

[1] See Kenneth Scott Latourette, *The Unquenchable Light* (New York: Harper and Brothers, 1941).

is the fact that the very idea and understanding of missions has changed radically from what it was during the last century. This new understanding has caused considerable doubt and self-examination in the churches concerning the missions and even the mission of the Church. Therefore, although the present period of Church history is not a period of recession since the Church is making advances in many areas, for example in the countries of Africa, it is a period of reflection on the part of the churches. Past successes are being evaluated and future strategies are being tentatively plotted.

In dealing with religion and with Christianity it is unwise to play a numbers game. Yet a few representative statistics can be helpful in understanding the present situation. With the Roman Catholic Church as an example, it can be shown that missionary work in the traditional sense seems to be entering a period of slowed growth.

First of all, although the number of Roman Catholics in the world is increasing, it is not increasing proportionately with the population. Thus, a study made in the nineteen-fifties showed that in 1954 the number of Roman Catholics in the world was approximately 19.1 percent of the total world population; whereas in 1956 it was approximately 18.3 percent, and in 1958 18.2 percent.[2] In a similar fashion, Hans-Werner Gensichen, a Protestant missiologist, estimated that in the middle of the nineteen-sixties 33 percent of the world's population was Christian, but that this is declining so constantly that it may be only 20 percent by the end of the century.[3]

During the last twenty-five years the number of United States Catholic missionaries rose steadily until the late 1960's and since then it has been falling. A study made in 1972 indicated that the number of United States priests, brothers, nuns, and lay people serving in the foreign missions had dropped over 20 percent between the years 1968 to 1972 from 9,655 to 7,649.[4] Furthermore, the number of those studying to be missionaries dropped from

---

[2] Cited in John Power, S.M.A., *Mission Theology Today* (Maryknoll, N.Y.: Orbis Books, 1971), p. 7.

[3] Hans-Werner Gensichen, *Living Mission: The Test of Faith* (Philadelphia: Fortress Press, 1966), p. 10.

[4] *National Catholic Reporter*, November 24, 1972, p. 5.

170 in 1960 to 90 in 1970.[5] A similar trend is manifest in the general statistics for the Catholic Church in America. There were 11,000 fewer men studying for the priesthood in 1970 than there were in 1960.[6]

In the Catholic Church in modern times, the religious orders have played the largest part in the expansion of Catholicism. Among the different male orders, the Society of Jesus — the Jesuits — has been one of the largest missionary-sending groups in the Church. A glance at the world-wide statistics for this order shows the same trends which appear in the Catholic Church in the United States. Although the number of Jesuits listed as working in mission areas increased from 4,954 in 1950 to 7,009 in 1975, the number of those preparing to be priests increased from 1,220 in 1950 to 1,566 in 1971, but it dropped to 1,283 by 1975.[7] Therefore, if the American Church and the Jesuit Order are valid indicators, missionary manpower in the Roman Catholic Church will drop in the coming years. Traditional forms of missionary work cannot but be affected.

This crisis of numbers, however, is but one concrete reflection of the more general crisis which confronts the Catholic Church and many other Christian churches today. Since John XXIII and the Second Vatican Council (1962-65) "opened the windows," the Catholic Church has begun to rethink and re-evaluate itself on almost every level. Traditional doctrines are being examined, questioned, and re-expressed — the Eucharist, original sin and the nature of sin in general, the nature of the Church and the exercise of authority and leadership in the Church, the relations among the Catholic Church, other Christian churches, and the world religions. Long-accepted moral teachings are being rethought; for example, the question of the meaning of marriage and the conception of children in marriage. Long-standing practices and devotions are being revised and relegated to less prominent positions with the revival of interest in the liturgy and a reawakening of concern

---

[5] *U.S. Catholics Overseas: Missionary Personnel, Jan. 1, 1960* (Washington: Mission Secretariat, 1960) p. xv; *United States Catholics Overseas in Missionary Service, Jan. 1, 1970* (New York: Society for the Propagation of the Faith, 1970), p. 51.

[6] *The Official Catholic Directory* for 1960 and 1970 (New York: P. J. Kenedy and Sons).

[7] These figures are taken from *Supplementum Catalogorum Societatis Jesu* for 1951, 1961, 1971, and 1975 (Rome: Curia Societatis Jesu).

for Scripture. Finally, pressures are being exerted for newer and different forms of the ministry.

In this situation, it should not be surprising that the missions are being questioned. This is expressed clearly in the writings of theologians who treat of the missions. Once considered as the greatest and holiest of the Church's works, the missions are now questioned as to their value and goal. Missionaries are asked to prove the usefulness of what they are doing.[8] As one theologian, Walter Freytag, has expressed it, formerly the missions had problems, now they have become a problem.[9] Whereas missionaries in the past worried about the tactics and techniques of mission, Christians today are concerned with the concept and purpose of missions. Perhaps never before have missionary aims and energies been so thoroughly examined.[10] Today we are asked to rethink the whole meaning and purpose of the missions, and this rethinking, which came to the front in the Catholic Church after Vatican II, is being continued by the theologians; it has upset missionaries, unsettled bishops, and has brought about a crisis of missionary vocation, motivation, and action.[11]

The crisis of identity and direction which has affected the missions in the Catholic Church during the last ten years has been felt for a somewhat longer time in the Protestant churches. Many in these churches will readily agree that the "great century" of missions, the nineteenth century, has long passed. It has been said that the Protestant missionary enterprise has undergone more radical change in the last several years than in the whole previous century.[12] At the Willingen meeting of the International Missionary Council in 1952, the leaders of the missionary movement in the Protestant churches affiliated with the Council were convinced that the time was right for a fresh formulation of the missionary mandate and for a revision of traditional mis-

[8] Power, *Mission Theology Today,* p. 3.

[9] Quoted in Ferdinand Hahn, *Mission in the New Testament,* Studies in Biblical Theology, 47 (Naperville, Ill.: Alec R. Allenson, 1965), p. 167.

[10] William B. Frazier, "The Church as Sign," *The Church as Sign,* ed. William J. Richardson, M.M. (Maryknoll, N.Y.: Maryknoll Publications, 1968), p. 13.

[11] Samuel Rayan, S.J., "Mission after Vatican II: Problems and Positions," *International Review of Mission,* 59 (October, 1970), 416; see also Joel Underwood (ed.) *In Search of Mission* in the IDOC publication *Future of the Missionary Enterprise* 9 (Rome: IDOC, 1974).

[12] Norman A. Horner (ed.), *Protestant Crosscurrents in Mission: The Ecumenical-Conservative Encounter* (New York: Abingdon, 1968), p. 10.

sionary policies. With a sense of urgency, they felt that there was need for a new missionary initiative and a reformulation of a theology of mission.[13] Willingen did not fully answer these problems and the basic uncertainties about the theological basis and purpose of the Church's mission have continued to arise. Writing in the early 1960's, Wilfred Cantwell Smith said that the missionary situation of the Church is in profound crisis in both practice and theory.[14] At the Uppsala meeting of the World Council of Churches in 1968, it was remarked that no common understanding of the nature and limitations of the Christian mission or of the method of its implementation was possible at that time.[15]

It should be noted, however, that if doubt, uncertainty, confusion, and a certain amount of pessimism exist within the Roman Catholic Church and some of the Protestant churches, this mood is not shared by all Protestant denominations. The conservative and evangelical denominations are decidedly more optimistic. In their estimation, the missions show positive signs that massive harvests are on the way in the world-wide expansion of Christianity.[16]

Causes for the Crisis in Missions

Except for this group of churches — and it is no small exception — there is widespread questioning and doubt today about the traditional form and function of the missions of the Church. There are many complex reasons which explain this transition from the optimism and confidence of the nineteenth century and early twentieth century to the present state of searching doubt and questioning. They can be divided into two general categories: the first

---

[13] International Missionary Council, *The Missionary Obligation of the Church: Willingen, Germany, July 5-17, 1952* (London: Edinburgh House Press, 1952), pp. iii-vi.

[14] Wilfred Cantwell Smith, *The Faith of Other Men* (New York: New American Library, 1963), p. 120. For other presentations of the crisis as seen by Protestant theologians, see: Wilhelm Andersen, *Towards a Theology of Mission: A Study of the Encounter between the Missionary Enterprise and the Church and Its Theology* (London: SCM, 1955), p. 10; Gensichen, *Living Mission*, p. 15; Hahn, *Mission in the New Testament*, p. 167.

[15] Norman Goodall (ed.), *The Uppsala Report, 1968: The Official Report of the Fourth Assembly of the World Council of Churches, July 4-20, 1968* (Geneva: World Council of Churches, 1968), p. 38.

[16] See, for example, Arthur F. Glasser, "The Evangelicals: World Outreach," *The Future of the Christian World Mission: Studies in Honor of R. Pierce Beaver*, eds. William J. Danker and Wi Jo Kang (Grand Rapids, Mich.: Eerdmans, 1971), pp. 102-106.

are historical, sociological, and cultural reasons; the second are theological developments, which come in part from the first set of reasons and in part from a newer understanding of the gospel message. In the following section of this chapter, I will list and comment on some of the reasons in the first category. I will develop the theological reasons in later chapters.

The first group of causes has been summarized well by Lesslie Newbigin in the second volume of the history of the ecumenical movement, *The Ecumenical Advance: A History of the Ecumenical Movement, 1948-1968*. During the twenty years covered by this history, Newbigin states that the foreign missionary movement in the non-Roman Catholic churches faced the most profound crisis of its history. He lists six factors which contributed to this crisis. Although he restricts his analysis to the missions of the Protestant churches, his observations apply as well to the missionary efforts of the Catholic Church. For example, the Catholic missiologist, Joseph Masson, lists similar phenomena concerning the Catholic Church's missions after the end of the Second World War.[17] In the following pages I will freely summarize Newbigin's six points, adding elaborations and comments of my own where I feel necessary.[18]

The first factor listed by Newbigin is the dismantling of the colonial empires in Asia and Africa with the result that many of the political and cultural proppings for the foreign missions have been removed. It has been estimated that, prior to 1945, 99.5 percent of the non-Western world was under some kind of colonial domination and that twenty-five years later the figures were completely reversed with 99.5 percent of the non-Western world independent.[19] Starting in the sixteenth century when the Catholic Church reached out from Europe to the Americas and to Asia, and culminating in the nineteenth and early twentieth

---

[17] Joseph Masson, "Missions," *Sacramentum Mundi: An Encyclopedia of Theology*, eds. Karl Rahner, S.J. et al., IV (New York: Herder and Herder, 1968), 76.

[18] Lesslie Newbigin, "Mission to Six Continents," *The Ecumenical Advance: A History of the Ecumenical Movement, Volume II, 1948-1968*, ed. Harold E. Fey (Philadelphia: Westminster, 1970), pp. 173-76.

[19] Ralph D. Winter, *The Twenty-Five Unbelievable Years, 1945-1969* (Pasadena, Calif.: William Carey Library, 1970), p. 12. Winter's figures may help to highlight the truth of political independence, but they overlook other factors such as economic domination which continue to deprive many former colonies of true independence and freedom.

centuries when the Protestant churches achieved their greatest enthusiasm for outreach, the missions of the Church in the modern period have been closely interwoven with colonialism. It is tempting to generalize about the colonial period and the relationship between colonialism and mission; but, as Stephen Neill has shown, the relationship between the missions and the colonial powers is beyond easy generalization since many positive and negative factors have to be balanced against each other. There are instances when missionaries, both Protestant and Catholic, have taken heroic stands against colonial suppression. Likewise, there have been missionaries and missions which have not been able to transcend the assumptions of superiority which they brought with them from the West.[20]

In any event, it can safely be said that just as the end of the era of persecution in the fourth century marked the change from one cultural situation to a new era in which the Church had to carry on its mission, and just as the discovery of new lands in the sixteenth century marked the end of European isolationism and the beginning of the modern mission period, so, too, the end of the colonial period in modern times marks the advent of a new context in which the Church will have to carry on its mission in our times. Because the context has changed, it is to be expected that repercussions will occur in the traditional, colonial period missionary structures, and that traditional reasons and motivation for mission will be affected.

Concomitant with the breakdown of colonial structures has been the rise of nationalism in the newer nations of the world community.[21] Since the demise of colonial structures, almost every linguistic and ethnic group of major importance has achieved some form of national independence. Democratic and socialistic ideals, which have their roots in Christianity and the West, are being experimented with in many different fashions. Although there is a growing cosmopolitanization in the family of nations, any future form of world unity is bound to be a unity amidst

---

[20] Stephen Neill, *Colonialism and the Christian Missions* (New York: McGraw-Hill, 1966), pp. 414-24. For an analysis of some of the nineteenth century assumptions in this regard, see Poikail John George, "Racist Assumptions of the Nineteenth Century Missionary Movement," *International Review of Mission,* 59 (July, 1970), 270-83.

[21] In this section I am partially dependent upon the analysis of David M. Stowe, "Strategy: The Church's Response to What God is Doing," *Protestant Crosscurrents in Mission,* ed. Horner, pp. 144-53.

proud national diversity. As a result, nationalism and nation building will be both an aid to, and a problem for, the expansion of Christianity in the decades to come. On the one hand, local churches will insist on their own customs, leadership, liturgical forms, and theological expressions; and, on the other hand, those who go to serve from one church to another will have to be men and women of great sensitivity and adaptability, using their own national identity where possible or submitting it if necessary to the desires of the church which they have come to serve.

The second crisis of the post-World War II period, Newbigin states, has been the closing of China to Western missionaries. From the time when Xavier died with his eyes on China, through the centuries when Jesuit missionaries were influential at the highest levels of the Chinese court and when the delicate issues of the Chinese rites were debated by the Catholic religious orders, and down to our own times, China exerted a hypnotic influence on the missionary imagination as a kind of Platonic ideal of what a true mission field is.[22] The American Catholic Church, led by groups like Maryknoll, invested heavily in manpower for the missions of China. The Protestant churches were no less devoted to China, and before the Second World War the Church in China seemed full of immense promise.

Just as the suppression of the Jesuits at the end of the eighteenth century marked a reversal in the expansion of Roman Catholic Christianity, so too the closing of China with the accession of a communist government has given the modern missionary-sending organizations, both Protestant and Catholic, much upon which to reflect. The big question, Newbigin says, is the fact that the communist government in China has been able to accomplish many of the reforms for which the missions were early advocates but which they were not strong enough to complete. The end of the China missions has raised profound issues regarding the relation of the Christian world mission to the world-wide process of secularization and to the exercise of political power.

The third crisis that Newbigin lists is the growth of global interdependence. This is the spiritual climate in which the people around the world feel that the human race is bound together more and more by common problems, common dangers, and com-

---

[22] Keith R. Bridston, *Mission: Myth and Reality* (New York: Friendship Press, 1965), p. 37.

mon goals. It is the process of world unification spoken of so much by visionaries like Teilhard de Chardin. With growing global interdependence, the frontiers of missions have become blurred. A breakdown has occurred in the distinction between sending and receiving nations. All will now have to send and all will receive. The question which this raises is whether foreign missions, as distinct from the general duty of witness which rests upon Christians everywhere, have any peculiar *raison d'être*. Obviously, this is a clear reason for the crisis of purpose and motive in missionary work.

A fourth crisis concerns the crucial subject of development. With the gradual secularization of development and aid projects in lands which were traditionally mission territories, the Church's role in this area has often been supplanted and a corresponding vacuum of purpose has been created. The time when the missionary was the only pillar of socio-economic development has passed and now international organizations and government agencies have moved in with technical and financial resources far beyond anything the churches could ever muster.[23] With regard to this point, it would be interesting to determine how many young men and women who formerly turned to the churches as missionaries now turn to various service organizations such as the Peace Corps and VISTA. The secularization of development has undoubtedly stolen some fire from traditional missionary enterprises. Again, the question of the purpose and goal of the missions is raised.

Newbigin's fifth point concerns the crisis of faith which has been present in the West for some time now. There has been a long-term questioning of the very foundations of faith which tends to produce a spiritual situation out of which missionaries simply do not come. Since the Second World War, a chronic bad conscience has seized the Western white man in his relations with the rest of the world so that he fears above everything else the charge of arrogance. Finally, the crisis of faith within the churches of the West has led to a loss of conviction that there is anything in the Christian faith which is so vital that without it men will perish. This brings up the all-important

[23] Power, *Mission Theology Today*, p. 6.

theological issue of salvation outside of the Church. Once more, however, the foundation of traditional missionary activity has been shaken.

Finally, the growth of the ecumenical movement has had repercussions on the missionary movement. A world-wide family of churches has been established and this calls for a re-examination of the nature of the missionary movement. Is not the work of missions done when the Church has been planted in every nation? Therefore, does not the task of mission now rest upon those in each nation rather than upon the foreign missionaries? What need is there, then, for missions in the traditional sense? Newbigin, of course, is speaking of the Protestant churches and the fact that these questions became inescapable after the formation of the International Missionary Council and its integration into the World Council of Churches. However, the same problem exists within the Catholic Church, which, since Vatican II, has started to become more closely affiliated with the different Protestant Churches and with the World Council of Churches, and which is attempting to become more international and less Roman in its organization.

In addition to these historical, cultural, sociological and economic developments which have affected the traditional missions of the churches, the last fifty years have seen the development of a new theological climate which has grown from the reflections of Christian theologians upon the happenings of our times and the meaning of the gospel message for these times. This theological climate will be discussed more thoroughly in later chapters. Briefly, it centers around a rethinking of the nature and purpose of the Church, the Church's role in salvation and its relation with other religious traditions, and the Church's place and function in the world today.

By way of summary, then, there are signs of, and reasons for, a crisis in missions today. The optimism of the "great century" of missions has come to an end both for most Protestant denominations and for the Roman Catholic Church. In the Catholic Church there is a vocation crisis which will be felt more and more in the years to come. Coupled with this, however, and more disturbing, is the fact that there is a crisis in meaning and purpose with regard to what has been the traditional mission activity of the churches. This crisis can be attributed to a number of definite cultural and theological developments.

The Need for A Spirituality for Mission

At this point something must be said about the missionary. Throughout the centuries those engaged in spreading the gospel have always had implicit or explicit motives, goals, and inspiration which formed the basis for their work of evangelization. In other words, they have had a definite, personal spirituality suited for mission. *The thesis proposed here is that because the context of mission work has changed, and because the theology of mission is developing and changing, the motivation, inspiration, and spirituality of those engaged in missionary work must also change.* Implicit in this thesis is the judgement that the spirituality of those engaged in missionary work in the past might be dated and suffer from limitations in the new cultural and theological situation. Therefore, a new spirituality for mission based on the present context of mission and, more importantly, on the newer theology of mission, is necessary.

The purpose of this book, then, is to propose some of the elements of a spirituality for mission suited to the present situation. It will not develop a comprehensive theology of mission for our times. Indeed, because of the present rate of change and development this would be an intricate, if not impossible, task. At the same time, however, Christians are engaged in missionary work and in bringing the gospel to all men, and, in spite of developing cultural and theological factors, these men and women require a spirituality suited for present-day missionary work. This book, then, is intended to be practical and personal. It will center upon that all-important area of the inner life of the Christian in mission and suggest some of the salient characteristics of a spirituality for mission.

In what has been written so far, several terms have been used which must be defined more clearly, for example, *church, mission(s)*, *missionary,* and *spirituality*. Accordingly, some preliminary definitions must be offered for these terms. It should be noted, first of all, that I am writing from within the Roman Catholic tradition. For the purposes of clarity and consistency then, *Church,* with a capital *C* will refer to two realities: first, the Roman Catholic Church; and, secondly, that larger yet definite reality which might be called the Christian Church, or the whole Church, which includes all the different Christian churches or communions. This use of the term *Church* seems consistent with the theology of Vatican II which sees the Catholic Church and other Christian churches related to each other in various ways.[24]

The terms *mission, missions,* and *missionary* must also be clarified. A problem presents itself here, however, for essential to the new theology of the Church is the fact that the meaning of these terms is changing. When the theology of mission is developed in later chapters, a clearer and more precise meaning for these terms will be developed. For present purposes, *Mission* with a capital *M* refers to the Mission of God and of the Trinity; *mission(s)* with a small *m* refers to the mission of the Church and the missions carried on by the Church. Vatican II gives a definition of *missions* which can serve as a preliminary description:

> "Missions" is the term usually given to those particular undertakings by which the heralds of the gospel are sent out by the Church and go forth into the whole world to carry out the task of preaching the gospel and planting the Church among peoples or groups who do not yet believe in Christ.[25]

Lesslie Newbigin has defined the term *mission* in a similar although slightly broader manner. Missionary work differs from other activities carried on by the Church inasmuch as it is concerned with crossing the frontier between faith in Christ as Lord and unbelief.[26] The *missionary,* therefore, is one engaged in this particular activity described by Vatican II and Lesslie Newbigin. A spirituality of mission or a spirituality for missionaries is that form of spirituality peculiar to men and women who are engaged in the activity of going forth to preach Christ and helping others to cross from non-belief to belief in Christ. The meaning of the term *spirituality* will be developed in the next chapter.

In conclusion it can be said that there is a crisis in the missionary work of the Church today, a crisis due to a new and changing cultural and theological situation. This situation calls for

---

[24] See "Dogmatic Constitution on the Church," *The Documents of Vatican II,* eds. Walter M. Abbott, S.J. and Joseph Gallagher (New York: Guild Press, American Press, and Association Press, 1966), Section 15; all references to the documents of Vatican II will be from this edition and will be indicated by the English title of the document and the number of the section.

[25] "Decree on the Missionary Activity of the Church," Section 6.

[26] Lesslie Newbigin, *One Body, One Gospel, One World; The Christian Mission Today* (New York: International Missionary Council, 1959), p. 29.

a re-examination of the meaning of missions and therefore a re-examination of traditional missionary motives, inspiration, and spirituality. The following chapter will discuss the nature of spirituality and the factors which form spirituality. Chapters III and IV will be historical — representative spiritualities of mission will be presented. These chapters will serve as a point of reference for Chapters V, VI, and VII which will discuss a present-day approach to the theology of mission, and the implications which this has for mission spirituality. Chapter VIII will relate the present historical-cultural situation to missionary spirituality. Finally, the concluding chapter of this book will synthesize these various historical, cultural, and theological factors into the groundwork of a spirituality for mission today.

II

CHRISTIAN SPIRITUALITY

Spirituality refers to the life of the spirit. This statement obviously presupposes that man is spiritual, that is, central to his being is the fact that he is an embodied spirit. This premise, expressed in one philosophical mode or another, and in no way implying any form of dualism, is essential to Christian anthropology. Man is spirit because he can transcend the material, biological limitations of his being. Of all creatures, man alone is a thinker. He is a being of consciousness and is conscious of the fact that he is conscious. He is a knower, one who becomes the other through knowledge, one who is and knows that he is, one who knows that he knows. Man is and possesses his being through self-consciousness.

Because he is a self-transcending being, man possesses motives and sets goals to direct his actions. Because he is self-transcending through knowledge, man expresses himself creatively—he is poet, musician, builder, and scientist. Poetry, music, technology, and science are the results of the life of the spirit. Writing poetry, working out hypotheses, and erecting skyscrapers are expressions of spirituality. They presuppose spirituality, but it would be incorrect to say that they form a spirituality. They are mentioned here to underscore the fact that man's ability for self-transcendence through knowledge, action, and the creation of culture means that he is a being of the spirit. This is the first presupposition upon which spirituality rests.

In its broadest extension, then, spirituality refers to the interior life of man the knower and doer, that inner life which makes it possible for him to grasp reality and express himself in the complexity of forms and symbols which make up human culture. The man who thinks, meditates, contemplates, wonders, desires, plans, projects, wills, and achieves is the man who lives the life of the spirit, the interior life. However, this is not the exact notion of spirituality with which this chapter is concerned.

A second presupposition concerning spirituality as it is understood here is the fact that man is religious. The reality which the term *religion* describes is extremely complex. It can be approached historically, anthropologically, sociologically, psychologically, philosophically, and theologically; and it can be elaborated in various ways according to the viewpoints of each of these disciplines. For example, Thomas Luckmann, writing from a sociological point of view, identifies religion with man's ability to transcend his biological nature and the social processes which lead to this.[1] Another sociologist, Peter Berger, identifies religion with man's self-externalization in the enterprise by which a *sacred cosmos* is established in an attempt to conceive the entire universe as humanly significant.[2] From a psychological stance, William James in his classic work on religious experience described religion as the feelings, acts, and experiences of individual men in their solitude, so far as they apprehend themselves to stand in relation to whatever they may consider divine.[3] This brings to mind the philosopher Alfred North Whitehead's definition of religion as solitariness — that which the individual does with his own solitariness. Whitehead, however, had a much more elaborate concept of religion than this rather individualistic formula would suggest.[4] A modern scholar of world religions, Wilfred Cantwell Smith, believes that the term religion is loaded with ambiguity and prefers that it be dropped entirely from discourse in preference to terms such as *cumulative tradition* to describe the positions held by Christians, Buddhists, etc., and *faith* to describe the personal stance of the believer.[5] Finally, from a more strictly theological point of view, religion is described as man's relation with the holy, a relationship with any kind of transcendent deity, real or supposed.[6] This

---

[1] Thomas Luckmann, *The Invisible Religion: The Problem of Religion in Modern Society* (New York: Macmillan, 1967).

[2] Peter L. Berger, *The Sacred Canopy: Elements of a Sociological Theory of Religion* (Garden City, N.Y.: Anchor Books, 1969), Chapter I.

[3] William James, *The Varieties of Religious Experience: A Study in Human Nature,* The Gifford Lectures, 1901-02 (New York: New American Library, 1958), p. 42.

[4] Alfred North Whitehead, "Religion in the Making," *Alfred North. Whitehead — An Anthology,* eds. F.S.C. Northrop and Mason W. Gross (New York: Macmillan, 1961), p. 472.

[5] William Cantwell Smith, *The Meaning and End of Religion: A New Approach to the Religious Traditions of Mankind* (New York: New American Library, 1964).

[6] Karl Rahner and Herbert Vorgrimler, *Theological Dictionary,* ed. Cornelius Ernst, O.P., trans. Richard Strachan (New York: Herder and Herder,

description, too, has its problems since some religions do not seem to have any notion of transcendent powers, and because it is difficult to define adequately what is meant by *the holy.*[7]

For present purposes it can be said that religion has to do with the activities of man's self-transcendence as they are related to the holy, to a deity, a sacred cosmos, or, in Paul Tillich's term, an *ultimate concern.* Religion, therefore, concerns man's total conception of the meaning of reality, his world view as it is determined by a relationship with a deity or an ultimate concern. Flowing from this total world view are definite ways of living and acting which are determined by it. Thus there is a subjective, practical aspect to religion. Spirituality is born from the marriage of such a world view related to the holy or an ultimate concern and the way of living which is in accordance with this world view. Spirituality, therefore, is the basic, practical, existential attitude of man which is the consequence and expression of the way in which he understands his existence and the meaning of reality. It is the way he acts or reacts habitually throughout life according to ultimate objectives which flow from his world view.

When spirituality is described in this way, it is obvious that there are as many forms of spirituality as there are religions and world views. In this sense, one could develop various spiritualities for Buddhism, Hinduism, Islam, and Marxism. Or one could say that there are Buddhist, Hindu, Marxist, and Maoist life styles which are determined by the ultimate concern and ethical demands of these world views as they are appropriated into a person's private life.

Christianity involves an elaborate world view concerning man and his relationship with God and with his fellow men. This world view stems from the Bible and has been developed by symbol, philosophy, and theology during the nearly two thousand years of Christian history. Essential to the Christian world view is the belief that God has assumed the world and its history to himself in the person of Jesus of Nazareth. This truth and the implications which follow from it form the basis of the Christian faith. Most fundamentally, Christianity is a life of faith, the

---

1965), p. 399; Louis Bouyer, *Introduction to Spirituality,* trans. Mary Perkins Ryan (New York: Desclée, 1961), p. 4.

[7] See Rudolf Otto, *The Idea of the Holy: An Inquiry into the Non-rational in the Idea of the Divine and Its Relation to the Rational,* trans. John W. Harvey (London: Oxford University, 1957).

acceptance of things unseen and not totally understood, which centers on the person of Jesus Christ who for the Christian is both God and man, God in a human way and human in a divine way.

Christian spirituality can be described as the daily life style of the believing Christian. It is the way a person lives in a definite historical situation according to his vision of faith, that is, according to his personal assimilation of the mystery of Christ under the direction of the Holy Spirit.[8] It is interesting to note that in the Acts of the Apostles one of the first names given to Christianity is *the way* (Acts 9:2, 19:9, 23; 22:4; 24:14, 22). It has been suggested that the phrase *Christian life style* may be regarded as a modern expression for *the way* of the Acts of the Apostles.[9] At the Uppsala meeting of the World Council of Churches in 1968, Mrs. Brigit Rodhe offered a description of what is meant by *style:* That "complex unity of shape and substance, of doing and being, of life and belief, of medium and message. It is about the outward manifestations of the inward convictions. It is about living on one's faith."[10]

Christian spirituality is an eminently personal affair. Given the world view common to Christianity and the concrete historical and cultural situations of different men, each Christian will live *the way* and conduct his life style in a manner which is peculiar to himself alone, although there will be common patterns in the lives of Christians in similar historical and cultural situations. This brings up an important distinction. Spirituality can be considered in the concrete or in the abstract. Concretely, it is that very personal and individual life style of this or that believing Christian. Viewed in this fashion, spirituality differs from person to person, for no two Christians have exactly the same vision

---

[8] For similar descriptions of Christian spirituality see Gabriel M. Braso, O.S.B., *Liturgical Spirituality,* trans. Leonard J. Doyle (Collegeville, Minn.: Liturgical Press, 1971), p. 3; Edward Carter, S.J., *Spirituality for Modern Man* (Notre Dame, Ind.: Fides, 1971), p. vii; Thomas M. Gannon, S.J. and George W. Traub, S.J., *The Desert and the City: An Interpretation of the History of Christian Spirituality* (London: Macmillan, 1968), p. 10; Joseph Sudbrack, "Spirituality," *Sacramentum Mundi: An Encyclopedia of Theology,* eds. Karl Rahner et al., VI (New York: Herder and Herder, 1968), 153.

[9] J. R. Chandran, "The Christian Style of Living," *Renewal for Mission,* eds. David Lyon and Albert Manuel (Madras: Christian Literature Society, 1968), pp. 86-87.

[10] Norman Goodall (ed.), *The Uppsala Report: Official Report of the Fourth Assembly of the World Council of Churches, Uppsala, July 4-20, 1968* (Geneva: World Council of Churches, 1968), p. 86.

of the Christian faith, and correspondingly no two persons have identical ways of living that faith. The lives of the saints and of outstanding Christians are the closest approximation to Christian spirituality in this concrete form. In this category would be biographies such as the *Life of St. Antony* by Athanasius, the writings of Teresa of Avila and John of the Cross, and autobiographical reflections such as Dag Hammarskjöld's *Markings*. Nevertheless, there are common elements in Christian spirituality, and there are trends and patterns of living *the way* in the Christian tradition. This is the area of theory in which generalizations can be made and common characteristics pointed out. Considered in the abstract, then, spirituality is a theory of living the faith culled from the gospel and the life styles of Christians who have lived and are living, and presented to others for imitation to direct their personal lives in Christ.

In these pages the terms *spirituality* and *life style* will be used almost interchangeably; however, each has a slightly different nuance. Christian spirituality refers more to the theory of Christian living; whereas Christian life style emphasizes the concrete expression of Christian living which, of course, always includes and is based upon the attitudes, values, and convictions of Christianity. This chapter will be more concerned with the former — the theory of Christian living. Chapters III and IV will give examples of the latter — the concrete life styles of those engaged in missionary activity.

In Roman Catholic theology since the sixteenth century it has been common to distinguish spirituality from dogmatic theology and moral theology. Thus, Pierre Pourrat in his four-volume history of Christian spirituality distinguishes these three in the following way: Spirituality is that part of theology which deals with Christian perfection and the ways that lead to it; dogmatic theology teaches what we should believe; and moral theology what we should do or not do to avoid sin. Spirituality is above moral and dogmatic theology although it is based on them both.[11]

Writing more than thirty years later, Louis Bouyer in the first volume of his history of Christian spirituality, *The Spirituality of the New Testament and the Fathers*, expresses a dissatisfaction with Pourrat's distinctions. Should Christian morality be defined by a

---

[11] Pierre Pourrat, *Christian Spirituality*, trans. W.H. Mitchell, S.P. Jacques, and Donald Attwater, I (Westminster, Md.: Newman, 1953-55), p. v.

merely negative idea, that of avoiding sin? Furthermore, Bouyer remarks, once one gets into Pourrat's history he is plunged into a medley of dogmatic or moral considerations and psychological analyses in which the definitions laid down at the outset of the work are constantly transgressed.[12]

There is no doubt that spirituality, dogmatic theology (systematic theology in today's terms), and moral theology (Christian ethics) are all closely interwoven. Bouyer distinguishes dogma from Christian spirituality by the fact that, instead of studying or describing the objects of belief in the abstract, Christian spirituality studies the reactions which Christian beliefs produce in the religious consciousness. Thus, dogmatic theology must always be presupposed as the basis of spirituality. Furthermore, he maintains that it is not by its concern with perfection that spirituality is distinguished from morality. Rather, morality examines all human actions in reference to their ultimate end, whether this reference be explicit or not; whereas spirituality concentrates on those actions in which the reference to God is not only explicit but immediate. Spirituality therefore, according to Bouyer, concentrates on prayer and on everything connected with prayer in the ascetical and mystical life, that is, on religious exercises as well as religious experiences. Therefore, just as a truly Christian morality is never really external to systematic or dogmatic theology, so spirituality is located far more within the heart of morality than alongside it.[13]

Pourrat is correct when he maintains that spirituality both stands above, and is based upon, moral theology and dogmatic theology. Bouyer, for his part, also makes an important point when he stresses the dependence of spirituality upon dogmatic theology and when he locates spirituality at the heart of moral theology. Christian spirituality, understood as a theory concerning the life style of the believer, is broader than, although it is based upon, both systematic theology and Christian ethics. Obviously, the life style of the Christian must be moral in the sense that he is concerned with the goodness of particular actions and situations. He must have a concern for Christian ethics, and, for example, the justice or injustice of this or that particular act

---

[12] Louis Bouyer, *A History of Christian Spirituality*, Vol. I, *The Spirituality of the New Testament and the Fathers*, trans. Mary Perkins Ryan (New York: Desclée, 1963), p. vii.

[13] *Ibid.*, pp. viii-ix.

or situation. But spirituality involves more than this. Obviously, too, Christian spirituality presupposes the positions and beliefs elaborated in systematic theology. Indeed, the different schools of Christian spirituality often flow from the great traditions developed in systematic theology. Therefore, it is impossible to make clear and watertight distinctions between systematic theology, Christian ethics, and Christian spirituality. The truth seems to be that spirituality cuts across and bridges all subjects and disciplines which are relevant to the Christian way of living. It has ethical dimensions; it is based upon systematic theology; and it must take account of psychology, anthropology, and sociology. If this is forgotten, a spirituality runs the danger of becoming defective.

The Sources of Christian Spirituality

Therefore, in order to understand the nature of Christian spirituality, it is necessary to outline the sources on which it depends. They are four: Scripture, theology, culture, and tradition. In every form of Christian spirituality, past or present, these elements are found. Among them there is a relationship of mutual influence and interdependence; one will never be found without the others, and each constantly acts upon and reacts to the others.

Scripture is the most important source for Christian spirituality. The Bible is a literary-historical, confessional document composed over hundreds of years in many complex and diverse literary forms. Different traditions have flowed into it; it was written in various cultural situations; and it contains multiple, and sometimes conflicting, theological points of view. To give a complete account of the spirituality which is contained in Scripture, one would have to take into consideration all of these diverse cultural and theological traditions that make up the Old and New Testaments. It would take a voluminous work simply to outline the spirituality contained in Scripture.

Therefore, in order to understand how Scripture is the essential element in the formation of Christian spirituality, it is necessary to arrive at one focal point upon which the whole depends. For the Christian, this is Jesus Christ, the fulfillment of the Law and Prophets of the Old Testament and the revealer of God's promises to man in the New Testament. Central, then, to the assertion that Scripture is the source of Christian spirituality is the fact that Christian spirituality is above all Christo-centric.

Recalling that spirituality is a way and a life style, it can be said that, most fundamentally, Christian spirituality is the way of Christ, that is, *imitatio Christi,* the imitation of Christ. Christian spirituality starts at this point, is centered upon it, and must constantly return to it. Bouyer says that the soul of Christian spirituality lies in the absolutely unique influence of Jesus' words and of his personality.[14] Christian spirituality starts from God's self-revelation and the faith and assent men give to the Word of God.[15] Pourrat says that Christian perfection consists in following Christ and in attachment to Jesus.[16] Christian spirituality is a partial re-enactment in our own lives of what happened once and for all in Jesus of Nazareth as the Incarnate Word. All authentically Christian piety is, consequently, an *imitatio Christi* — not a mechanical, servile, mawkish imitation, but one which is spontaneous and free, proportioned to one's unique personality and life situation.[17] It is a participation in the paschal mystery of Christ, the putting on of the mind of Christ, a living of the life of Christ.[18]

These statements echo the spiritual theology of Paul's epistles. For him, the baptized Christian is clothed in Christ and becomes a new creation in Christ (Gal. 3:27-28; 2 Cor. 5:17). Being in Christ means that the Christian reflects the brightness of the Lord, that he is called to be an image of the Son, that he must live the good life (2 Cor. 3:18; Rom. 8:29; Eph. 2:10). The writer of the First Epistle of John expresses the same idea: one can only claim to be in Christ when he walks in the same way in which Christ walked (1 John 2:5-6).

By acknowledging the fact that Christian spirituality is Christo-centric, and therefore that all Christian spirituality consists in an imitation and appropriation of the life of Christ to one's own life, we have the starting point for Christian spirituality; but in no way should this be interpreted in a simplistic manner. For the Christian, Jesus is the central figure in Scripture, but who he was

---

[14] Bouyer, *A History of Christian Spirituality,* p. 35.
[15] Bouyer, *Introduction to Spirituality,* pp. 6-7.
[16] Pourrat, *Christian Spirituality,* I, 304.
[17] Gannon and Traub, *The Desert and the City,* p. 9.
[18] Jordan Aumann, O.P., Thomas Hopko, and Donald G. Bloesch, *Christian Spirituality East and West* (Chicago: Priory Press, 1968), p. 18.

and what he stood for come to us only through intermediaries. Jesus left nothing in writing. His words and teachings are available only in the writings of the authors of the various books of the New Testament. Immediately, therefore, with the very person of Jesus, we are involved in the other elements which form spirituality — theology, culture, and tradition.

Jesus was a man who lived in the Jewish culture of Roman-dominated, first-century Palestine. He read and prayed the Old Testament. He thought of God as Father, prayed *Abba,* and followed the Jewish cultural and religious customs of his times. Finally, those who wrote of him did so according to their own theological points of view. Paul's interpretation of the mystery of Christ differs from John's, which differs again from that of the writer of the Epistle to the Hebrews; and all three of these great New Testament witnesses differ from the interpretations given by the Synoptic writers.

In spite of these complexities in the New Testament witness concerning Jesus, the broad outline of a spirituality based upon the New Testament can be determined. The following summary is not intended to be comprehensive, nor will it discuss all the strands of New Testament spirituality and the different interpretations given by the writers of the gospels and the epistles.[19] It concentrates on seven important elements which form the foundation of all Christian spirituality as based upon the New Testament.

First of all, there is the absolute demand for faith and a change of heart — belief in Christ and the God who sent him, and *metanoia.* "Repent and believe" are among the first recorded words spoken by Jesus (Mark 1:15). This demand presupposes a theology of sin, forgiveness, and reconciliation on the one hand, and, on the other, the corresponding notions of justification and sanctification which result from faith. Both of these areas have a long and much discussed history in Christian thought and spirituality.

Closely allied with faith and *metanoia* is the Christian interpretation of history — the reason Jesus gives for belief and repentance is that the kingdom of God is at hand. A second important element in Christian spirituality, therefore, is the notion of the kingdom. This is the area of Christian eschatology which is con-

[19] See, for example, Bouyer, *The Spirituality of the New Testament and the Fathers,* pp. 3-164.

cerned with the interpretation and meaning of the final times inaugurated by the coming of Christ. From the New Testament down to our own times, much theological concern has been given to the notion of the kingdom of God, its presence among us, and its final manifestation in time. The life style of the believer differs radically according to whether he believes that Christ's final coming is imminent or will be delayed for some time. Finally, intimately connected with any interpretation of the kingdom of God is hope, next to faith the second great Christian virtue.

A third element which is central to Christian spirituality as it is illustrated in the life of Jesus and presented in the New Testament is the fact that Christian spirituality is trinitarian. The Christian by his commitment is brought into the life of the Trinity, Father, Son, and Holy Spirit. This has special importance for the spirituality of mission, as will be shown. In what seems to be an ever developing and deepening fashion, Jesus realized his mission as sent by the Father to bring men to the Father. When his ministry was complete, he promised the Spirit to guide those who would accept him. Christian spirituality is trinitarian inasmuch as man is caught up in the very life of God the Father by incorporation into Christ and possession by the Holy Spirit.

The paschal mystery is the fourth key element in Christian spirituality presented in the New Testament. This mystery concerns the life, suffering, death, resurrection, and glorification of Jesus Christ. By professing faith in Christ, Christians are incorporated into the paschal mystery. They are baptized into his death and possess new life by his resurrection (Rom. 6:1-11, 2 Cor. 4:7-15, 1 Peter 1:3-2:10). The mysteries of suffering and death confront every human person. The Christian suffers the harshness of these elements the same as every other human being. Participation in the paschal mystery of Christ does not lessen the evils of suffering and death for the Christian, but it does give them a meaning and purpose which transcend their immediate negativity.

Charity or love is the greatest Christian virtue. Love and the service which flows from love must be listed as the fifth important area forming the basis of New Testament spirituality. Jesus left one commandment with a double thrust—love of God and love of neighbor (Mark 12:28-34, Matt. 22:34-40, Luke 10:25-28).

He manifested this love in service and enjoined those who would follow him to do the same (John 13:1-15). Love and service in imitation of Christ have always been central to Christian spirituality. The way of loving and the mode of serving, however, have differed vastly over the centuries. Here is an instance where theological interpretation and cultural adaptation have had great influence on the basic gospel values.

It would be superfluous to say that Christian prayer is based on the New Testament. Prayer and meditation are central to every form of religious and faith experience. The whole of Scripture not only contains many parts which are themselves prayers, for example, the Psalms; but it also gives the Christian many forms and motives for praying — glory, praise, thanksgiving, and petition. Perhaps what is most significant about the New Testament's influence on prayer is the fact that Christian prayer is directed to the Father through Christ, the one mediator between God and man. The Christian's life of prayer and worship, therefore, is the sixth element of New Testament spirituality.

It should also be noted that Christian spirituality as it is presented in the New Testament is sacramental. Just as God was mediated to man through the person of Jesus Christ, so the love and presence of Christ continues to be mediated to the people of God through the sacraments, material signs of Christ's saving love. Baptism, forgiveness, the Eucharist, orders and ministry in the Church, all these sacraments central to the life of prayer, worship, and ritual, have their foundation in the New Testament and in the life of Christ. What is being said here is tantamount to saying that New Testament spirituality is ecclesial. God encounters man in Scripture and in the sacraments, but these are mediated to the believer in the Christian community, the Church. It is impossible to have any Christian spirituality which is not ecclesial at least to the minimal extent that the believer owes his knowledge of Christ to the community, the Church, which has preserved that knowledge by handing on the Word of God in Scripture.

Finally, asceticism is the last key New Testament factor which might be mentioned in this overview. Throughout the centuries Christian asceticism has taken many different forms, some of them, perhaps, rather dehumanizing and un-Christian. The person of Jesus Christ as he appears in the New Testament is the picture of a man who is both a humanist and an ascetic. He came "eating and drinking" (Luke 7:34) and called upon his followers to deny themselves (Mark 8:34).[20] Basic to Christian spirituality is the fact that a certain amount of self-control and self-discipline is essential. This has been spoken of by the writers of the New Testament in terms of carrying one's cross after Christ. The self-control and self-discipline necessary to imitate Christ and live one's Christian life style in whatever form it may take is the basic meaning of asceticism in Christian spirituality. In the simplest of terms, asceticism is the cost of Christian love and service.

Faith and a change of heart, the kingdom of God and the meaning of time, Christian hope, the Trinity, the sending of the Son by the Father, the mediative role of the Son, the gift of the Holy Spirit and the indwelling of the Spirit, the mystery of suffering, death, and resurrection, Christian love and service, prayer and the sacramental life, self-discipline and asceticism — these form the outline of Christian spirituality as found in the New Testament. They make up the Christian world view which existentially affects believers, their life styles, and their way of living the faith.

The second foundation upon which Christian spirituality rests is *theology*. As we have already mentioned and implied in this brief enumeration, even with these basic Scriptural elements we are from the very start engaged in theology. As understood here, theology is the science of faith, that is, the conscious and methodological explanation of the divine revelation received and grasped in faith. The New Testament contains many theologies inasmuch as its various authors interpreted Christ, man, and the world in differing ways. For example, Jesus is given various titles and names in the New Testament, each with different theological implications — Servant of God, Messiah, Lord (*Kyrios*), Son of David, Son of Man, Son of God, Word of God (*Logos*). In Scripture, likewise, there are several interpretations of eschatology, and this question has been debated down to our times: Is Christ's second coming to be considered as imminent, or only at the end of time, or is there an "already" and "not yet" character to it? Volumes have been written on this one point, even with regard to Jesus' own understanding of it. Scripture also gives and presupposes various interpretations of man and his world. One cannot speak of repent-

[20] E.R. Hardy, "Asceticism," *Dictionary of Christian Ethics*, ed. John Macquarrie (Philadelphia: Westminster, 1967), p. 20.

ance without a theology of sin and evil. Paul does this in terms of *flesh* and *spirit;* John speaks in terms of *light* and *darkness* and the *world.* Examples from the New Testament could be multiplied. The point is that the Word of God given in revelation is always mediated through human understanding and interpretation, that is, through theology. The role of theology, therefore, is essential in Scripture itself and its importance for Christian spirituality has continued throughout the history of the Church.

With the end of New Testament times a unique phase in the history of Christian theology and spirituality also came to an end. Everything that followed in the history of the Church had to live on the elements presented in the New Testament. In a sense, nothing new can be added. What has happened, and what continues to happen, is that one or another aspect of the apostolic teaching develops and reveals its implications according to the historical and cultural needs of the moment and the problems of the times.[21] Theology is thus challenged to be faithful both to the biblical revelation and to historical circumstances in order that the Christian interpretation of life and, therefore, the Christian way of living the faith may be true to Christ. On the other hand, when theology becomes defective and erroneous, the Christian way, Christian spirituality, will also be adversely affected.[22]

Perhaps the effects of theology upon spirituality come into sharpest focus when this negative influence of a defective theology is seen. In the Christian world view and in Christian anthropology a constant tension must be maintained between man as embodied spirit and man as part of the material world. Likewise, a balance must be kept between the world as God's creation sanctified by the Incarnation and the *world* in the Johannine sense as the sphere dominated by the power of evil. A theology which overemphasizes either side of these tensions, or a theology which overlooks one side of either of these polarities will be defective and will, accordingly, have inhuman and un-Christian consequences upon spirituality. For example, early in its history, Christian spirituality was affected by Neo-Platonic dualism and a two-layer conception of man as body and soul. This view of man rests on an ontological misinterpretation of the Pauline tension between *spirit* and *flesh.* A great part of spiritual literature has been consciously or unconsciously

[21] Bouyer, *The Spirituality of the New Testament and the Fathers,* p. 163.
[22] See Pourrat, *Christian Spirituality,* I, 68.

dominated by the ideal of the "spiritual" man who, purified of all material concerns, strives to attain to the pure realm of the soul and the spirit.[23] This has led to the charge that Christians do not take man and his world seriously. It has also given an enfeebled and dematerialized connotation to the notion of Christian spirituality and Christian asceticism.

Another theological tension which must be maintained because of the far-reaching repercussions which it has upon spirituality is the relation between man's freedom and the gratuitous bestowal of God's love, that is, grace. This mystery of the interaction of grace and freedom came into sharp outline at the time of Augustine and the Pelagian controversy. If heavy stress is given to man's freedom, then the gratuity and power of God's grace is impaired. The result is a spirituality of the will in which man can, through personal effort, pull himself to God and perfection by his own boot straps. Pelagian spirituality is a spirituality of pride and rigorism.[24] On the other hand, if a pessimistic view of man is taken and God's grace is given sole consideration, man's freedom is wrecked. The result is Quietism, a do-nothing form of spirituality which leads to absolute disinterest in any form of human effort. The tension between grace and freedom has been at the heart of innumerable theological wrangles during the history of the Christian Church; and the failure to keep a balance between these two has led to not a few deformities in Christian spirituality and the way men live their faith commitment.

It has been said that the most profound differences in spirituality are of the intellectual order.[25] From these two examples, it is easy to see how a particular theological interpretation of God, man, and the world can have far-reaching implications on how men live their faith. Theology, therefore, is an important determinant in any spirituality. If God is viewed not as a father but as a hard master, saving only the elect who are predestined, the Christian life style becomes one of severe, fearful austerity, pessimism, and joyless moralism. The best illustration of this would be the Jansenistic spirituality of seventeenth-century France.[26] This form of spirituality differs greatly from that of the Middle Ages which might be repre-

---

[23] Sudbrack, "Spirituality," *Sacramentum Mundi,* VI, 150.

[24] Pourrat, *Christian Spirituality,* I, 169-73.

[25] Braso, *Liturgical Spirituality,* pp. 4-5.

[26] Pourrat, *Christian Spirituality,* IV, Chapter I; Gannon and Traub, *The Desert and the City,* pp. 233-36.

sented by Bernard of Clairvaux's loving devotion to the humanity of Christ as our way to the unseen God.[27] It differs, too, from the Renaissance spirituality of Ignatius of Loyola and the Jesuit Order, the great enemy of Jansenism, which is characterized by a kind of chivalrous, personal commitment to Christ and service under his standard. Likewise, the Augustinian view of man wounded in natural gifts (*homo vulneratus in naturalibus*), differs from the Thomistic view of man deprived of gratuitous gifts (*homo gratuitis spoliatus*). Some will contend that the former naturally results in a more pessimistic way of living the Christian life. Finally, the Neo-Platonic view of the world as a threat to the spiritual man will result in a Christian pattern of living which stands in marked contrast to a more modern conception which sees the world as sanctified by the Incarnation and offered as a challenge to be developed and perfected by man who becomes, as it were, a co-creator with God. A spirituality in this latter vein would be that of the Christian evolutionist, Pierre Teilhard de Chardin.

Culture is the third determining factor for spirituality. Here again, as with the notion of religion, we are confronted with an extremely rich and complex reality. Nearly a century ago, Sir Edward Tylor described culture as "that complex whole which includes knowledge, belief, art, morals, law, custom and any other capabilities and habits acquired by man as a member of society."[28] Culture, then, is the whole range of human activities which are learned and not instinctive, and which are transmitted from generation to generation through various learning processes.[29]

Theology and spirituality are part of culture — they both form and are formed by culture. They are part of culture inasmuch as they are two of the many interlocking elements which compose that "complex whole" which is handed on from generation to generation in society through the process of learning. An example of a culture formed by Christian theology and spirituality would be the Christendom of the Middle Ages. Theology and spirituality are formed by culture because God's revelation of himself and his plan for man and the world are by necessity enculturated. Jesus was Jesus of Nazareth, a Jew who was born into, and grew

---

[27] Pourrat, *Christian Spirituality,* II, Chapter II.

[28] John Beattie, *Other Cultures: Aims, Methods, and Achievements in Social Anthropology* (New York: Free Press, 1966), p. 20.

[29] *Ibid.*

to maturity within, the cosmopolitan Jewish-Greco-Roman culture of first-century Palestine. The New Testament was written by men of that same culture, in Greek, the lingua franca of the Mediterranean world. Throughout the centuries, the Word of revelation has been received, understood, and interpreted according to the thought patterns and institutions of the various cultures to which it was presented. Today Christianity is sometimes criticized because it is a Western religion, and the Catholic Church is called the *Roman* Catholic Church. This is the case because the main thrust of Christianity in its expansion was westward into the Roman Empire. It is interesting to speculate what the characteristics of the Christian religion and Christian theology would be if the main current of expansion had flowed southward through Egypt into Africa or eastward through Persia and into India.

The effect which culture and society have upon theology and spirituality is extremely important; indeed, it is difficult to overestimate its importance. This has been made clear, for example, by recent developments in the field of the sociology of knowledge. This discipline deals with a description and structural analysis of the ways in which social relationships influence thought.[30] It maintains that man's understanding or appreciation of reality, and therefore his way of acting, is determined by the style of life followed by the type of society in which he lives.[31] A quick glance at the history of Christian spirituality will show how this linkage between society's life style and thought structures influences Christian theology and the Christian life style.

I have already mentioned the influence which Neo-Platonic dualism and anti-materialistic pessimism had upon Christian theology and spirituality. I shall not discuss here the much debated problem of the Hellenization of Christianity or the Christianization of Hellenism which occurred in the early Church, although this is one of the prime examples of the influence of the intellectual life

---

[30] See Karl Mannheim, *Ideology and Utopia: An Introduction to the Sociology of Knowledge*, trans. L. Wirth and E. Shils (New York: Harcourt, Brace, and World, 1936), Chapter V; Peter L. Berger, *A Rumor of Angels: Modern Society and the Rediscovery of the Supernatural* (Garden City, N.Y.: Anchor Books, 1970); *idem, The Sacred Canopy: Elements of a Sociological Theory of Religion* (Garden City, N.Y.: Anchor Books, 1969); Harvey Cox, *The Secular City: Secularization and Urbanization in Theological Perspective* (New York: Macmillan, 1965).

[31] See B.N.Y. Vaughn, *Structures for Renewal: A Search for the Renewal of the Church's Mission to the World* (London: A.R. Mowbray, 1967), p. 11.

of a particular era upon theology and the Christian way of living. Bouyer in his history of spirituality maintains that the last Hellenistic philosophy and Christian culture developed simultaneously at Alexandria and present a symbiosis in which it is extremely difficult, however desirable, to seek to define the interchanges of influences and stimulations.[32]

In the realm of culture and society there is another phenomenon in the early Church whose importance for Christian spirituality is difficult to exaggerate — martyrdom. Until it became the state religion in the fourth century, Christianity was officially proscribed and Christians in the Roman Empire underwent continuous persecutions of differing intensity and magnitude. Bouyer estimates that after the elements of the New Testament no other factor has had more influence in constituting Christian spirituality than martyrdom. There is hardly any other instance where doctrinal development is so clearly bound up with the experience of the Church in the world.[33]

Bouyer and Pourrat in their histories are quick to point out how persecution and martyrdom affected the interpretation given to the Scriptural elements of Christian spirituality.[34] As I mentioned, the imitation of Christ is at the core of Christian spirituality. Writers such as Ignatius of Antioch, Polycarp, and Origen offer the martyrs as supreme examples of the imitation of Christ. Martyrdom also led to a distinctive interpretation of Christian eschatology. In the view of Ignatius of Antioch, it offered the Christian the possibility of attaining and anticipating the *parousia* of Christ by assimilation into Christ dead and risen.

Martyrdom was linked with the sacraments of baptism and the Eucharist. The Eucharist was seen to begin the process of union with Christ which was fulfilled by martyrdom. Tertullian, Origen, and Augustine saw martyrdom as a baptism of blood, taking the place of water baptism for those unbaptized. Finally, the virtues necessary for living in a situation of persecution were constantly preached by the writers of the first three centuries. The Christian had to be a fighter and possess those qualities which guarantee victory: courage, energy, patience, self-abnegation, and hope in the rewards which flow from suffering and death.

---

[32] Bouyer, *The Spirituality of the New Testament and the Fathers*, p. 260.
[33] *Ibid.*, p. 190.
[34] *Ibid.*, Chapter VIII; Pourrat, *Christian Spirituality*, I, 48-59.

Persecution and the ever-present possibility of martyrdom are not only central to an understanding of the spirituality of the early Church, but they also lead into a second great phenomenon in the history of Christian spirituality — monasticism. From the moment when the persecutions ceased and martyrdom was no longer so much an actual possibility, the main line in the progress of Christian spirituality flowed through monasticism.[35] During the first part of the fourth century, starting with Constantine and Licinius' rescript of Milan in 313, Christianity was first tolerated and then gradually started to develop into the state religion of the Empire. The socio-cultural situation in which Christians found themselves shifted from one of proscription and persecution to acceptance and privilege. In this new milieu large numbers of converts entered the Church and it was feared that as the world became Christian many Christians would become more worldly.[36] With martyrdom removed as a possibility, devout Christians sought other forms within which to live their lives of faith.

Monasticism is not only a Christian phenomenon. It has existed and continues to exist in other religious traditions. Christian monasticism has a pre-history in Judaism, for example, the Qumran community; and it undoubtedly owes something to the philosophic climate of Neo-Platonism. These facts, however, in no way endanger the truth that monasticism as it developed was also thoroughly Christian in its motivation and inspiration. The apostolic community in Jerusalem as described in the Acts of the Apostles exemplifies a quasi-monastic form of life in the very earliest days of the Church.

Without a comprehensive examination of the origins of monasticism, it can be said, for the purpose of illustrating the influence which culture has upon spirituality, that the development of monasticism owes something to the theology of martyrdom and the new cultural situation which the Church inherited in the fourth century. As Bouyer suggests, it was not by chance that anchoritism spread so suddenly after the state made its peace with the Church. There was a close connection between these two contemporaneous historical facts. When a world in which Christians as such were separated and proscribed was succeeded by a world in which they came to be in honor, but a world whose spirit had hardly changed for

[35] Bouyer, *The Spirituality of the New Testament and the Fathers,* p. 523.
[36] Pourrat, *Christian Spirituality,* I, 74-75.

all that, the best Christians, by instinct, freely chose the state of proscription no longer imposed on them by circumstances. Although the world no longer treated them as enemies, they felt obliged to live as enemies of the world lest they become its slaves.[37] Even before this situation occurred, theologians of the Church were thinking about the continuity from martyrdom to monasticism. This is exemplified by Origen's *Exhortation to Martyrdom* in which the transition is made from the ideal of martyrdom as prepared for by asceticism to the ideal of asceticism as the equivalent of martyrdom.[38]

Martyrdom and monasticism are but two instances in which the influence of society and culture had important effects upon the Christian life style. As Christianity progressed through the centuries other instances appeared. The Benedictine form of monasticism flourished after the Patristic Era and during the so-called Dark Ages in Europe. The monastery was a center of stability and learning in a society which was fractured by invasions and fragmented by feudalism. By the opening of the thirteenth century, Europe was in the throes of another major change — the shift from an essentially rural, agrarian culture to an urban and commercial society. Feudalism, the basic framework of society, broke apart to be replaced by the medieval towns and cities. In this situation a new, free, middle-class man emerged. The mendicant orders of Dominic and Francis rose to meet the challenge of this new bourgeoisie, the new cities, the new commerce, and the new intellectual life of the university.[39] The mendicants reforged the traditional monastic way of life and spirituality to gain more mobility and adaptability to preach and teach in the contemporary situation.

Examples could be multiplied as we enter into the modern period. I shall briefly mention one more — Catholic spirituality following the sixteenth century religious upheavals in Europe. It has been said that post-Reformation Catholic spirituality took direction more from its fight against the supposed and real heresies of the Protestants than from the entire Christian tradition. In a context of reaction and defensiveness, the spiritual writers of this period expressed themselves more than ever in the battle and combat imagery which the desert fathers had first popularized.

---

37 Bouyer, *The Spirituality of the New Testament and the Fathers,* pp. 305-306.

38 *Ibid.,* pp. 208-10; 305.

39 Gannon and Traub, *The Desert and the City,* pp. 81-82.

The martial tactics of Laurence Scupoli's *Spiritual Combat* (1589) illustrate this trend. So successfully did the Catholic Church foster this spirit of defensiveness that it was able to remain relatively untouched by the outside world until the present century.[40]

These selective examples demonstrate the impact which the cultural situation in which the Church finds itself has upon Christian spirituality. The particular style of life and the thought structures of a certain milieu by necessity affect the way Christian revelation is received, understood, and lived in that milieu; they cannot but have repercussions upon Christian thought and theology and the ensuing Christian life style. The Church and culture are mutually interpenetrating dimensions of God's activity in the world. This is the conclusion reached by Norman K. Gottwald in his study of Church and culture based upon the relationship between Israel and the nations.[41] This truth will have great implications when a spirituality for the contemporary world is discussed, be it Christian spirituality in general or a spirituality for mission. In Chapter VIII, I shall outline some of the more important cultural factors of the present-day world which will have to be considered in any relevant Christian spirituality and mission spirituality for our times.

The fourth source which forms Christian spirituality is *tradition*. Lest there be confusion on this point, the term tradition is used here in a wide sense as the sum and total of what man has inherited from the past. It consists of the matters of importance from the past which have special significance for the society concerned: the events, legal forms, art, customs, language, religious beliefs and practices, and the way of life, all of which give a particular society its roots in the past.

The Christian faith is lived in a community, the Church, which stands in a tradition. Scripture, theology, and cultural elements are handed down from generation to generation within the Church to form a tradition. Some elements from tradition are common to all Christians; for example, acceptance of the New Testament and liturgical worship of one form or another. Other elements are peculiar to the different forms which Christianity has taken during history, that is, to the churches; for example, a hierarchical structure, legal traditions, and certain theological positions.

---

40 *Ibid.*, pp. 227-30.

41 Norman K. Gottwald, *The Church Unbound* (Philadelphia: J.B. Lippincott, 1967), p. 170.

Therefore, there are traditions in Christian spirituality. Martyrdom was a dominant tradition in the early Church; monasticism is another such tradition. The monastic ideal has developed and taken many forms in the Church from the anchorites and cenobites of the Eastern Church, to the enclosed Benedictine form, to the mendicant orders in the Middle Ages, and down to the more active, apostolic orders of the modern period. Monasticism, or as it might more properly be called today, the religious life, forms one tradition, albeit with many facets, within Roman Catholic spirituality. The *devotio moderna* of the fourteenth and fifteenth centuries in northern Europe is another tradition within Christian spirituality. In Protestant spirituality, Pietism, which was in many ways a reaction against the dryness of Lutheran scholasticism in the seventeenth century, is another example of a tradition in spirituality. It is an important one for our purposes here inasmuch as the modern missionary movement in Protestantism is in many ways the fruit of Pietism. There are also traditions within Christian mysticism; for example, the mysticism of the Middle Ages in northern Europe as exemplified by Meister Eckhart, John Tauler, and John van Ruysbroeck stands in the traditions of the world-denying mysticism of Evagrius and Pseudo-Dionysius of the early Church. Finally, the traditions of Roman Catholic spirituality and devotional life differ from those of Protestantism which, in turn, differ from those of the Orthodox Churches.[42]

The notion of traditions of spirituality is of special importance in a consideration of a spirituality for mission. In the history of Christian spirituality basic changes in the socio-cultural situation have led to new theological insights and new forms of Christian living. Such was the case when Christianity became the state religion in the Empire and again when a society of towns began to develop in the Middle Ages. There comes a time, then, when the tradition must be re-evaluated in order to make the faith relevant to present cricumstances. Mission theology and mission spirituality in the Roman Catholic Church and in the Protestant churches have been the children of the discoveries of the sixteenth century, the reactionism of the post-Reformation era, Pietism, and the colonial patterns of Western dominance. The modern mission movement inherited these traditions. Today the cultural and theological climate has under-

[42] For a comparison, see Aumann et al., *Christian Spirituality East and West.*

gone significant change, and, accordingly, the theology and spirituality of mission, once valid, must now be reappraised.

Different Christian Spiritualities

The mention of different traditions within Christian spirituality and a specific spirituality for mission brings up one final point which should be mentioned in this chapter. It is the question of whether there is one or whether there are many Christian spiritualities. There has been some discussion in Roman Catholicism as to whether or not there are different Christian spiritualities.[43] Louis Bouyer has great reservations about speaking of Christian spirituality in the plural. His concentration is on the essential gospel spirituality as found in the New Testament. The gospel is one — there is but one faith, one baptism, one Lord, one Spirit, one God and Savior of all. For Bouyer, then, there can be but one Christian spirituality, and all differences in various spiritualities are on a relatively external and secondary level.[44]

It cannot be denied, however, that differences do exist within Christian spirituality, that there are great patterns of religious conduct and Christian living, and that there are definite schools and trends within Christian spirituality. The life style during times of persecution differed substantially from monastic spirituality; and, as the monastic form of life in the Church evolved into the religious life, certain definite schools and trends became manifest. Thus, Franciscan, Dominican, and Jesuit spiritualities can be distinguished. In modern times, spiritualities for various classes in the Church have been elaborated, for example, a spirituality for the laity as opposed to the religious form, spirituality for married people, and spirituality for working men. The position taken here is that these different schools and emphases can be called distinct spiritualities.

Christian spirituality is the life style of the Christian. Its goal is holiness, union with God, and full possession by the Father, through Christ in the Spirit.[45] Ultimately all Christians are called

---

[43] See, for example, Bouyer, *Introduction to Spirituality*, pp. 20-23; Jean Daniélou, "A propos d'une introduction à la vie spirituelle," *Etudes*, 108 (February, 1961), 270-74.

[44] Bouyer, *The Spirituality of the New Testament and the Fathers*, pp. x-xi: *idem*, *Introduction to Spirituality*, pp. 20-23.

[45] Gannon and Traub, *The Desert and the City*, p. 9.

to glorify God, and, imitating Christ, to be united through love and service with the Father. This is the one, ultimate goal of all Christian spirituality, and there is no form of Christian spirituality which does not aim at this. Furthermore, in order to attain this ultimate goal, any form which Christian spirituality takes must include those New Testament elements outlined above. In this sense, it is correct to say that there is but one Christian spirituality.

But there are different ways to reach the goal of Christian life. John Courtney Murray is recorded as having said that God would have each man wholly to be his witness, but not necessarily a witness to the whole of him.[46] Different spiritualities can be distinguished, then, as different ways of living the Christian faith and various means towards union with God. These differences are as distinct and important as the difference which exists between the contemplative monk in his monastery and the married man working in a factory. Ultimately, the same basic Christian elements will shape the life of each, but the way these values are concretized and lived in each case is quite distinct. In this sense, it can be said that they possess different spiritualities.

The Christian life does not exist in the abstract. It is lived in the interchange which takes place between the basic New Testament vision, the particular theological insights of an age, the very diverse demands and forces of particular cultural situations, and the traditions that men inherit. The way a person lives his life of faith, the way he chooses to imitate Christ and attain union with God, must differ, therefore, according to particular situations and circumstances of life. What distinguishes different spiritualities, then, is the way and the means they employ in order to attain the common goal towards which all Christians are oriented.[47] One may refer to these different means as external and secondary, as Bouyer does, but in the concrete, historical and cultural order the distinctions are quite clear and important. For example, the asceticism of the early centuries which stressed a flight from the world and pessimistic mistrust of matter differs vastly from modern forms of asceticism which are characterized by involvement in the world and an optimistic evaluation of the material universe. The love

---

[46] Gannon and Treub, *Ibid.*

[47] Joseph de Guibert, S.J., *The Jesuits: Their Spiritual Doctrine and Practice*, ed. George E. Ganss, S.J., trans. William J. Young, S.J. (Chicago: Institute of Jesuit Sources, 1964), p. 6.

and sacrifice entailed in building the world and bettering the lot of mankind can be just as demanding, if not more so, than the love and sacrifice required on the part of one who rejects the world.

In view of these distinctions, it is legitimate to speak of a spirituality for mission and a spirituality suited to Christians engaged in mission. Mission spirituality will be formed by all the elements outlined in this chapter. This book will stress the theological and cultural factors since it is in these areas that change has occurred and development is taking place, and, because of this, traditional forms of mission spirituality have become dated. The motives and goals for mission will have an important place in this study. Some of the past reasons for justifying missions have to be examined and re-expressed to fit the present situation. The next two chapters will offer examples of mission spirituality from the past. They will elaborate the theological positions and cultural situations of missionaries in the past and show the traditions of spirituality in which they lived. They will also offer points of contrast and comparison for a present-day theology and spirituality of mission which will be developed in later chapters.

III

MISSIONARY SPIRITUALITY: THE APOSTOLIC ERA TO THE RENAISSANCE

Both a unity and a diversity in Christian spirituality have been pointed out. Its unity resides in the fact that all Christians are called to glorify God by becoming one with the Father through Christ in the Spirit. The diversity of Christian spirituality comes from the fact that there are many ways of living one's life according to the basic Christian world view encompassed by these New Testament elements. Stated in another way, the unity of Christian spirituality would answer the question *what* a Christian does in order to attain his salvation in Christ; the diversity of Christian spirituality becomes manifest in answer to the question *how* the Christian does this — how he lives and expresses his faith, how he imitates Christ, how he loves and serves, how he prays and partakes in the sacramental-liturgical life of the Church, how he practices asceticism.

The missionary, one who desires to tell others of Christ to help bring them from non-belief to belief, lives his life in a way which differs from one whose primary role in life is not to engage in mission. For the greater part of the Church's history, Christianity has expanded through the efforts of men and women who have dedicated their lives completely to this goal. Accordingly, their spirituality and life styles possess characteristics which set them apart from those who have not chosen mission work.

The purpose of this and the following chapter is to examine the spirituality of some of the outstanding figures in mission history. It is not a history of mission spirituality; such a history, to the best of my knowledge, remains to be written. My intention is to present paradigms and models of mission spirituality as it has flourished in the Church. I shall discuss, first, some of the qualities of mission spirituality which marked the early centuries of the Church, since it is difficult to focus on any one personality in this era; then I shall present the spirituality of seven key figures in mission history: Columban, Boniface, Ramon Lull, Francis Xavier, Nikolaus Ludwig von Zinzendorf, William Carey, J. Hudson Taylor, and Charles de Foucauld. The reasons for concentrating on these men are two: first, they were all deeply spiritual men; second, each in his own way was a seminal, path-breaking figure in mission history who set a pattern which was followed by others.

Chapter II outlined four constitutive elements which blend to make up Christian spirituality — Scripture, theology, culture, and tradition. Christian spirituality is a complex reality which sees these elements concretized in the lives of individual Christians. In the models and patterns of mission spirituality presented here, I shall indicate how these elements influenced the missionary life style. Since motivation is highly important in determining how a missionary lives and what he does, I will, when possible, trace the motives of each of the figures discussed.

I have also mentioned the fact that spirituality can be considered in the concrete and in the abstract. Concretely, it is that incommunicable manner in which each Christian lives *the way* of faith, his Christian life style. Abstractly, spirituality consists of those generalized principles, patterns, and characteristics which govern one's Christian life style. In this and the following chapter, I will present both elements, but will place stress on the latter in order to determine what the important qualities of mission spirituality have been over the centuries so that they can be evaluated in the present-day situation.

Finally, something should be said about the method followed in this chapter and the next. Both primary and secondary sources have been used for most of the figures considered. Where possible, autobiographies, books, letters, sermons, and diaries written by each of the men discussed have been consulted. This presentation, however, is not intended to be a comprehensive study of each man. Rather, from the sources consulted I have outlined an adequate description of the salient characteristics of the spirituality of each of these outstanding missionaries.

Mission Spirituality After the Apostolic Age and Before Constantine

The Apostle Paul is the missionary par excellence in the first century. From his letters and the Acts of the Apostles, we have inherited an outline of the teaching, methods, successes, problems, and failures of the most outstanding missionary in the history of Christianity. What is more, these sources have left a magnificent description of Paul's spiritual life, a spirituality which is not only at the heart of missionary spirituality but also basic to all Christian spirituality. This chapter will not deal with the apostolic mission of Paul and the other early disciples of Jesus.[1] This decision might seem rather arbitrary. Is it possible at all to speak of Christian missions and mission spirituality without giving attention to Paul? Obviously, the answer is that it is not, any more than it is possible to consider Christianity without giving place to the mission and teachings of Jesus. However, respecting the uniqueness of the apostolic witness, I have chosen to prescind from the first century of Christianity and devote my attention to the spirituality of those who were engaged in spreading the gospel after the close of the age of the apostles.

The first section of this chapter, then, will consider mission in the second and third centuries before Constantine. This is a unique period in the growth of the Church, for, during it, Christianity moved from a sect within Judaism to become a universal religion confronting men in the different regions of the Roman Empire and in many places beyond the boundaries of the Empire. The period is important for two other reasons. First of all, it was the era of persecutions. I have already commented on the impact which persecution and martyrdom had upon Christian spirituality. At the end of this period with the reign of Constantine in the fourth century, the situation of Christians and the Church changed radically from one of proscription and persecution to one of acceptance and privilege. Speaking in broad generalizations, the period following Constantine was marked by whole groups of people becoming Christians; whereas, during the first three centuries, conversion to the faith seems to have been by individuals and families. It was individual change rather than the complete transformation of society which Christians envisaged.[2] The

---

[1] For a classic discussion of St. Paul the missionary, see Roland Allen's study first published in 1912: *Missionary Methods, St. Paul's or Ours?* (London: Lutterworth, 1968).

[2] James Thayer Addison, *The Medieval Missionary: A Study of the Conversion of Northern Europe, A.D. 500-1300,* Studies in the World Mission of Christianity, 11 (New York: International Missionary Council, 1936), p. 71; Kenneth Scott Latourette, *A History of the Expansion of Christianity,* I (New

second and third centuries, then, present a very different social and cultural situation for the Church when they are contrasted with the period following Constantine.

The second reason which makes the two pre-Constantinian centuries unique concerns those who were engaged in mission. It has been estimated that during this time Church and mission were largely identical.[3] Although there is evidence of full-time missionaries, the second and third centuries were not yet the era of professional missionaries in the sense in which the term has come to be understood traditionally. During these centuries, the ordinary Christian played a large role in the propagation of the faith. During the fourth century, monks and other professional missionaries began to take a prominent place in the spread of Christianity, and for the next thousand years these professionals dominated in the expansion of Christianity.[4]

As noted, spirituality is an extremely individual matter. In speaking of the second and third centuries, however, it is difficult to focus upon individuals. The reason is because very little is known about the actual persons who were engaged in the spread of Christianity during these years. Adolf Harnack, in the preface to his study of the expansion of Christianity in the first three centuries, was forced to observe that the primitive history of the Church's missions lies buried among legends which are largely worthless to the critical historian. When it comes to the second century, Harnack observed, we know next to nothing of any details concerning the missionaries and their labors.[5]

York: Harper and Brothers, 1937-44), 296, 365; hereafter this work will be cited: Latourette, *Expansion,* plus the volume number and page.

One notable exception to individual conversions and a prominent example of group conversion in the early Church is the Armenian Church. Towards the close of the third century, the people of this territory were converted en masse under the leadership of Gregory the Illuminator and with the support of the state. See Latourette, *Expansion,* I, 223; and Harold R. Cook, *Historic Patterns of Church Growth: A Study of Five Churches* (Chicago: Moody, 1971), Chapter I.

[3] Joseph Schmidlin, D.D., *Catholic Mission History,* trans. Matthias Braun, S.V.D. (Techny, Ill.: Mission Press, S.V.D., 1933), p. 59; M.H. Marrou, "L'Expansion missionnaire dans l'Empire romain et hors de l'Empire au cours des cinq premiers siècles," *Histoire universelle des missions catholiques,* ed. S. Delacroix, I (Paris: Librairie Grund, 1956-58), 62.

[4] Latourette, *Expansion,* I, 201-05; II, 9.

[5] Adolf Harnack, *The Expansion of Christianity in the First Three Centuries,* trans. James Moffatt, Theological Translation Library, 19, I (New York: G.P. Putnam's Sons, 1905), viii-ix, 440.

Kenneth Scott Latourette acknowledges the same lack of information concerning the period before Constantine. Our knowledge of this period, he says, is scant and meager and it is impossible to reconstruct even the main outlines of the manner in which the faith spread during these centuries. Concerning Asia Minor, which according to Harnack's judgement was the most Christian of all the Roman provinces at the time of Constantine,[6] Latourette says that, except for the work of Paul about which we have only imperfect knowledge, there is almost no information of the processes by which Christianity spread or of the missionaries who propagated it.[7] By and large, then, it is impossible to arrive at the personal spirituality of those who engaged in mission during these centuries.

Despite this frustrating lack of information, however, it is worthwhile to examine what historical evidence there is, and so pick out the trends and directions which can be observed and reflect upon the spirituality and motivation which are present. It was a unique period of Church history, a period when the Church was not accepted by, and had few and very tenuous links with, the centers of political power in the world. In this respect, it was a period which might be similar to what the Church will have to live with in many places in the present century and, therefore, it is a period which can enlighten us concerning the Christian life style and witness in a situation where believers are a cultural minority.

Those who have studied evangelization in the early Church acknowledge the fact that there is evidence of *wandering, full-time missionaries* or apostles who went from place to place during the second and third centuries preaching the faith.[8] Most of the evidence for the existence of this class is based upon the *Didache* (c. 160-170) and Hermas (c. 100-140). It is corroborated by Origen (c. 184-254) and Eusebius (263-339). Thus, Origen writes: "Christians do all in their power to spread the faith all over the world. Some of them accordingly make it the business of their life to wander not only from city to city but from township to township and village to village, in order to gain fresh converts for the

---

[6] Harnack, *ibid.*, 11, p. 457.

[7] Latourette, *Expansion,* I, 84-89.

[8] See Harnack, *The Expansion of Christianity in the First Three Centuries,* I, 398-458; Latourette, *Expansion,* I, 114-16; Michael Green, *Evangelism in the Early Church* (Grand Rapids, Mich.: William B. Eerdmans, 1970), pp. 167-69.

Lord."[9] The historian Eusebius speaks of those who divided their goods among the needy and "set out on long journeys, performing the office of *evangelists,* eagerly striving to preach Christ to those who as yet had never heard the word of faith, and to deliver to them the holy gospels."[10] Concerning the lives of these wandering preachers, two characteristics are set down by the *Didache* and mentioned by Origen and Eusebius: they were to be penniless and were to engage in indefatigable missionary activity by never settling down.[11] From early sources, therefore, it is known that there were a number of wandering missionaries totally dedicated to the propagation of the faith. Lost in the shadows of antiquity, however, are the identification of these itinerant preachers and further details concerning their life styles.

Since mission and Church were closely integrated in the early centuries, the lack of information concerning full-time missionaries, in the sense in which modern churchmen have understood them, is not surprising. *All classes of Christians* seem to have been engaged in the task of forwarding the faith. As the offices of bishop and presbyter evolved in the second century, the men who held them could not but become directly engaged in the spread of the faith. Ignatius of Antioch tells his fellow bishop Polycarp to press on and exhort all men that they may be saved. Irenaeus, as bishop, preached in the villages as well as the towns of Gaul both in Greek, the language of the educated, and in the vernacular.[12] Pantaenus, the founder of the school at Alexandria in the second century was first a missionary to "India." Justin operated a school at Rome and his pupil Tatian set up another school. These schools were not exclusively devoted to the cultivation of Christian learning within the Church; they were also intentionally set up as pastoral and evangelistic agencies.[13]

To approach the early centuries of the Church and attempt to identify those who were professionally engaged in spreading Christianity is to operate from a set of categories and presuppositions which are more those of modern Christianity than early Christianity. One point that the historians of the early Church's

---

[9] Quoted from Harnack, *The Expansion of Christianity in the First Three Centuries,* I, 436.

[10] *Ibid.,* p. 437.

[11] *Ibid.,* pp. 435-38.

[12] See Green, *Evangelism in the Early Church,* p. 170.

[13] *Ibid.,* pp. 171-72.

mission agree upon is the fact that the greatest force in the spread of Christianity through the Roman Empire was the ordinary, non-ordained Christian. Harnack states that the most numerous and successful missionaries of the Christian religion were not the regular teachers but the Christians themselves by dint of their loyalty and courage. Everyone who confessed the faith proved of service to its propagation; therefore, the great mission of Christianity was in reality accomplished by means of informal missionaries.[14] Latourette agrees with this: the chief agents in the expansion of Christianity were not those who made it a profession or a major part of their occupation, but men and women who earned their livelihood in some purely secular manner and spoke of their faith to those whom they met in this natural fashion.[15] Michael Green concludes his study of evangelism in the early Church with the same idea:

> One of the most striking features in evangelism in the early days was the people who engaged in it. Communicating the faith was not regarded as the preserve of the very zealous or of the officially designated evangelist. Evangelism was the prerogative and the duty of every Church member. We have seen apostles and wandering prophets, nobles and paupers, intellectuals and fishermen all taking part enthusiastically in this the primary task committed by Christ to his Church. The ordinary people of the Church saw it as their job: Christianity was supremely a lay movement, spread by informal missionaries. The clergy of the Church saw it as their responsibility, too: bishops and presbyters, together with doctors of the Church like Origen and Clement, and philosophers like Justin and Tatian, saw the propagation of the gospel as their prime concern. They seem not to have allowed the tasks of teaching, caring and administering to make them too busy to bring individuals and groups from unbelief to faith. The spontaneous outreach of the total Christian community gave immense impetus to the movement from the very outset.
>
> What is more, this infectious enthusiasm on the part of such diverse people of differing ages, backgrounds, sex, and cultures was backed up by the quality of their lives. Their love, their joy, their changed habits and progressively transformed characters gave great weight to what they had to say. Their community life, though far from perfect,

[14] Harnack, *The Expansion of Christianity in the First Three Centuries,* I, 458-61.

[15] Latourette, *Expansion,* I, 116.

> as Christian writers were constantly complaining, was nevertheless sufficiently different and impressive to attract notice, to invite curiosity, and to inspire discipleship in an age that was as pleasure-conscious, as materialistic and as devoid of serious purpose as our own. Paganism saw in early Christianity a quality of living, and supremely of dying, which could not be found elsewhere.[16]

Green's reference to the quality of living and dying gives an important clue concerning the life styles and spirituality of those who spread the gospel in the early centuries of the Church. Christian theology proclaimed that they were new men in Christ, and this belief could not but determine the way they lived the faith. John Chrysostom in the fourth century was convinced that the most effective means for furthering the Christian mission was the example of Christian living. There would be no more heathens if Christians would be true Christians.[17] This strong connection between Christian belief and behavior runs through Christian literature.[18] The Christian mission, Harnack observes, was reinforced and positively advanced by the behavior of Christian men and women.[19]

How can the *life styles* of these countless men and women who did so much to spread Christianity in the early centuries be described? There is no lack of testimony and evidence on this point. It can be summarized under five categories: the transformation and moral uprightness of their personal lives, their fellowship and social concern for others, their joy, their endurance under hardship and persecution, and the power which they exercised by virtue of their faith.[20]

Cautious of simplified generalizations, Latourette remarks that, although the experience of thoroughgoing moral and spiritual renewal was probably shared by only a minority of Christians, enough of them had it to give a tone to the Christian community.[21] A whole series of illustrations can be produced to indicate that the high level of morality enjoined by Christianity directly promoted

---

[16] Green, *Evangelism in the Early Church*, pp. 274-75.

[17] See Latourette, *Expansion*, I, 192.

[18] See Green, *Evangelism in the Early Church*, pp. 179-80.

[19] Harnack, *The Expansion of Christianity in the First Three Centuries*, I, 479.

[20] Green, *Evangelism in the Early Church*, pp. 178-93.

[21] Latourette, *Expansion*, I, 167.

the interests of the Christian mission.[22] Christians stood out for their sharing of material goods, their restraint in sexual matters, their love for others and hatred of cruelty, their civil obedience and good citizenship. They did not expose infants; they did not swear; they refused to have anything to do with idolatry and its by-products. Such lives had great impact on a society and culture which often held values which were quite the opposite.

The piety and spirituality of the early Christians were not merely personal. The fellowship and social concern with which the Church went out to others transcended the barriers of race, sex, class, and education. This was an enormous attraction. With copious citations from early sources, Harnack lists ten areas of the Church's humanitarian concern during this period: almsgiving, the support of teachers and officials, the support of widows and orphans, care of the sick, infirm and disabled, concern for prisoners, burial of the dead, the care of slaves, help for those visited by calamities, providing employment, hospitality for travelers.[23] Such works were important means of attracting converts to the Church.[24]

It is to be remembered that this took place during two centuries of cyclic harassment and persecution. The endurance which Christians displayed during these times and the joy to which their lives gave witness were other powerful forces leading to the spread of the gospel. Tertullian's famous dictum is often quoted in this regard: "Plures efficimur quotiens metimur a vobis; semen est sanguis Christianorum," "The oftener we are mowed down by you, the larger grow our numbers. The blood of Christians is seed."[25] The Acts of the Martyrs record that the deaths of Christians sometimes resulted in their executioners becoming Christians, and, even when this did not occur, the way they died convinced men of the innocence of their creed. The sheer joyous enthusiasm of the early Christains enhanced their absolute claims for Jesus Christ. If Christ really was the only way to God, if there was salvation in no other, it is not surprising that Christians should commend him with such enthusiasm. Jesus had promised joy as a permanent possession, a joy which no man could take from the Church, and

---

[22] See Harnack, *The Expansion of Christianity in the First Three Centuries,* I, 263 ff.

[23] *Ibid.,* pp. 190-249.

[24] Latourette, *Expansion,* I, 186.

[25] Quoted from Harnack, *The Expansion of Christianity in the First Three Centuries,* I, 458.

the Christians of the early centuries seemed to demonstrate that this was true. The joyous death of Ignatius of Antioch is one outstanding example of this spirit. If the gospel could inspire men with such perseverance, enthusiasm, and joy, Christianity was assured of a very serious hearing.

One final point which deserves mention in a description of the life styles of those early Christians is the power that went with the proclamation of the Christian message, a power which seems to have proved itself in healings and exorcisms. Christians of those times went out into the world as exorcists and healers as well as preachers. This was a factor of incalculable importance for the advance of the gospel during times which had inadequate medical services and among peoples who believed in the presence of demonic forces of every kind. Harnack observes that exorcism was a very powerful method for mission and propaganda in a world which was seen to be filled with demons. In this situation Christians had at their command weapons which were invincible.[26]

The final question which might be asked regarding the missionary efforts of the early Christians concerns their *motivation*. Michael Green outlines the outstanding motives. In his judgement, the main motive for evangelism in the early Church was a sense of gratitude, devotion, and dedication to the Lord who had rescued men and given them a new life. This is definitely a theological rather than a merely humanitarian motive — they spread the message because of the overwhelming experience of the love of God which they had received through Jesus Christ.[27] The second motive which stands out is the responsibility which Christians felt before God to live lives consistent with their profession of the faith.[28] Finally, the Christians of the pre-Constantinian centuries had a great sense of concern for those who did not accept Christ. In second-century writings there is a greater emphasis on rewards and punishments and the desire for eternal life. Green notes that this lively awareness of the peril of those without Christ was a major evangelistic motive during this period.[29]

In this description of the missionary motives of the early centuries it should be observed that the "Great Commission" in

---

[26] Harnack, *The Expansion of Christianity in the First Three Centuries*, I, 152-80, especially pp. 160-61.

[27] Green, *Evangelism in the Early Church*, pp. 236-43.

[28] *Ibid.*, p. 243.

[29] *Ibid.*, p. 251.

Matthew 28:18-20 receives relatively little attention. Among the Apostolic Fathers it appears only in a spurious recension of Ignatius, and Irenaeus quotes it once in a context where he is speaking about the descent of the Spirit on the Church.[30] This is interesting in view of future developments in missionary motivation. What was important during these times, Green notes, was the example of Christ and the privilege and the responsibility which Christians felt to speak of him to others.[31]

Medieval Missions

In his *History of the Expansion of Christianity,* Kenneth Scott Latourette describes the period between the years 500 and 1500 as the "thousand years of uncertainty," a period usually referred to as the Middle Ages. As for most historical periods, these dates are chosen rather arbitrarily. The time under consideration is that period between the decline of classical Roman and Greek civilization and the expansion of European influence around the globe following Columbus' voyage in 1492. In any account of the history of Christian missions, this period stands in contrast to the spread of the Church in the early centuries before Constantine and the missions of the Church which followed the discoveries of the fifteenth and sixteenth centuries. The remainder of this chapter will be devoted to key examples of the Church's mission from Western Europe. Nothing will be said about the missions and missionaries from the Eastern branches of Christianity: the Greek Orthodox churches, the Jacobites, the Armenians, and the Nestorians.[32]

There is considerably more information about the men and women who spread Christianity in the Middle Ages than there is concerning their counterparts in the first three centuries of the

---

[30] Green, *Ibid.,* pp. 239-40.

[31] *Ibid.,* pp. 240-43.

[32] Although they did not have the same long lasting effects as the missions in the West, the missionary enterprises carried on in the East are a fascinating study. There is, for example, the remaıkable mission of the Nestorians in China from the seventh to the ninth centuries. Inaugurated by A-lo-pên about the year 635, this mission continued until its eradication in the middle of the ninth century. See Kenneth Scott Latourette, *A History of Christian Missions in China* (New York: Macmillan, 1929), pp. 51-60; Raymond L. Oppenheim, *The First Nestorian Mission to China and Its Failure* (Berkeley, Calif.: Shires Bookstore, 1971).

Church. Latourette has described this period as the time of the professional missionaries. Although our knowledge is incomplete with regard to all the ways in which Christianity spread during these centuries, it is certain that men who gave the major part of their time to missionary work played a much larger role during this period than during the first three centuries.[33] Significantly, most of these full-time missionaries were monks. Although initially missionary work was not an integral part of monasticism, because most men and women entered monasteries to be free of the world and to labor towards their own perfection, as monastic life came to be considered the ideal form of Christian living, the monks almost naturally if not by necessity became evangelists among non-Christian peoples.[34]

Monastic spirituality was characteristic of the life styles of these medieval missionaries. They led lives marked by prayer and austere discipline, celibacy, devotion to the hours of the Office and the Mass, a tradition of learning, and an appreciation of manual labor. In many cases the monk-missionaries established monasteries which became centers not only for the propagation and strengthening of the faith but also for the education and the economic and social welfare of the people in the nearby territories.

The merger of the monastic vocation and the missionary vocation is important in the history of Christian missions. Just as until the modern period after 1500 the main current of development in Christian spirituality in the West flowed through the monastic tradition, so too missionary spirituality in the Church followed the monastic tradition. This tradition was inaugurated in the West by the Benedictines, rendered more suitable for active work by the mendicants of the Late Middle Ages, and perfected again by the active orders in the modern Church such as the Jesuits. There is no underestimating its contribution. The missionaries from the orders led lives of prayer, self-discipline, and scholarship in centrally organized communities which gave them the ability and freedom to range over the world in witness to the gospel.

On the other hand, one can question whether the merger of the monastic and missionary vocations did not have some draw-

---

[33] Latourette, *Expansion,* II, 9.

[34] *Ibid.,* pp. 17, 152, 227; Schmidlin, *Catholic Mission History,* p. 123.

backs. For example, the form of Christianity instilled by the monks in the Middle Ages had a strong monastic flavor to it. The perfect Christian was the ideal monk.[35] Not until the Protestant Reformation in the sixteenth century and until more recent times in the Catholic Church did a lay spirituality develop.[36] Furthermore, the merger of these two vocations created a separate class in the Church whose responsibility, among others, was to engage professionally in the propagation of the faith. The necessity and privilege of spreading the gospel, therefore, was taken from those Christians, both clergy and laity, who were not monks. It is interesting to speculate how Christianity would have spread and what forms of Church order might have existed had the missionary vocation not become identified with the tradition of the monastery and religious orders.

In addition to the fact that the majority of missionaries during the Middle Ages were monks, several other characteristics of the Church's missions during this period can be pointed out. The first is the fact that, in contrast with the early Church, mass conversions became more the rule than the exception during this period. Preachers of Christianity would often concentrate upon the kings or leaders of a particular people, and, once they had accepted the faith, the people under them would follow. Although this form of acceptance of Christ is not the ideal, since deep personal commitment on the part of those entering the Church was often non-existent, it would be precipitous to condemn the phenomenon too hastility. In truth, conversion en masse offers an example of how the social and cultural structures of a society influence its religious life and grasp of the faith. Many of the people whom the medieval missionaries encountered were living in societies in which the individual was dominated by the tribe or clan. In this setting, religion was an affair of the whole people and it was natural for them to enter Christianity in a group led by those whom they were accustomed to follow. Given this

---

[35] Latourette, *Expansion*, II, 18.

[36] In the Catholic Church it was Vatican II which officially resolved the problem of the religious life being a higher state of life than the lay state. The Council affirmed the fact that all Christians are called to the state of perfection and to the apostolate. See "Dogmatic Constitution on the Church," Section 40; "Decree on the Apostolate of the Laity," Section 2, *The Documents of Vatican II*, eds. Walter M. Abbott, S.J. and Joseph Gallagher (New York: Guild Press, America Press, Association Press, 1966).

context, it was practical for the missionary to concentrate his attention upon the leaders in the hope that once converted they would bring their people into the Church with them.[37]

Because conversion to the faith tended to be in terms of groups instead of individuals, a second characteristic of the missions of these centuries is the fact that the faith received was shallow and superficial, often little more than a veneer over the more deeply rooted indigenous religious beliefs and practices of the people brought into the Church in large numbers.[38] Columban and Boniface were constantly confronted with this problem. One historian estimates that from fourth century Italy to tenth century Yorkshire or Normandy the religious and social attitudes of the *pagani* were unaffected by the essentials of the Christian faith, and, in reality, a Christian paganism existed. By the year 1000 Europe was Christian, but only a shadow of the Christian symbol had been cast; the real conversion was still to follow.[39] Yet it is important to note, as Schmidlin does, that, although the motives for accepting Christianity were often shallow in character and conversion was superficial and incomplete, the process of Christianization in Europe continued without any serious opposition from paganism.[40]

Joseph Schmidlin distinguishes two divisions of the mission and missionary methods of the Early Middle Ages in Europe: the vocational mission and the Frankish imperial mission.[41] The former type which was carried on by the Irish and Anglo-Saxon missionaries is distinguished by the fact that, although these missionaries sought the approval and support of kings and rulers, they were relatively independent of their power and carried on their work in a more individual and spiritual fashion through apostolic preaching. Boniface is an outstanding example of this type. In the imperial mission, on the other hand, it was not the work

---

[37] Addison, *The Medieval Missionary,* Chapter II; Latourette, *Expansion,* II, 15-16; Schmidlin, *Catholic Mission History,* pp. 123, 181.

[38] Latourette, *Expansion,* II, 18; Schmidlin, *Catholic Mission History,* pp. 181, 188.

[39] L.G.D. Baker, "The Shadow of the Christian Symbol," *The Mission of the Church and the Propagation of the Faith,* ed. G.J. Cuming, Papers read at the Seventh Summer Meeting and the Eighth Winter Meeting of the Ecclesiastical History Society (Cambridge, England: At the University Press, 1970), pp. 27-28.

[40] Schmidlin, *Catholic Mission History,* p. 182.

[41] *Ibid.,* pp. 181-82.

of the missionary but the will of the ruler that predominated. In this form, every method of conversion seemed justified — lures, threats, compulsion, and force. The use of compulsion by rulers, usually with a view towards political dominance, marked a new and unfortunate stage in the methods used to spread Christianity.

Charlemagne was a classic example of this type of mission when he conquered and "converted" the Saxons at the end of the eighth and beginning of the ninth centuries. Latourette estimates that never before had the adherence of people to the Christian religion been brought about by so drastic a use of the mailed fist.[42] Not long afterwards, the same methods were used in central Europe where baptism was imposed by the sword in the clash between races and peoples, Teutons and Slavs, Teutons and Finns.[43] Finally, in the thirteenth century this method was employed most harshly by the Teutonic Knights in the north of Germany where it was stipulated in at least one treaty between conquerors and the conquered that those not baptized should receive the rite within a month, that those who declined should be banished from the company of the Christians, and that any who relapsed into paganism should be reduced to slavery.[44] The marriage of cross and sword was performed and consummated in the Middle Ages.

Last of all, something should be said about the role of the papacy in medieval missions.[45] Much has been made of Gregory the Great's sending of Augustine to England in the year 596 as an example of the papacy entering directly into the inauguration of missionary work. During the greater part of the Middle Ages, however, the part played by the papacy was neither creative nor dominant, save for a few exceptions such as Gregory and Innocent III and his followers in the twelfth century.[46] This is not to say that the pope did not have an important role in the missionary work of the Church. Rome acted as a center of reference and unity throughout the period. A good illustration of this is Boniface's correspondence with four different popes in the eighth

---

[42] Latourette, *Expansion,* II, 105; Schmidlin, *Catholic Mission History,* 172-78.

[43] Latourette, *Expansion,* II, 153.

[44] *Ibid.,* p. 205.

[45] For a study of the role of the papacy in early missionary work see André V. Seumois, O.M.I., *La Papauté et les missions au cours des six premiers siècles: methodologie antiques et orientations modernes* (Paris: Eglise Vivante, 1951).

century, letters which contain concrete and vivid examples of the problems and questions posed to Rome and answered in detail by the popes.[47]

Celtic Monasticism and Columban

In the history of the Church's missions, the missionary movement from Ireland to Europe in the seventh century offers one of the most interesting studies. For reasons which are not too clear, the Church in Ireland in the Early Middle Ages developed in a way which was different from the Roman form of Christianity on the Continent. In creed and allegiance it was one with Rome, but in structure and practice it was centered around the monastery rather than the bishop and the diocese, and it developed traditions and practices different from those of Roman Catholicism. Some historians conjecture that Irish monasticism owes something to the pre-Christian clan structure of Irish society which, with the advent of Christianity, lent itself to focus upon the monastery instead of the bishop. Bishops there were, but their role was to ordain priests who were usually subject to the local abbots. Irish Christianity, then, was dominated by a monasticism which was distinguished by several characteristics: an esteem for scholarship; a rather severe yet vigorous religious discipline; traditions which differed from Rome, for example, the celebration of liturgical feasts and seasons and the discipline of penance; and an intriguing phenomenon which makes the Irish unique in the history of missions — a wanderlust which urged men to leave home to pilgrimage in other lands for the sake of Christ and in imitation of Christ.

It is this last characteristic which is important for mission spirituality in the sixth and seventh centuries. The Irish monks left home not primarily to preach the gospel and bring others into the Church, but to practice asceticism and achieve self-perfection. They viewed Christ himself as a pilgrim upon the earth, and, in imitation, they became pilgrims for Christ in foreign places. Caught up in love for Christ and following the injunction given to Abraham (Gen. 12:1), they left all for Christ to bring

---

[46] Addison, *The Medieval Missionary*, Chapter IV.

[47] See Ephraim Emerton (trans. and ed.), *The Letters of Saint Boniface* (New York: Columbia University, 1940).

their form of monastic Christianity to the European continent. Columban (543-615) is the foremost example of this type of missionary.[48]

He was born about the year 543 in the province of Leinster in Ireland. Little is known about his early years except that, following the advice of an aged anchoress who regretted that she herself could not undertake a pilgrimage for Christ, Columban left home to become a monk notwithstanding the protestations of his mother, who threw herself on the floor in front of him in a vain attempt to stop him. He was eventually accepted at the famous monastery of Bangor where he was ordained and became a lecturer in the monastic school. Jonas, his biographer, says that at about the age of forty-five he began to desire to go abroad into strange lands in obedience to the command of the Lord to Abraham. Accordingly, with twelve monks he left Ireland for the Continent and the lands of the Merovingians in France. About the year 591, Columban founded his most famous monastery at Luxeuil in the Vosges. Others were founded before and afterwards. Because of his passionate and uncompromising nature, he gradually ran into difficulties both with the bishops of Gaul due to his free-lancing, Irish type of apostolate and such issues as the tonsure and the date of Easter, and with the Merovingians because he refused to condone King Theuderich's concubinage. Eventually he was forced into exile in the year 610 to the lands of the Lombards in Northern Italy where he died on November 23, 615.[49]

---

48 For the Irish missionaries see: Addison, *The Medieval Missionary*, pp. 4-7; Eleanor Duckett, *The Wandering Saints* (London: Collins, 1959); *idem, The Gateway to the Middle Ages* (New York: Macmillan, 1938), Chapter IX; Latourette, *Expansion*, II, 36-39; Brendan Lehane, *The Quest of Three Abbots: Pioneers of Ireland's Golden Age* (London: John Murray, 1968), pp. 101-11, 184.

49 For Columban see: Jonas, *The Life of St. Columban*, in *Translations and Reprints from the Original Sources of European History*, II, No. 7 (Philadelphia: University of Pennsylvania, c. 1902); Marguerite Marie Dubois, *Saint Columban: A Pioneer of Western Civilization*, trans. James O'Carroll (Dublin: M.H. Gill and Son, 1961); Duckett, *The Wandering Saints*, pp. 118-39; Lehane, *The Quest of Three Abbots*, pp. 147-88; Francis MacMannus, *Saint Columban* (New York: Sheed and Ward, 1962); G.S.M. Walker (ed.), *Sancti Columbani Opera*, Scriptores Latini Hiberniae, 2 (Dublin: Dublin Institute for Advanced Studies, 1957); G.S.M. Walker, "St. Columban: Monk or Missionary?" *The Mission of the Church and the Propagation of the Faith*, ed. G.J. Cuming, pp. 39-44.

It has been stated that the missionary work of the Irish monks has been exaggerated inasmuch as their travel to other lands was primarily for ascetic motives rather than for evangelistic purposes, and their main contribution resides in the fact that they founded monasteries.[50] This observation makes a point, but it does not seem to lessen the importance of the missionary contribution made by the wandering Celts such as Columban. Although they were primarily interested in personal perfection, the historical situation forced them to become missionaries.

G. S. M. Walker, who has edited the works of Columban, sums up the man in this way: "He was a missionary through circumstance, a monk by vocation; a contemplative, too frequently driven to action by the vices of the world; a pilgrim, on the road to Paradise."[51] In the case of Columban, Walker estimates, the vocation of monastic pilgrim and missionary merged and both became subordinate to the spiritual perfection of the monk. Walking the road of life towards eternal glory, the pilgrim Columban could not but reach out to others on the journey.[52] There is ample evidence that he engaged in direct evangelization when he saw the debilitated state of Christendom and the practices of paganism both in Gaul and in Lombardy.[53] Columban, then, exemplifies the merger of the monastic and missionary vocations.

The importance of Columban's monasticism for the faith and spirituality of Europe is hard to overestimate. For example, it is certain that the practices of personal, auricular confession and detailed, rigorous penances owe their origin to Luxeuil and the monasteries which stood in the Celtic tradition. These practices had great influence upon Roman Catholicism. Walker estimates that in the seventh century no less than fifty-three abbeys, nunneries, and hermitages observed the rules set down by Columban.[54] Although his form of Celtic monasticism would gradually be re-

---

[50] Lucien Musset, "La Conversion des Germains," *Histoire universelle des missions catholiques*, ed. S. Delacroix, I, 111-12.

[51] Walker (ed.), *Sancti Columbani Opera*, p. xxxii; *idem*, "St. Columban: Monk or Missionary?" *The Mission of the Church and the Propagation of the Faith*, ed. G.J. Cuming, pp. 39-40.

[52] Walker, "St. Columban: Monk or Missionary," *The Mission of the Church and the Propagation of the Faith*, ed. G.J. Cuming, pp. 41-44.

[53] See Columban, Letter 4.5; references to Columban's Letters, Sermons, and Rules are from Walker (ed.), *Sancti Columbani Opera;* see also Jonas, *The Life of St. Columban*, Nn. 10, 56; Dubois, *Saint Columban*, pp. 20-21, 68-69.

[54] Walker (ed.), *Sancti Columbani Opera*, p. xxxiii.

placed by the less harsh Benedictine form, its effect upon Europe was considerable. One biographer says that to Columban must certainly be given the honor of raising up countless saints, civilizers, scholars, and apostles to whom France, Switzerland, and Italy owe their rebirth in the faith.[55]

The key theme in Columban's life style and spirituality, and in the lives of those monks who followed his rule and example, is the theme of pilgrimage (*peregrinatio pro Christo*). Jonas states that this was the motivating factor behind his departure for Gaul; and Columban himself states in one of his letters that he entered Gaul as a pilgrim for the sake of Christ.[56] Again and again in his writings, Columban compares life to a roadway towards eternity upon which men travel and suffer for a time while looking constantly towards the end of the journey, eternal glory. Like a roadway, life is doubtful and uncertain; it is full of deceptions, shadows, and mirages. Therefore, man must not look on what he is but upon what he shall be. The traveller is not to love the road more than the homeland to which he is moving. Everything earthly is foreign to man and nothing here is to be loved since nothing lasts. The pilgrim in life, therefore, must travel lightly and poorly and not become entangled in worldly things since all earthly things are foreign to him.[57]

At other times, the theme of warfare complements the theme of pilgrimage — men are on pilgrimage for the Lord; life is like a battle; but Christ is the Captain of our war and after a brief period of struggle we will be crowned forever.[58] There is one line in his second letter which sums up the spirituality of Columban the monk-pilgrim-missionary: "He who says that he believes in Christ, ought also himself to walk even as Christ walked — that is, both poor and humble and ever preaching the truth under the persecution of mankind."[59] Fascinated by Christ, Columban walked the pilgrimage of life letting the light of his example as much as his missionary preaching attract non-believers to Christianity and believers to better Christian lives. This prayer appears at the end of one of his sermons:

---

[55] Dubois, *Saint Columban*, p. 99.
[56] Columban, Letter 2.6.
[57] Columban, Sermons 3.2, 4.2, 6.1, 8.2, 9.2.
[58] Columban, Sermons 4.3, 10.3; Letter 4.6.
[59] Columban, Letter 2.3.

> Lord, grant me, I pray Thee in the name of Jesus Christ Thy Son, my God, that love which knows no fall, so that my lamp may feel the kindling touch and know no quenching, may burn for me and for others may give light. Do Thou, Christ, deign to kindle our lamps, our Saviour most sweet to us, that they may shine continually in Thy temple, and receive perpetual light from Thee the Light perpetual, so that our darkness may be enlightened, and yet the world's darkness be driven from us.[60]

The specifics of the life style of this monk-pilgrim-missionary are set down in his Rules — a life of mortification following the injunction laid down by Paul to empty oneself as Christ emptied himself (Phil. 2:5-8); a life of fasting and penance; a life of daily prayer, daily toil, and daily reading; a disdain of riches; the purging of vices; cultivation of the most perfect and perpetual love of God, and affection for divine things which follows on the forgetfulness of earthly things; a life of complete denial of one's own will: not disagreeing in mind, not speaking as one pleases, not going anywhere with complete freedom.[61]

In summary, then, Columban's spirituality offers a clear example of the Celtic monk-missionary. From Scripture he had gained an intimate love and knowledge of Christ. From the tradition and culture of Ireland and Celtic monasticism he inherited a way of life suited to personal holiness and concern for reaching out to others. From the same source he received and developed a theology which placed great importance on the transitoriness of this life and a longing for eternity. This eschatology may not be totally acceptable to men of our times, but for his times and in his tradition it did much to bring men to Christ and set their values on him above all. Until recent times, it has always been a strong undercurrent in much missionary theology and spirituality.

Boniface

The next figure I shall consider is a man who, according to Christopher Dawson, "had a deeper influence on the history of

[60] Columban, Sermon, 12.3.

[61] Columban, Rules, in Walker, *Sancti Columbani Opera*, pp. 123-43.

Europe than any Englishman who has ever lived"[62] — Winfrid, better known as Boniface (675-754). If Columban is the outstanding figure in mission history during the early seventh century, Boniface deserves this title for the first half of the eighth century. The probable date of his birth is 675, at Exeter in England. He entered the abbey of Nursling in the diocese of Winchester when he was rather young. After his years of study, he was placed in charge of the abbey school and ordained priest in 705. As was the case with so many of his monastic brothers and predecessors in England and Ireland, he felt a desire to join the stream of missionaries going from the British Isles to the Continent. Unlike the Irish monks, however, Boniface's motives seem to have been primarily evangelistic and not ascetic. His first mission to the Continent was undertaken when he was about forty years old. He traveled from London to Frisia where Willibrord, another Englishman, was laboring. The stay was frustrating and lasted about a year and a half.

Boniface undertook his next mission trip to Europe convinced of the necessity of diplomacy and set upon getting the approval of Rome and Pope Gregory II as well as the support of the Carolingian Mayors of the Palace. In May of 719 he received a papal commission to go forth with God's guidance "to those peoples who are still in the bonds of infidelity . . . to teach them the service of the kingdom of God by persuasion of the truth in the name of Christ, the Lord our God."[63] Boniface traveled through Bavaria and Thuringia and eventually evangelized in Hesse where he is said to have baptized large numbers. In 722 he again went to Rome, was consecrated bishop by Pope Gregory III, and returned to Germany where he received an extensive diocese with no fixed boundaries. The famous incident of felling the oak dedicated to Thor occurred in Hesse in 723. Laboring in Thuringia a year later, Boniface found the Christianity which existed there to be in a sorry state and he labored for reforms. His methods were not new but his genius for organization rendered them more successful. He addressed himself to the leaders

---

[62] Quoted from George William Greenaway, *Saint Boniface: Three Biographical Studies for the Twelfth Centenary Festival* (London: Adam and Charles Black, 1955), p. 2.

[63] Boniface, Letter 4; references to Boniface's Letters are from Ephraim Emerton (trans. and intro.), *The Letters of Saint Boniface* (New York: Columbia University, 1940).

and upper classes; once these groups were won, the masses followed. He was able to attract others to help him, and with these companions he traveled the rivers and roads spreading the faith, founding monastic centers, and enlisting others in the mission. In the meantime Rome made him an archbishop. In 738 Boniface paid his third visit to Rome and then left to organize the Bavarian Church in 739, and the Frankish Church starting about 742. In 744 it was proposed that he become Archbishop of Cologne, but this fell through and he was made Archbishop of Mainz a little later. Nearing the end of his life, he returned to Frisia, the territory where he began his missionary career years before. There, about the year 754, shielding himself with a copy of the Gospels, Boniface was martyred by the non-Christian Frisians.[64]

Like Columban, Boniface was a monk, and, similar to Columban, Boniface was not sent on his mission to Germany — it was a personal enterprise. There is only a hint of the Irish wanderlust about his journey to Europe. Willibald, his biographer, notes that, although he had an outstanding career before him in England, Boniface "began, with great care and solicitude, to hasten more intently to other things, and to shun the society of his relatives and connexions, and to desire foreign places more than those of the lands of his paternal inheritance."[65] In his mission Boniface was not motivated by the penitential urge nor a desire for personal perfection but by a drive to spread the gospel.[66]

He had genius both as an apostle and as an administrator. This latter quality might have been his forte; it certainly distinguishes him and his work from the wandering monk-missionaries of Ireland and the loosely structured church organization they established. His contribution was to all levels of ecclesiastical life: as a priest he labored to convert non-believers to Christ, as a bishop he concerned himself with the establishment of high priestly standards and the training of candidates to continue his

---

[64] For the life of Boniface see: Addison, *The Medieval Missionary,* pp. 9-15; Greenaway, *Saint Boniface;* Latourette, *Expansion,* II, 85-99; Musset, "La Conversion des Germains," *Histoire universelle des missions catholiques,* ed. Delacroix, I, 119-24; C.H. Talbot, "St. Boniface and the German Mission," *The Mission of the Church and the Propagation of the Faith,* ed. G.J. Cuming, pp. 45-57; George W. Robinson (trans.), *The Life of Saint Boniface by Willibald* (Cambridge, Mass.: Harvard University, 1916).

[65] Robinson (trans.), *The Life of Saint Boniface by Willibald,* p. 42.

[66] Talbot, "St. Boniface and the German Mission," *The Mission of the Church and the Propagation of the Faith,* ed. G.J. Cuming, p. 45.

work, and as an archbishop he worked to organize dioceses, choosing candidates for episcopal office, and convoking councils to impose discipline in the Frankish and German churches.[67] The force behind his long life of missionary work, his spirituality, appears in his Letters. These give the core of his sanctity: a habit of prayer and meditation on Scripture, a constant and regular practice of the sacramental life, strict self-discipline, faith in God whose will he accepted with unquestioning obedience, and complete confidence in God's purpose for him and in the reality of his vocation.[68]

For Columban, the theme of pilgrimage for Christ dominated all he did. In Boniface's Letters the central theme is the success of his mission of bringing others into the Church.[69] Although we have no trustworthy accounts of the exact content of his preaching to non-Christian people, Boniface's Letters do outline the theological view of man, the world, and the Church which formed his spirituality. In accordance with the Christian anthropology of his era and the monastic tradition in which he was nurtured, it is not surprising to find him warning a young friend about the vanity of all worldly riches which "pass away like shadow, vanish like smoke, disappear like foam."[70] He advocated a mistrust and contempt for the body.[71] Indeed, the body was but the prison for the soul.[72] The Church for Boniface was seen as the Ark of Salvation and his mission was to free pagans from the snares of the devil in which they are bound and gather them among the children of Mother Church.[73] Those who corresponded with Boniface strengthened him in this vision of the Church. His mission was "to reap the harvest of God, gathering in sheaves of holy souls into the storehouse of the heavenly kingdom."[74] Pope Gregory II reminded him that the Church was the "haven of safety" for eternal life,[75] and without baptism there could be only damnation.[76] Anyone who rejected Boniface, Gregory felt,

[67] *Ibid.*, p. 56; Latourette, *Expansion*, II, 91.
[68] See Greenaway, *Saint Boniface*, p. 75.
[69] See Emerton (trans. and intro.), *The Letters of Saint Boniface*, p. 10.
[70] Boniface, Letter 1.
[71] Letter 2.
[72] Letter 40.
[73] Letter 36.
[74] Letter 7.
[75] Letter 9.
[76] Letter 10.

was subject to eternal punishment.[77] For Boniface, the fire of hell was a strong reality.[78]

In addition to the motive of saving souls from damnation by bringing them into the safety of the Church, there are other clear motives for the missionary's life in Boniface's writings. One is the glory of God. He asks for prayers that the Word of God might be accepted, that pagans might be rescued from idols, become sons of the Church, and thereby bring praise and glory to God.[79] Another motive is the missionary's own eternal happiness. Boniface exhorts others to help in the mission to ensure their own eternal reward.[80] And he is reminded more than once by Pope Gregory II and others that conversion of non-believers is linked with his own salvation, and that the reward for his missionary labor will be the hundredfold of heaven.[81] Finally, the Pope offers a third motive to Boniface when he reminds him that his mission is really Christ's mission and when he cites the "Great Commission" to go forth, teach, and baptize all peoples.[82]

Boniface was a monk and a bishop, but for most of his career he was a monk without a monastery and a bishop without a fixed episcopal see. He remained rooted in the monastic way of life in which he had grown to maturity; and he founded several monasteries as centers for advancing the gospel, although he never allowed himself the luxury of settling down in any one of them. If Columban can be described as a monk who engaged in mission, Boniface can be characterized as a missionary who was a monk. He was commissioned and exhorted by the popes in Rome to wander and to preach, and this he never ceased doing.[83] He saw the value of prayer as an essential for the success of his mission and asked for prayers in more than one letter.[84] Finally, he was convinced of the absolute necessity of good example on the part of Christians, especially priests and bishops, if others were to be brought into the Church.[85] This was the substratum under his constant anguish concerning the scan-

[77] Letter 9.
[78] Letter 2.
[79] Letters 36, 53.
[80] Letter 38.
[81] Letters 16, 17, 35, 37, 74.
[82] Letters 9, 17.
[83] Letters 4, 9, 16, 35.
[84] Letters 36, 53.
[85] Letter 62.

dalous lives of priests and bishops and his persistent labors towards Church reform.

Ramon Lull

It is not possible here to devote attention to several of the other outstanding figures in medieval mission history in the Western Church. Among these would be Anskar, a monk from the Columban tradition who worked in Scandinavia in the ninth century; Cyril and Methodius, champions of the indigenization of Christianity among the Slavs in the ninth century; and Otto of Bamberg, a man not of the monastic tradition, who labored at a relatively late age of his life so successfully among the Pomeranians in the twelfth century.

The High Middle Ages witnessed the birth of two new orders in the Catholic Church, the Franciscans and the Dominicans, who were to carry on the missionary work of the Church so successfully for many centuries to come. The outstanding characteristic of these orders was the fact that they were founded explicitly for apostolic labors in contrast to the older orders which were dedicated primarily to personal perfection.[86] Dominic broke with the past in this respect when he wanted his friars to be concerned with preaching and conversion; everything else in his rule became subservient to this end.[87] Motivated by a love for the Church, compassion for souls, and the example of Christ sending his followers to preach the kingdom of God, Dominic sent his men not only throughout Christian countries but also to preach among non-Christians in Russia, Hungary, Sweden, and the Near East.[88] Francis, for his part, sent friars to work in Morocco and attempted himself to labor there.[89] One of the most fascinating missionary studies of the Middle Ages is the work of the Franciscans in China which was started by John of Montecorvino in the late thirteenth century.[90] There is, however, one figure in the High Middle Ages

---

86 Latourette, *Expansion,* II, 320-21.

87 G.R. Galbraith, *The Constitutions of the Dominican Order: 1216-1306* (Manchester: The University Press, 1925), pp. 175-76.

88 M.H. Vicaire and C. Vansteenkiste, "L'Inspiration missionnaire de saint Dominique," *Histoire universelle des missions catholiques,* ed. Delacroix, I, 198-99; Schmidlin, *Catholic Mission History,* pp. 227-28.

89 Schmidlin, *Catholic Mission History,* p. 228.

90 For the Franciscans in China see: Kenneth Scott Latourette, *A History of Christian Missions in China;* A. C. Moule, *Christians in China before the*

who was in the Franciscan tradition and who is worth considering in more detail. That man is Ramon Lull (1232-1316).

Ramon Lull was born about the year 1232 on the island of Majorca which had recently been captured from the Saracens. After a youth which was not outstanding for its Christian quality, he had a profound conversion experience at about the age of thirty. This experience, which centered on the cross of Christ, so transformed him that he left his possessions, wife, and children to dedicate himself totally to the service of Christ. The rest of his life can be summarized as a love story between Christ the Lover and Ramon the beloved. His burning passion and interest was to bring the knowledge and love of God to other men and to convert non-believers, especially the Moslems, to Christ.

Ironically, Lull is not important in mission history because of the number of people he converted and baptized; he made only three (possibly four) relatively brief missionary journeys to North Africa and to the Near East, and it seems that he had little success in spreading the faith. He was never ordained priest and only when he was in his sixties did he become a Franciscan tertiary. Lull's importance rests in the fact that he was one of the first great publicity men, idea men, and theoreticians for the missions. During the fifty-odd years after his conversion, he traveled constantly back and forth from Spain, through France, and down into Italy and Rome to lobby with the Franciscans and Dominicans, with popes and princes for the cause of spreading the faith to non-believers. Writing incessantly and voluminously on philosophy, theology, science, and mysticism, he was one of the intellectual, religious, and literary geniuses of the Middle Ages. After a life spent pleading the cause of missions, he was martyred during his last journey to Africa in Bugia, a town near Algiers, about the year 1316.[91]

Lull is a seminal figure in the history of the missions and in several ways was centuries ahead of his times. There

Year 1550 (London: Society for Promoting Christian Knowledge, 1930); *idem,* "Documents Relating to the Mission of the Minor Friars to China in the Thirteenth and Fourteenth Centuries," *Journal of the Royal Asiatic Society,* (July, 1914), 533-99; Anastasius Van de Wyngaert, O.F.M. (ed.), *Itinera et relationes FratrumMinorum: saeculi XII et XIV*, Sinica Franciscana, I (Florence: College of St. Bonaventure, 1929), lxix-xc.

91 For Ramon Lull see: E. Allison Peers, *Ramon Lull* (London: Society for Promoting Christian Knowledge, 1929); Liam Brophy, *So Great a Lover* (Chicago: Franciscan Herald Press, 1960); J.N. Hilgarth, *Ramon Lull and*

are four notable things about his life style. The first is a significant fact, not often mentioned by those who comment on him — he was a layman. In an era during which missionary work was almost exclusively a clerical and monastic preserve, and was to remain such for centuries to come, Lull represents an outstanding example of the influence open to laymen. Secondly, the consistent, obsessing, and driving motive behind all Lull did was a profound experience of, and love for, Christ. There is no doubt about this.[92] The heart of his mission program was the conviction that no one can give greater service to Christ than by giving his life for him by working for the conversion of non-believers. This love was so strong and deep that he was willing to die in order to preach Christ, to give up his life to save any soul.[93] He lived this love by dying a martyr's death. Thirdly, it should be noted that Lull was a man of his times in his evaluation of the non-Christian religions. He was a contemporary of Pope Boniface VIII who had written *Unam Sanctam* in 1302 reaffirming that outside the Church there was neither salvation nor forgiveness of sins. Lull for his part shared this theological position, believing that non-Christians were condemned to eternal punishment.[94] Naturally, this belief gave all the more force to his drive to bring the saving love of Christ to those outside the Church.[95]

Despite this position, which one can hardly expect Lull to transcend since it was a common tradition of the Medieval Church, what is outstanding is the attitude he took towards those not in the Catholic Church. This is the fourth point of his theology and spirituality worthy of mention. Conversion was seen as a work of love accompanied by penance, prayer, suffering, devotion, sacrifice, understanding, and intelligence.[96] He wrote, "Missionaries will convert the world by preaching, but also through the shedding of tears and blood with great labor, and through a bitter death."[97]

Lullism in Fourteenth-Century France (Oxford: Clarendon, 1971); Latourette, *Expansion,* I, 321-23; Stephen Neill, *A History of Christian Missions,* The Pelican History of the Church, VI (Baltimore, Md.: Penguin Books, 1966), 134-37; Ramon Sugranyes de Franch, "Raymond Lulle, ses idées missionnaires," *Histoire universelle des missions catholiques,* ed. Delacroix, I, 207-20.

[92] Peers, *Ramon Lull,* pp. 24-25.

[93] *Ibid.,* p. 245; Sugranyes de Franch, "Raymond Lulle," *Histoire universelle des missions catholiques,* I, 210.

[94] Peers, *Ramon Lull,* pp. 68, 253. [95] *Ibid,* pp. 68, 74.

[96] Sugranyes de Franch, "Raymond Lulle," *Histoire universelle des missions catholiques,* I, 216; Hilgarth, *Ramon Lull and Lullism in Fourteenth-Century France,* pp. 24-25.

[97] Quoted in Neill, *A History of Christian Missions,* p. 137.

Lull felt that conversion should be an act of freedom carried on peacefully. This attitude of respect and good faith is something which was ahead of his times. In some ways his methods were a return to those of primitive Christianity.[98]

Lull was convinced that philosophy and reason could prove the faith and that peaceful discussion with non-believers could win them over. There is, therefore, a strong current of rationality in his missionary program. In his writings he strove to develop a general science and method of thought which would be able to bring all men to Christ.[99] Perhaps he was too sanguine in those hopes, but, nevertheless, he was a forerunner of the scientific study of religions inasmuch as he stressed the necessity of thoroughly knowing other religions, and having their philosophers thoroughly understand Christianity, so that he could convince them of the truth of the faith. It is not surprising, then, that one of the essentials to his program, a goal which he worked for constantly, was the establishment of language schools at the universities of Europe where the best preachers of Christianity could learn the language and thought of Islam.

Finally, something should be mentioned about the use of force towards conversion since it does not seem to square with the ideas above. Lull is ambivalent on this point. A man of the Middle Ages living at the time of the Crusades, he could not but be confronted with the possibility of using military methods for spreading the faith. It seems that early in his career he took a position of restraint with regard to the use of a crusade to spread Christianity.[100] Later in his life, however, he favored force as an auxiliary means for evangelization.[101] This is hard to reconcile with his ideas of love and understanding, but it demonstrates how great men, despite their far-reaching ideas, find it difficult not to trade in the methods and practices which are the common currency of their times.

Perhaps the best summary of his missionary program appears in the petitions he made to the Holy See concerning the missions. In 1294 Ramon petitioned the saintly, tragic hermit-pope, Celes-

---

[98] Sugranyes de Franch, "Raymond Lulle," *Histoire universelle des missions catholiques*, I, 216; Peers, *Ramon Lull*, p. 73.

[99] Peers, *Ramon Lull*, pp. 70, 261; Sugranyes de Franch, "Raymond Lulle," *Histoire universelle des missions catholiques*, I, 209.

[100] Peers, *Ramon Lull*, p. 73.

[101] *Ibid.*, pp. 200, 253, 351.

tine V, that the Church open her temporal and spiritual treasures for the sake of conversions. For every Christian, he wrote, there are a hundred or more that are not Christians who are journeying towards everlasting fire. Therefore, the Church should assign a tithe of her wealth to crusades and missionary work until the world is won for Christ. One cardinal should be assigned to spend his life searching for the best preachers, holy men, religious and secular alike, who would be willing to suffer death to honor the Lord. These should be prepared for mission by being taught all the languages of the world in colleges founded for this purpose both at home and abroad.[102] Almost twenty years later, the same program was still foremost in his thought. In 1311 he petitioned the Council meeting at Vienne that three language schools be started so that missionaries could bring the gospel to all nations, that an order of knights be formed to conquer the Holy Lands, and that men of learning devote themselves to refuting the errors of non-Christians such as Averroes who opposed the Catholic Faith.[103] The Council decreed that five schools for the instruction of Hebrew, Arabic, and Chaldean were to be started at Rome, Bologna, Paris, Oxford, and Salamanca, and that these were to be funded by the Church and secular rulers. Unfortunately, it seems that this grand design was never fully executed.[104]

Ramon Lull was both a man of his times and a man ahead of his times. He was very much a man of his times when he advocated, after some preliminary reluctance, the advancement of Christianity by the use of force. Again, he was a man of his times with regard to his notions of the impossibility of salvation outside the Church. There is no doubt, though, that he was ahead of his times in his attitudes toward non-believers, his respect for their language and thought, and his interest in sending the most well-equipped missionaries to discuss religion with them, missionaries who would be thoroughly versed in the languages, beliefs, and modes of thought of non-Christians. The heart of his spirituality, however, shows him to be a man for all times. The love of Christ was the dominant passion of his life and because of this love, and for the sake of it, he spent over fifty years wandering, writing and arguing for the cause of missions.

---

[102] Peers, *ibid.*, pp. 252-53.

[103] *Ibid.*, pp. 350-58.

[104] *Ibid.*, p. 360; Sugranyes de Franch, "Raymond Lulle," *Histoire universelle des missions catholiques,* I, 219.

Francis Xavier and Jesuit Spirituality

Kenneth Scott Latourette observes that at the beginning of the sixteenth century the outlook for the expansion of Christianity was unpromising; yet the next three centuries proved quite the opposite.[105] During these centuries Christianity enjoyed one of its greatest periods of expansion, second only to the nineteenth century. The discovery of new lands offered the field for this expansion. A revitalization of Roman Catholicism caused tens of thousands of missionaries to go out to preach the gospel in the newly opened territories. The Society of Jesus — the Jesuits — was the foremost missionary sending group in the Catholic Church during this period. The spirituality of the Jesuits is a spirituality for the apostolate and for mission. Missionary service was thought to be the highest expression of the Jesuit vocation.[106] The Basque nobleman Ignatius Loyola (1491-1556) who founded the Jesuits was a transitional figure in Church history: one who in many ways was a man of the Middle Ages, yet one who founded an order and forged a spirituality suited to the world of the modern period.

Jesuit spirituality, which bears the stamp of Ignatius' own profound personal religious experience, is best summarized in his *Spiritual Exercises,* and is elaborated in the *Constitutions* he wrote and in his personal correspondence. Joseph de Guilbert has summarized the spirituality of Ignatius as a combination of surging enthusiasm and reason — a passionate love of Jesus Christ for the service of God and a powerful supernatural logic.[107] Ignatius' supernatural logic is expressed in the "Principle and Foundation" of the *Spiritual Exercises:* man was created to praise, reverence, and serve God and by this means to save his soul; all other things are created to help towards this end; therefore, man is to make himself indifferent and maintain balance and equipose with regard to all created things, using them insofar as they help him to attain his end and ridding himself of them if they prove to be a hindrance.[108] But unlike many of the earlier monastic tradi-

---

105 Latourette, *Expansion,* III, 373-74, 450.

106 Joseph de Guibert, S.J., *The Jesuits: Their Spiritual Doctrine and Practice,* trans. William J. Young, S.J., ed. George E. Ganss, S.J. (Chicago: Institute of Jesuit Sources, 1964), pp. 208, 238, 287, 438.

107 *Ibid.,* p. 175.

108 See Louis J. Puhl, S.J. (trans.), *The Spiritual Exercises of St. Ignatius* (Westminster, Md.: Newman, 1957), p. 12.

tions, the spirituality of Ignatius is not centered on self in the sense that his followers are to work only for their own salvation and perfection; rather, they are to labor "strenuously" for the salvation and perfection of their neighbor.[109]

It is here that passionate love for the service of Christ enters. Writing in the tradition of medieval chivalry, Ignatius proposes that his followers meditate upon the Kingdom of Christ and the call by Christ to service. The follower of Ignatius is urged to become caught up in the love of Christ who emptied himself for men out of love, and in imitation to follow Christ's footsteps. To achieve his own perfection and to make himself an apt instrument for the salvation of his neighbor, he is asked to lead a life of radical self-abnegation which stresses a rejection of ease, honor, riches, and even his own judgement in obedience. He is challenged to be a man of profound prayer, not secluded contemplation however, but the type of prayer which finds God's presence in all things — contemplation in action.[110] All this is to be done for the one primary motive of the "greater glory of God" or "the service of God." These phrases, and ones similar to them, appear hundreds of times in the writings of Ignatius.

Finally, Ignatian spirituality is ecclesial spirituality inasmuch as the Jesuit is to be a man of the Church, working in obedience to his superiors and to the head of the Church, the pope, to whom Jesuits take a special vow of obedience. In short, Ignatian spirituality is a spirituality of service through love, apostolic service for the greatest possible glory of God, a service given in generous conformity to the will of God, especially as it is expressed through superiors, a service expressed in abnegation and sacrifice of all self-love and personal interest in order to imitate Christ who is ardently loved, and to bring other men to Christ.[111] Animated with this spiritual vision, Ignatius founded an order which has been a leading presence in the missionary work of the Church, and in our own times continues to be the largest male missionary sending body in the Catholic Church.

---

[109] George E. Ganss, S.J. (trans. and ed.), *Saint Ignatius of Loyola: The Constitutions of the Society of Jesus* (St. Louis: Institute of Jesuit Sources, 1970), pp. 77-78.

[110] See, for example, Ignatius' "Contemplation to Attain the Love of God," *The Spiritual Exercises of St. Ignatius,* trans. Puhl, pp. 101-03.

[111] See De Guibert, *The Jesuits,* pp. 83-85, 132, 176.

Francis Xavier (1506-1552) was among the first group of men who gathered around Ignatius Loyola at the University of Paris in the 1530s. Even before the Society of Jesus was officially approved by the pope, Xavier was sent by Ignatius to India as a missionary. He departed from Portugal on April 7, 1541, and after a peril-filled journey lasting a year arrived at Goa on May 6, 1542. His missionary career was to last a scant ten years, but during that time he traveled and preached the faith incessantly in India, the East Indies, and Japan. He longed to continue his work in China, but death overtook him at the age of forty-six on the island of Sancian off the coast of the mainland on December 3, 1552.

Xavier offers an outstanding example of Ignatian spirituality for mission. His life style was one dominated by enthusiasm for Christ and union with the Lord in hardship and suffering for the salvation of souls to the glory of God. It is remarkable that during his unrelenting travels, at a time when travel and communication were not easy, he was able to write one hundred and forty-one letters and documents, some thousands of words in length, to his friends, fellow workers, and confreres in the Far East and in Europe. This body of correspondence contains descriptions of the places and people among whom he labored; it offers fairly clear accounts of his missionary methods; and describes the tremendous need he felt for fellow missionaries to join him in the Far East. When read and copied in Europe, his letters had no little influence in arousing interest and volunteers to do missionary work. More important for the purposes of this chapter, however, is the fact that his letters outline the spirituality of Xavier the missionary. In Joseph de Guibert's judgement, they lay down the almost complete principles of a whole missionary spirituality.[112] If the key figure for Jesuit spirituality is Loyola, Xavier is the outstanding model for the missionary spirituality of the Jesuits.

The spirituality of Francis Xavier was first of all Ignatian inasmuch as it was dominated by that same supernatural logic and passionate love for Christ which is at the heart of Ignatian spirituality. Union with God, enthusiasm for Christ, and personal holiness are the characteristics which are at the heart of the Jesuit apostolate. Xavier's life was marked by these and he exhorted his

[112] *Ibid.*, p. 189.

fellow workers to strive for the same deep personal sanctity. True to Ignatian principles, however, this overarching necessity for personal holiness was not for purely personal reasons but for the success of the apostolate and the good of souls.[113]

In the unique mission context, several other themes appear in Xavier's writings which give his basic Ignatian spirituality a distinctively missionary cast. The one quality which stands out most clearly perhaps is Xavier's profound trust in God and deep sense of dependence upon God as the source of any good he might achieve. Coupled with this trust and dependence is a sense of his own personal limitations. On his way to India, Xavier expressed the feeling that he lacked every talent for preaching the gospel and that all the good results which he achieved were totally due to God.[114] Near the end of his career, he reminded a fellow Jesuit that the gift of preaching is to be attributed solely to God and that it is God who gives people the grace to listen and respond.[115] He refers to himself as a *triste peccador,* powerless alone but trustful that God will use such a broken reed and dust and ashes to plant the faith.[116] He begs God to make him his instrument for spreading the faith in spite of his own great unworthiness and sinfulness.[117] He frequently keeps before his eyes the advice of Ignatius that one must strive to conquer himself and cast aside all fears which impede faith, hope, and loving trust in God.[118] Finally, amid the totally alien culture and language of Japan, Xavier confesses that it was God's great mercy which brought him there and gave him the realization that he had nothing in which to trust but God alone.[119] It can safely be said that for Xavier dependence upon God and unlimited trust and confidence that mission is God's work and any successes are only to be attributed to him, coupled with a sense of one's own un-

[113] See Xavier, Letters 80.1, 117.1; citations from the Letters of Xavier are from George Schurhammer, S.J. and Joseph Wicki, S.J. (eds.), *Epistolae S. Francisci Xaverii aliaque eius scripta,* Monumenta Historica Societatis Jesu, 67-68 (Rome: Monumenta Historica Societatis Jesu, 1944-45); translations of the Letters are those of James Brodrick, S.J., *St. Francis Xavier (1506-1552)* (New York: Wicklow Press, 1952).

[114] Xavier, Letter 12.2, 4.

[115] Letter 116.1-2.

[116] Letters 15.5, 48.1.

[117] Letter 68.2.

[118] Letter 85.13.

[119] Letter 90.42.

worthiness, and balanced with unstinting labor in preaching are the absolute requisites for missionary spirituality.

During his missionary career Xavier worked with all classes of people: the Catholic hierarchy, his fellow Jesuits and priests, the Portuguese of wealth and power and those of more humble circumstances, the poor of India, the better educated and more sophisticated in Japan, and the sick and suffering of all nations and classes. In all these dealings he labored to be a man of patience and love, and he exhorted others to cultivate these characteristics. Writing to Europe for helpers, he asks for men of humility, kindness, and patience.[120] Again and again he encourages others to acquire a great love for people and to deal with them lovingly and patiently, pardoning and supporting them in their weaknesses.[121] He asks others not to be discouraged with failures on the part of those to whom they are presenting the faith, but to have the patience of God who does not weary of the pagans.[122] He encourages those under him not to become dejected because of the amount of work facing them, but patiently to do what they can.[123] Finally, he does all this with a tremendous spirit of joy. So great are the consolations given by God to those working for conversions, he wrote to Rome in 1544, that if there be joy on earth this is it.[124] He encourages others to take great joy in the fact that so many baptized infants are in paradise because of their labors.[125]

This last point brings up one of the strong motivating factors in Xavier's spirituality. Like most of his missionary predecessors, Xavier was quite pessimistic about goodness and the possibility of salvation outside the Church. There is no doubt that this conviction was one of the driving forces in his life. One of the reasons for this was his almost complete ignorance of the religions of the people to whom he came.[126] The Jesuits who followed him in India, Japan, and China spent lifetimes informing themselves of, and attempting to conform themselves to, the beliefs and practices of the peoples of the East. In a mere ten years, Xavier could hardly have absorbed much of the rich religious heritage of the major countries in the Far

---

[120] Letter 79.22.
[121] Letters 23.2, 24.5, 28.3, 116.3.
[122] Letter 22. [123] Letters 22, 28.2.
[124] Letter 20.13. [125] Letter 68.3.
[126] Brodrick, *St. Francis Xavier,* pp. 112-13.

East. Although there can be no doubt that Xavier tried to deal lovingly and patiently with non-Christians, he is unrelenting in his condemnation of their vices and their religious practices. As his biographer James Brodrick notes, this is ironic in view of the pity, understanding, and tolerance Xavier could show to the vices and corruption of Portuguese soldiers, sailors, traders, and officials. Brodrick attributes Xavier's position in this regard to the "overwhelming prejudice bred in his Spanish bones."[127] It certainly proves the strong cultural influence upon Xavier who was born not too many years after the reconquest in Spain.

In all events, Xavier in the Far East felt that he lived among peoples devoid of God and ingrained in sin.[128] He believed that God did not abide with infidels and took no pleasure in their prayers since their gods were devils.[129] He accused the Brahmins in India of being the mainstays of heathenism and the most pernicious people in the world.[130] He was convinced that few in India go to heaven except those who were baptized under the age of fourteen.[131] In one of his letters to Rome, he tells how multitudes fail to become Christians merely because there is no one to preach to them and that he would love to visit the universities of Europe and cry like a madman for help telling how many miss heaven and go to hell because of this.[132]

Of course, the deeper motive behind all Xavier did and the underlying reason for his labors to convert souls was always his Ignatian concern for the glory of God. This is well expressed early in his career when he wrote while on his way to India that anything he did was to glorify God and that he had hope and confidence that God would give abundantly what is needed to promote his glory.[133]

Finally, it might be observed that in his labors to glorify God and serve him there is a faint echo of the pilgrimage theme in Xavier's writings. To a fellow Jesuit in India he wrote that to be good in this life we have to be pilgrims prepared for journeys

---

[127] Brodrick, *ibid.*, pp. 108-09.
[128] Xavier, Letter 70.1.
[129] Letters 15.8, 19.3.
[130] Letter 20.10-11.
[131] Letter 68.3.
[132] Letter 20.8.
[133] Letter 13.4.

to any and all places where we can best serve God.[134] And in a letter to Europe he states that this life is not life at all but a drawn-out death and exile from the glory for which we were created.[135]

Xavier's missionary methods were primitive to say the least. In his famous letter of 1545 to his companions at Rome, a letter which was copied and passed all over Europe and which inspired many to follow Xavier's example, he gives one description of his methods:

> My method, on arriving in a heathen village, was to assemble the men and boys apart, and to begin by teaching them to make the Sign of the Cross three times as a confession of faith in Father, Son, and Holy Ghost, three Persons in one only God. I then recited in a loud voice the General Confession, the Creed, the Commandments, the Pater Noster, the Ave Maria, and the Salve Regina. Two years ago, I copied out those prayers and formulae in the Tamil language which is spoken here, and know them by heart. I put on a surplice for the occasion. All, little and big, then repeated the prayers after me, and that done I gave them an instruction on the articles of faith and the Commandments, in Tamil. Next, I required them one and all to ask pardon from God for the sins of their past lives, and that publicly and loudly, in the presence of heathens who did not desire to become Christians. This was done for the confusion of bad men and consolation of the good . . . . When they had finished, I asked them severally, young and old, whether they believed sincerely each article of the Creed, to which they replied that they did. I then went again through the Creed article by article, asking after each if they believed it, and they answered me, with their arms folded on their breasts in the form of a cross, 'I do believe.' Thereupon I baptized each one, and handed him his new Christian name written on a slip of paper. It was next the turn of the women and girls, and these I instructed and baptized in the selfsame way. The baptisms over, I told the new Christians to demolish the shrines of the idols, and saw to it that they crushed the images into dust. I could not express to you the consolation it gave me to watch the idols being destroyed by the hands of

---

[134] Letter 50.2.
[135] Letter 85.14.

> those who so recently used to worship them. I went thus from village to village making Christians, and in each place I left a written copy of the doctrine and prayers in their language, with instructions that they were to be taught daily, each morning and evening. My joy in doing all this was greater than I could ever tell you by letter or even explain to you, were we face to face.[136]

In this same letter, Xavier mentions that in the space of a single month he baptized ten thousand men, women, and children. Convinced of the absolute necessity of baptism by water for salvation, Xavier made it a special point to baptize children and he encouraged others to do the same even though grown-ups had no desire for it.[137] Like the early medieval missionaries of Western Europe, Xavier employed mass baptism; but, unlike them, it seems that he did not concentrate upon converting the leaders to the faith, a fact which made for the success of the spread of Christianity in Europe and which undoubtedly hindered its spread in the East. While in India and the East Indies, Xavier was working mostly with the lower classes of society and he felt that great learning was not essential for those engaged in missionary work. He requested men who were strong of constitution and well grounded in the spiritual life.[138] Several years later, after he had experienced the more sophisticated people of Japan, he did request men of deeper learning who would be able to discuss religious matters with their peers.[139]

Xavier is another pioneer, a ground-breaking figure of mission history. Although he baptized thousands and founded numerous Christian communities, his greatest achievement seems to be the example he set and the spirit he aroused for missionary work. He was a man of personal holiness and constant self-abnegation who traveled and preached incessantly for the good of souls, always to the glory of God. The dominant characteristic of his mission spirituality would be his sense that missionary work is ultimately God's work which must be done in complete dependence upon God with trust and hope that he will see the missionary

---

136 Quoted from Brodrick, *St. Francis Xavier*, pp. 207-08; other similar examples are found in Letter 20 and in Letter 53 which is Xavier's "Instructio pro catechistis."

137 Xavier, Letter 29.

138 Letters 47.2, 52.7.

139 Letter 110.2.

as his instrument for the spread of the faith. All this is done with great love, patience, kindness, humility, and joy.

There is no reason to doubt that Xavier's Jesuit successors in the Far East were men equally fired with the principles and vision of Ignatian spirituality. Perhaps their most significant contribution was the imaginative advances they attempted in missionary methodology. In India, Robert de Nobili (1577-1656) sized up the Indian caste system and became a Brahmin *sannyasi* in life style and thought in order to bridge the cultural gap between Western Christianity and Indian religious thought and practice. His work was imitated by Constantine Josephus Beschi (1680-1746), the great Tamil scholar. In Japan and China, Alessandro Valignano (1539-1606), Matteo Ricci (1552-1610), Adam Schall (1591-1666), and Ferdinand Verbiest (1623-1688) labored with some initial success to incarnate Christianity in oriental forms and to approach the learned classes of society.

Their methods were ultimately frustrated due to nationalistic rivalries and the myopic theological vision of those who opposed them. These Jesuits carried the humility demanded by Xavier for the missionary to its necessary and logical conclusions and came to the East to enculturate themselves in language and custom and to learn from the rich religious and philosophical heritage of the countries there, something which Xavier was unable to do and, indeed, scarcely had the time or temperament to work at. There is no space here to mention the many hundreds of other Jesuits who, inspired by Ignatian spirituality, carried Christianity to other parts of the world during the sixteenth, seventeenth, and eighteenth centuries. They worked around the globe with varying degrees of success, in the Philippines, in North America, and in many areas of Latin America. The Jesuit reductions of Latin America in Paraguay, for example, represent a fascinating experiment to create a Christian society based on gospel principles and work for the common welfare of the people.

The Society of Jesus represents but one tradition in the missionary work of the Roman Catholic Church following the European expansion during the sixteenth century. The older religious orders, particularly the Dominicans and Franciscans, were no less active in their missionary labors. They, too, produced outstanding missionaries. One of the most notable was Bartolomé de las Casas (1474-1566), a long-lived contemporary of Xavier and Ignatius who was an *encomendero* in Hispaniola, priest, Dominican friar, missionary in Venezuela, Guatemala, and Nicaragua, and bishop of Chiapas in Mexico. Las Casas' peregrinations perhaps outdid those of most of his missionary predecessors including Xavier, Lull, and the medieval missionaries. He made at least four trips between the New World and Spain to plead the cause of the natives, demanding that they be treated justly and humanely by the Spaniards. Deploring the cruelties of the conquistadores, he argued that the Indians were human beings with rights of their own (which some denied!) and that the only scheme for their evangelization was one of peace, love, and good example. Las Casas played a great role in much of the humanitarian legislation contained in *The Laws of the Indies* and he stands out in mission history as one of the great examples of a mission theory and spirituality dominated by justice, love, and compassion towards less developed peoples.[140]

[140] See Bartolomé de las Casas, *History of the Indies,* trans. and ed. Andrée Collard (New York: Harper Torchbook, 1971); Lewis Hanke, *Aristotle and the American Indians: A Study in Race Prejudice in the Modern World* (London: Hollis and Carter, 1959); *idem, Bartolomé de las Casas: An Interpretation of His Life and Writings* (The Hague: Martinus Nijhoff, 1951).

IV

MISSIONARY SPIRITUALITY: THE MODERN PERIOD

Contemporaneous with the development of the Society of Jesus in the sixteenth century was the formation of the churches of the Protestant Reformation. Historians of the missions usually note that the Protestant churches were slow to engage themselves in missionary work during the sixteenth and seventeenth centuries. Latourette lists a number of causes for this, his main reason being that the churches of the Reformation had relatively little contact with non-Christian peoples until the rise of British and Dutch sea power.[1] There are exceptions. The Puritans, for example, displayed interest in converting the natives of New England during the seventeenth century.[2]

The movement which gave Protestantism the impetus towards foreign missions was Pietism which developed in the latter half of the seventeenth century in Germany. The outstanding figure in the missionary movement inspired by Pietism was August Francke (1663-1727) who was a member of the theology faculty at the University of Halle from 1698 until his death. From Halle came the first two Protestant missionaries to India, Bartholomäus Ziegenbalg (1683-1719) and Heinrich Plütschau (1678-1747), who worked in Tranquebar. As a young man, Ziegenbalg entered into the following covenant with a student friend: "We will seek nothing else in the world but the glory of God's name, the spread of God's kingdom, the propagation of divine truth, the salvation of our neighbor, the constant sanctification of our own souls, wherever we may be and whatever of cross-bearing and suffering it may occasion us."[3] Although the comparison might be odious

---

[1] See Latourette, *Expansion,* III, 25-26.

[2] See Sidney H. Rooy, *The Theology of Missions in the Puritan Tradition: A Study of Representative Puritans: Richard Sibbes, Richard Baxter, John Eliot, Cotton Mather, and Jonathan Edwards* (Grand Rapids, Mich.: Eerdmans, 1965).

[3] Henry C. Vedder, *Christian Epoch-Makers: The Story of the Great Missionary Eras in the History of Christianity* (Philadelphia: Griffith and Rowland, 1908), p. 233.

to Pietists, it is interesting to note how similar this covenant is to the spiritual foundation of the Jesuit Order.

Nicolaus Ludwig Zinzendorf

One of the reasons for the slow entry of the churches of the Reformation into missionary work was the fact that they lacked the organizational structures which for centuries had been the mainstays of Roman Catholic missionary work — the monastic and religious orders.[4] When Count Nicolaus Ludwig Zinzendorf (1700-1760) helped to renew the Moravian Brethren in the first half of the eighteenth century, he formed a missionary-sending community which in some ways was similar to the religious orders in the Catholic Church. Although in later life he fell into disagreement with the Pietists,[5] Zinzendorf was from a Pietist family background and he studied at Halle under Francke during his early years. In 1722, together with a group of exiled refugees from Moravia, he organized the community of Herrnhut (the "Lord's Watch") on an estate he had recently acquired at Bethelsdorf in Saxony. In ten years the Herrnhut colony had sent its first missionaries to the West Indies, and by the time of Zinzendorf's death these had been followed by over two hundred others who worked from Greenland to South Africa and in both North and South America.

Pietism developed in reaction to Lutheran orthodoxism with its stress on intellectual assent to correct doctrine and a dry sacramentalism. It stressed a religion of the heart and feeling, right *belief* as opposed to *right* belief.[6] One drop of love, the Pietists declared, was worth more than a sea of knowledge. Pietists insisted upon a conscious conversion experience and a living faith relation to Jesus as the one personal saviour from sin. Conversion had to show itself in a changed life and in outward manifestations of this change. Many Pietists insisted upon a strict asceticism which shunned worldly pleasures such as theatre, cards, and dancing. Not unlike the organized ascetic discipline of the

---

[4] Latourette, *Expansion,* II, 26.

[5] See, for example, the discussion of Zinzendorf in A.H. Oussoren, *William Carey: Especially His Missionary Principles* (Leiden: A.W. Sijthoff's Uitgeversmaatschappij N.V., 1945), pp. 224-26.

[6] See Martin J. Heinecken, "Pietism," *Dictionary of Christian Ethics,* ed. John Macquarrie (Philadelphia: Westminster, 1967), pp. 256-57.

monastic orders of old, they developed a program for like-minded people, sometimes from different denominations, to meet in schools of piety (*collegia pietatis*) to form little churches within the Church (*ecclesiolae in ecclesia*) in order to increase their spiritual fellowship in prayer, Bible study, meditation, family worship, and conversation. In this atmosphere Zinzendorf was nurtured.

From his earliest days, Zinzendorf was devoutly religious. Moreover, the thrust of his faith was outgoing and missionary — he had a passion to win souls for Jesus Christ, even in the midst of contempt and reproach. The conversion of souls became the chief object of the community at Herrnhut.[7] The particular symbol which formed the center of his devotional life, and which he proposed to his followers, was Jesus Christ as the Lamb of God. Adoration of the Lamb, especially the slaughtered Lamb, was central to the spiritual life of Herrnhut. Its theological foundation stressed redemption through the sufferings of Christ, a "blood and wounds" soteriology which sought to bring deliverance and salvation to all men through the scandal of the cross. Zinzendorf taught the Moravians to look to the cross with joy because there they would find the covering for all their sins.

Devotion to the slaughtered Lamb became the impelling force and chief motive for their missionary enterprises. It led the Moravians joyfully to sacrifice themselves in order to carry the power and fellowship of the crucified Christ across the world. Their missionary message, according to Zinzendorf, was to tell about the Lamb until they could tell no more. Only this blood and wounds theology of the slaughtered Lamb could bring non-Christians to Christ.[8] The emphasis is slightly different, affection for the Lamb of God and the suffering Christ becomes the touchstone of devotion and motivation, but the impelling force for Zinzendorf and the Moravians is not unlike the vision of generations of missionaries who went before them and who have followed them — a passionate love for Christ and interest in telling others of him.

Three ideas are central to Zinzendorf's missionary thought and to the life styles of the Moravian missionaries who went out

---

[7] A.J. Lewis, *Zinzendorf, the Ecumenical Pioneer: A Study in the Moravian Contribution to Christian Mission and Unity* (Philadelphia: Westminster, 1962), pp. 12, 54-55, 133.

[8] *Ibid.*, pp. 69-70, 73-74, 91.

from Herrnhut — his notions of *tropus* and diaspora and his concern for Christian unity. Zinzendorf believed in the manifoldness of life and revelation, that every nation and religion had a thought of God and natural religious genius of its own, its own "jewel" of truth, ritual, or order. Therefore, according to his *tropus* idea (from the Greek *tropoi paideias,* methods of training), each church was a *tropus* or school of wisdom with something particular to contribute to the Body of Christ. In each *tropus,* be it Lutheran, Calvinist, Anglican, Moravian, or Catholic, the Lamb was preparing his "Christed ones" for membership in the one universal Church. No *tropus* was to be destroyed and the members of each were to remain faithful to their own tradition, although no one *tropus* was to be considered as an end in itself.[9] The purpose of missions, therefore, was not so much to found local churches, although Moravians did this, or simply to convert non-believers; but to gather together the particular souls who were the first fruits of the Spirit into the congregation of God in the Spirit.[10]

It is easy to see that such a concept made Zinzendorf a missionary and ecumenical thinker ahead of his times. He looked askance on proselytism, attempting to make men change from denomination to denomination. He conceived of his community at Herrnhut as being a facilitating agent which would enkindle the flame of devotion to the Saviour in the existing denominations of Christianity. When he began his experiment at Herrnhut, Zinzendorf intended to have it remain an *ecclesiola in ecclesia,* but with the passing of time he was faced with a dilemma: on the one hand, there was his strong ecumenical thrust which saw seeds of goodness in all denominations and impelled him to remain within the Lutheran tradition; and, on the other, he felt that it was his God-given task to renew the Moravians, the ancient *Unitas Fratrum,* the Unity of Brethren. In the end, historical factors, especially the opposition of the state authorities and the needs of his growing missionary projects, caused him to turn his commu-

[9] *Ibid.,* pp. 104, 139-140; R.A. Knox, *Enthusiasm: A Chapter in the History of Religion* (New York: Oxford University, 1950), p. 403; S. Baudert, "Zinzendorf's Thought on Missions Related to His Views of the World," *International Review of Missions,* 21 (1932), 397.

[10] Lewis, *Zinzendorf, the Ecumenical Pioneer,* pp. 88, 99; Baudert, "Zinzendorf's Thought on Missions," p. 399; Laurids Kristian Stampe, "The Moravian Missions at the Time of Zinzendorf: Principles and Practices" (unpublished S.T.M. dissertation, Union Theological Seminary, 1947), pp. 58-60.

nity into a full-fledged church which became known as the Moravian Church.[11]

From the *Unitas Fratrum* of the fifteenth century Zinzendorf inherited the notion of the invisible church. All the visible churches have only a relative validity and point to the invisible church of God which is found both within and without the visible churches. According to Zinzendorf, there is to be no organic unity among the existing churches based on intellectual agreement, creed, worship, or organization, since the unity of which Jesus spoke (John 17:21) is an internal, spiritual unity. The "Christed" souls spread throughout the world and in all denominations are those who compose the great Invisible Church of Christ. Their bond of unity rests in the fact that they call Christ Lord and Saviour and this heart-to-heart devotion to Christ is above all barriers of creed, worship, and organization. The purpose of mission both among non-Christians and amid the different confessions is to build up the invisible church, partially now, and fully when it is revealed at the end of time.[12]

Zinzendorf's grand purpose, therefore, was to make present the unity of the "Christed ones" in all the world. Towards this end, he devised two kindred ventures: the Pilgrim Congregation and the diaspora. The first was a temporary measure, but the latter became permanent in the Moravian Church. As seen above, the notion of the missionary as pilgrim appeared early in the Church's history. Zinzendorf's thought corresponds partially with this tradition. August Gottlieb Spangenberg (1704-1792), his successor, said that Zinzendorf regarded it as a privilege to be a pilgrim on earth. Especially during his ten years of exile from Herrnhut (1736-47), Zinzendorf traveled widely on the Continent and in England carrying on a campaign of evangelism and ecumenical witness. True to his principles, he preached devotion to the Lamb but aimed not so much to make converts to Moravianism as to awaken slumbering Christians in their own churches.[13]

The diaspora movement began soon after a great pentecostal experience at Herrnhut in 1727. Zinzendorf saw it as the means through which the Moravian Church could fulfill her self-denying

[11] Lewis, *Zinzendorf, the Ecumenical Pioneer,* pp. 94-95, 103, 109-10.

[12] *Ibid.,* pp. 25-27, 98-101; Stampe, "The Moravian Missions at the Time of Zinzendorf," pp. 58-60; Baudert, "Zinzendorf's Thought on Missions," p. 397.

[13] Lewis, *Zinzendorf, the Ecumenical Pioneer,* pp. 116-18.

task of being a servant to all churches. Itinerant messengers went out from Herrnhut in twos and threes to give witness to the Lamb. They went from house to house holding meetings for prayer and exhortation, stressing Christian experience more than theological debate. They were instructed by Zinzendorf to be cautious not to give any occasions of offense to other churches. These messengers traveled all over Europe but made a special contribution in Great Britain where they were midwives to the Evangelical Revival and the Methodist movement. Once more, their motive was not to spread Moravianism, but to be of service to other churches by directing souls to Christ within their own denominations. It has been estimated that never before in history has a band of witnesses made such a successful effort to discourage the growth of their own church.[14]

Ronald Knox has observed that Moravianism is essentially a spirituality.[15] The spirituality of Herrnhut was Pietism as interpreted and developed by Zinzendorf. It stressed conversion and deep personal affection for Christ the Lamb, a theology which at times seemed to approach Christo-monism. It was also a spirituality for mission which insisted on winning souls, be they among Christians or non-Christians, for the fellowship of the Lamb. But a spirituality which does not evolve a practical, structural framework is useless for mission. Therefore, perhaps one of the greatest contributions which Zinzendorf made to the missionary enterprise rests in his developing an organizational structure for his theory of mission. Viewed in this light, Moravianism is a life style rather than merely an interior spirituality.

I have mentioned the fact that the community at Herrnhut was not unlike the religious orders which had for centuries carried the burden of missionary work in the Roman Catholic Church. Functionally speaking, Zinzendorf's community filled the structural vacuum left in the Protestant churches when they rejected religious orders. In a way, however, he goes beyond the orders of the Catholic Church because the church into which his community evolved was totally committed to mission. The church was mission and for mission; missionary work was not merely one of the activities carried on by the church. Of course, the relatively small size of his church community facilitated this unity. Never-

---

[14] Lewis, *ibid.*, pp. 116-33.
[15] Knox, *Enthusiasm*, p. 408.

theless, the total dedication of the Moravian Church to mission makes Zinzendorf important because he put mission into the life style of every church member.

Also of importance is the fact that Zinzendorf used laymen in his missionary enterprises. How could it be otherwise when the whole church was for mission? No longer, then, was missionary work to be considered a clerical preserve which, except for a few examples like Lull, it had been for more than one thousand years. Finally, his notions of diaspora and *tropus* gave the Moravians an extremely open theoretical framework for their missionary life styles. They traveled to spread the fellowship of the Lamb and at the same time they were sensitive to the workings of the Spirit who had already preceded them and prepared Cornelius souls (see Acts 10), "Christed ones," among the peoples they approached.

Traveling in diaspora, spreading the fellowship of the Lamb, going abroad to win non-Christians for the Lamb, being sensitive to the God-given "jewel" or *tropus* of each religion and nation, and performing a servant role to awaken Christian life in other churches — this is the theory which was at the heart of early Moravian mission spirituality. Because of the intense personal conversion and commitment to Christ which Zinzendorf insisted upon, it is almost needless to say that, besides preaching, the primary means for spreading devotion to the Lamb was the personal example of the missionary. His life was to be missionary itself.[16] The qualities which Zinzendorf insisted upon for the missionary's life were humble faith and a burning spirit to witness, caution against pride, faintheartedness and impatience, and finally courage and perseverance.[17]

Last of all, as already noted in the case of Xavier, there was the context of joy. Zinzendorf taught the Moravians to look at the cross and rejoice because there they found forgiveness for their sins, and they were to sacrifice themselves and carry the fellowship of the crucified Christ around the world in happiness and joy.[18] August Spangenberg (1704-1792), Zinzendorf's successor, saw joyfulness, *Freudigkeit,* as one of the necessary qualities for those engaged in work among non-Christians.[19]

---

[16] Lewis, *Zinzendorf, the Ecumenical Pioneer,* pp. 91-92.
[17] Stampe, "The Moravain Missions at the Time of Zinzendorf," p. 73.
[18] Lewis, *Zinzendorf, the Ecumenical Pioneer,* pp. 73-74.
[19] Stampe, "The Moravian Missions at the Time of Zinzendorf," p. 74.

Zinzendorf can be criticized because of some of his personal foibles, and Moravian spirituality can be criticized for the saccharine sentimentality in the excesses of their devotion to the Lamb and the "blood and wounds" theology, and their occasional overdependence upon lots to find the divine will. I have not taken this course purposely, in order to stress the positive contribution which Zinzendorf made to missionary thinking. In both missionary and ecumenical matters he was a man ahead of his times.[20] Indeed, it is difficult to estimate the debt which Protestant missions owe to the evangelists who went out from Herrnhut. A. J. Lewis estimates that Zinzendorf's conception of the missionary, his message, and his strategy were the first coherent contributions to the vast enterprise of Protestant missions in the modern era. Moravianism had an influence on the great John Wesley in Britain, and there was a direct influence from it in the foundation of the London Missionary Society, the Basel Mission, and the Leipzig Missionary Society. Finally, William Carey, sometimes called the father of modern Protestant missions, was challenged by what the Moravians had done when he formed the Baptist Missionary Society in 1792.[21]

William Carey

Count Zinzendorf died on May 9, 1760. A little more than a year later, on August 17, 1761, in Paulespury, a village in Northampton in the English Midlands, William Carey (1761-1834) was born. Of Carey, Stephen Neill has said that "in the whole history of the church no nobler man has ever given himself to the service of the Redeemer."[22] After a conversion experience and rebaptism, William Carey performed the functions of village cobbler, Baptist pastor, teacher, student of languages, and botanist. Like Zinzendorf, Xavier, Lull, and the others considered above, William Carey is a pioneer figure in mission history. His genius rested on the fact that he had both missionary vision and a concrete plan for implementing this vision. In 1792 as a result of his

[20] See Baudert, "Zinzendorf's Thought on Missions."

[21] Lewis, *Zinzendorf, the Ecumenical Pioneer*, p. 94; Oussoren, *William Carey*, p. 33.

[22] Stephen Neill, "William Carey," *Concise Dictionary of the Christian World Mission*, eds. Stephen Neill et al. (Nashville: Abingdon, 1971), p. 83.

monograph *An Enquiry into the Obligations of Christians to Use Means for the Conversion of the Heathen,* and his vision expressed in conversations and one famous sermon on Isaiah 54:2-3, Carey was instrumental in founding the Particular Baptist Society for Propagating the Gospel among the Heathen. In November of 1793, Carey arrived in Bengal as one of the first missionaries of the Society. There followed several frustrating years during which he had to accept a position as a manager of an indigo plantation in the interior to help support himself and his companions in order not to be expelled by the East India Company. During this time he preached the gospel when opportunity afforded and labored incessantly to master the Bengali language.

In 1800 he and his fellow Baptists moved to the Danish settlement of Serampore, sixteen miles from Calcutta, which was to be the center from which he worked for the next thirty-four years. Although not an intellectual genius, Carey possessed an extraordinary gift for languages and unstinting perseverance in mastering them. From Serampore the work of the Baptist mission proceeded along several lines: widespread preaching of the gospel in towns and villages; careful study of the Indian languages, religions, and customs; the translation, printing and distribution of the Scriptures in several languages; the formation of a church on Baptist principles; and the foundation of Serampore College for the education of Indian ministers and preachers.[23]

Although Carey was deeply and personally devoted to preaching the gospel and making converts, and although he had some success in this area, his great contribution to the Bengali mission was his interest in translating and propagating Scripture. In a letter written in 1797, he saw only two obstacles to missionary work in any part of the world: the want of the Bible, and the depravity of the human heart.[24] William Carey spent his life attempting to remove the first impediment. He produced himself complete translations of the Bible in Bengali, Sanskrit, and Marathi; and he directed the production of translations in a score of other languages.

It is significant and says much of Carey's organizational abilities to realize that before leaving England he developed an outline

---

[23] *Ibid.,* pp. 82-83.

[24] Eustace Carey, *Memoir of William Carey, D.D.* (Boston: Gould, Kendall, and Lincoln, 1836), p. 199.

of the theological foundation for mission, proposed a practical plan for its implementation, and sketched the spiritual qualifications necessary for missionaries. He published these ideas in his *Enquiry* of 1792, a work which ranks as one of the greatest missionary treatises in the English language.[25] His life was a living out of these ideas. Carey's reading had given him a broad vision of the numbers of men who had never heard the gospel preached to them. Furthermore, he reacted against the position held by some of the eighteenth-century Calvinists and Lutherans that God would convert the non-believers in his own due time. Accordingly, Carey proposed whether the commission given by the Lord to preach the gospel to all nations (Mark 16:15; Matt. 28:18-20) was binding on men of his own time as well as upon the disciples of Jesus. He concluded that it was and called loudly for all possible exertion to preach the gospel among non-believers.[26] Obedience to the command of Christ, therefore, is the primary motive and foundation for missionary labor in Carey's mind. After summarizing the history of Christian missions to his times, giving special praise to the work of the Moravians, and after twenty-three pages of statistical analysis on the population of the different sections of the globe, Carey concludes that, although the non-Christians are capable of knowing divine things, the vast majority of the human race is as destitute of civilization as they are of religion and that they are without any means of knowing the true God and utterly lacking in the knowledge of the gospel of Christ and of any means of obtaining it.[27]

The *Enquiry* goes on to argue that distance, language, the uncivilized ways of many less advanced peoples, dangers to life and limb, and the difficulty of being without the necessities of life cannot be advanced as arguments against engaging in mission work abroad. On the contrary, it would be against the spirit of the gospel to let these things stand in the way, for the commission of Christ is sufficient reason to venture all and, like the Christians of the early Church, to go everywhere preaching the gospel.[28] To this end, he proposed the formation of a society

[25] William Carey, *An Enquiry into the Obligations of Christians to Use Means for the Conversion of the Heathens* (New Facsimile Edition with an Introduction by Ernest A. Payne; London: Carey Kingsgate, 1961).

[26] *Ibid.*, pp. 13, 77.

[27] *Ibid.*, pp. 62-63.

[28] *Ibid.*, pp. 67-73.

of serious Christians, ministers and private persons, to set up rules and regulations, raise funds, and send missionaries abroad.[29]

I have noted that the Moravians were outstanding because of their identification of mission and Church. Functionally, Carey's Society is similar to the religious orders of the Roman Church which are missionary societies within the Church but not totally identifiable with the Church. It seems that for Carey mission was the function of the society within the church, although he suggested that the whole body of Christians enter heartily into the spirit of the divine command, and he thought that all church members had to pray for, and contribute to, the work of the missions. Most likely the question of society or Church as the responsible organ for missionary work did not enter into Carey's thoughts.[30]

Carey stressed obedience as a motive for the missionary, but this should not displace other reasons which he mentions in his *Enquiry*, especially the motive of compassion. Carey was concerned for the uncivilized state of non-Christians in many parts of the world. He conforms to the nineteenth-century pattern of those who readily identified civilization with European or Anglo-American culture. He stated that pity and humanity, as well as Christianity, call believers to go out to the non-Christians, and that the gospel is, perhaps, the most effective means for civilization.[31] In his *Enquiry* Carey does not fret, as Xavier did, over the millions of souls who are going to hell, but he does allude to the perishing state of non-Christians.[32] In a later document, "The Serampore Form of Agreement," drawn up in 1805 by Carey and his co-workers as a summary of their missionary principles, this motive comes more to the fore. The first point of this document states that missionaries should fix in their minds the awful doctrine of eternal punishment and the dreadful loss sustained by an unconverted soul launched into eternity.[33] Therefore, although it is not central to his missionary motivation, saving souls from damnation does have a place. Another motive often offered in the past for missionary work is the glory of God. This, too, does not stand out

---

[29] *Ibid.*, p. 82.

[30] See Oussoren, *William Carey*, p. 144.

[31] Carey, *Enquiry*, pp. 13, 70. [32] *Ibid.*, p. 70.

[33] William Carey et al., "The Serampore Form of Agreement," in Walter Bruce Davis, *William Carey: Father of Modern Missions* (Chicago: Moody, 1963), pp. 110-11.

in Carey's *Enquiry*. It has been suggested that Carey's motives are more anthropocentric than theocentric, for example, the motive of compassion rather than the motive of the glory of God.[34] This is not entirely the case, however, for in at least two places in his Journal, Carey expresses the desire that he may live entirely for God and that all of his concerns might be for his glory.[35] Nevertheless, the motive of the glory of God does not rank as high as obedience to Christ's command and compassion for the unconverted.

Carey's *Enquiry* of 1792 is an exhortation to action. Accordingly, it is more concerned with missionary motivation than with the content of missionary preaching. In fact, it says little about this subject. The dominant theme of Carey's preaching is found expressed in the "Serampore Form of Agreement": following the example of Paul, the missionary is to make Christ crucified the subject of his preaching. The grand means of conversion, therefore, is the doctrine of Christ's expiatory death and all-sufficient merits.[36] In his personal Journal and in his letters, Carey affirms that Christ crucified is the theme of his conversations and sermons in India.[37] The following excerpt from his Journal for 1795 is one example of Carey's preaching:

> In the afternoon I was much cheered by a considerable number of the natives coming for instruction, and I endeavored to discourse with them about divine things. I told them that all men were sinners against God, and that God was strictly just, and of purer eyes than to approve of sin. I endeavored to press this point, and to ask how they could possibly be saved if this was the case. I tried to explain to them the nature of heaven and hell; and told them that, except our sins were pardoned, we must go to hell. They said, that would be like the prisoners in Dinagepore gaol. I said, no; for in prison only the body could be afflicted, but in hell the soul; that in a year or two a prisoner would be released, but he never would be freed from hell; that death would release them from prison, but in hell they would never die. I then told them how that God sent his own Son to save sinners; that he came to save them from sin; that he died in the

---

[34] See Oussoren, *William Carey*, p. 217.
[35] See E. Carey, *Memoir of William Carey*, pp. 105, 133.
[36] Carey et al., "The Serampore Form of Agreement," p. 144.
[37] See E. Carey, *Memoir of William Carey*, pp. 111, 157, 160, 172, 194.

> sinner's stead; and that whosoever believed in him would obtain everlasting life, and would become holy. They said they were all pleased with this, but wished to know what sin and holiness were. I told them that there were sins of the heart, the tongue, and the actions; but as a fountain cast out its waters, so all sin had its source from the heart; and that not to think of God, not to wish to do his will, not to regard his word, and also pride, covetousness, envy, &c. were great sins; and that evil and abusive language was very sinful; that not to be strictly upright in their dealings was very sinful. I told them that God was under no obligation to save any man; and that it was of no use to make offerings to God to obtain the pardon of sin, for God had no need of goats, kids, sheep, &c., for all these are his at all times; and that if God forgave them, it must be from his own will; but that he was willing to save for the sake of Jesus Christ. After this, part of the 5th chapter of Matthew was read by Mounshi, and explained to them, and they went away promising to return next Lord's day; and my spirits were much revived.[38]

Carey's writings give an explicit outline of missionary spirituality. I have already mentioned the reasons he advanced for missionary work — obedience to Christ's command, compassion, salvation of the unconverted. These are the motivational factors in his spirituality. Carey's *Enquiry* and the "Serampore Form of Agreement" list other requirements for the missionary. In the former document, he states that missionaries must be men of piety, prayer, and orthodoxy, endowed with prudence, courage, and forbearance. They must be ready to enter with all their hearts into the spirit of their mission, constantly laboring and traveling, applying themselves to understanding the people and to mastering their language. Humility, a recurring missionary virtue, also has its place — they are not to resent injuries, nor to think highly of themselves or despise the people they are with. Carey was tough-minded and uncompromising when he looked forward to the hardships of mission life in his *Enquiry*. No hardship, even death itself, was too great, for the goodness of the cause, and their duties as children of God and Christians should compel missionaries to give themselves entirely. Christ's commission is sufficient reason to go anywhere. Hardship should be the

---

[38] *Ibid.*, pp. 148-49.

object of the missionary's expectations. Servanthood also has a place in his mission spirituality. In Carey's mind, the minister is not his own person, but the servant of God, one who must forsake friends, pleasures, and comfort to be totally dedicated to God by engaging himself in the Lord's work by going where the Lord pleases.[39]

The *Enquiry* sketches the spirituality of one who had not engaged himself in missionary work. The "Serampore Form of Agreement," written in 1805, represents the principles of missionaries who had gone through seven years of frustration (Carey's first convert was baptized in 1800) and five years of limited success. I have already mentioned that the "Agreement" stresses the value of immortal souls as a motive for mission and Christ crucified as the content of missionary preaching. It also says much about the life style and spirituality of the missionaries.

First of all, it is acknowledged that God alone can bring men to conversion, but this does not free missionaries from personal zeal in reconciling men to God. The missionaries, therefore, were to bend all efforts to know the language, thinking, habits, and propensities of their people. They should be humble — he who is too proud to stoop to others in order to draw them to him is ill-qualified. Missionaries should abstain from such things as cruelty to animals which would increase prejudice against the gospel. The real conquests of the gospel were to be conquests of love — the same theme which Lull advocated. The people must be treated as equals, should feel at home with the missionaries, and their gifts should be used to advance the gospel. The "Agreement" advocated the formation of separate churches with indigenous pastors and deacons without the interference of the missionaries, although these would continue to oversee the new communities. Carey and his friends advocated that newly won Christians should be treated with patience, tenderness, and forbearance, with a realization of the sacrifices they had made to become Christians and the "gross darkness" in which they were so recently involved. The "Agreement" gave women an important role in approaching their counterparts in India. Finally, it states that the means towards the ends proposed by the missionaries are to be prayer, both private and communal, and the "cultivation of personal religion." All worldliness, indulgence, and

---

[39] Carey, *Enquiry,* pp. 67-76.

personal profit were to be rejected. The missionaries were to realize that their time, gifts, strength, families, and even their own clothes were not their own, but were to be sanctified to God and his cause. At Serampore, Carey and the others lived in a community of families with all things in common, and, in this situation, they acknowledged that they enjoyed a greater portion of happiness than any private family ever enjoyed.[40]

The best source for understanding a person's spiritual life is a diary or journal. Carey kept such a diary and it contains a wealth of information about his personal spirituality. It would be worth study in itself as an illustration of missionary spirituality. However, I limit myself here to the extensive portions of Carey's Journal included in Eustace Carey's *Memoir of William Carey, D.D.* The Journal covers the period of Carey's trip to India in 1793, continues through the days of struggle before he had a fixed residence and source of income, and concludes during the time he settled as manager of the indigo plantation three hundred miles from Calcutta in 1794.

The first thing of note is the source to which Carey turned for spiritual support. The first of these, of course, was Scripture, which Carey constantly read and which constantly fed his soul.[41] A second source of spiritual strength was the writings of Jonathan Edwards. Carey mentions that he read them frequently.[42] He was especially impressed with Edward's life of David Brainerd (1718-1747), who worked as a missionary to the Indians in Massachusetts, Pennsylvania, and New Jersey and who died at twenty-nine, exhausted by his labors.[43] Finally, Carey's Journal shows him to be a man of constant prayer, prayer sustained in times of dryness and consolation, prayer which frequently had for its theme the conversion of the people of India, and prayer in common with his friends and family which gave him a sense of the communion of saints.[44]

What appears most clearly in Carey's Journal during these early years is the struggle which goes on within the soul of a missionary. He described most perceptively the movements of consolation and desolation that he experienced. On the one hand,

---

[40] Carey et al., "Serampore Form of Agreement," pp. 109-28.
[41] See E. Carey, *Memoir of William Carey*, pp. 74, 114, 116.
[42] *Ibid.*, pp. 73, 112. [43] *Ibid.*, pp. 88-89.
[44] *Ibid.*, pp. 75, 106, 107, 124, 125, 136.

there were times of barrenness and aridity in which he was overwhelmed by the limitations of his own spirit and character; and, on the other hand, there were moments of joy and happiness centered on an impelling desire to preach Christ crucified. Amid this struggle he constantly turned to God as the only center of trust and strength.

In 1793, on his way to India, one month he feels serene and tranquil, impressed by the work towards which he is traveling; the next month he feels nothing but barrenness of soul and wonders how so dead and stupid a person can be of any use to the people of India.[45] Once in India, he is consumed with material concerns and feels less ardor for divine things because of this. He longs to be able to live entirely for God.[46] A few months later, in March of 1794, the barrenness and foolish wanderings of his mind still plague him and he continues to feel that, since he has so little goodness in himself, he can be of no use to non-Christians. He searches for wisdom to know how to direct all his concerns for the glory of God, faith, and holiness.[47] Again that same month, he laments the wanderings of his prayer, his lack of devotion, and the fact that he does not walk with God and find himself in his sight. Discouragement persists, yet there is some consolation in reflecting that he is in the hands of God. "What is there in all this world worth living for," he writes, "but the presence and service of God?" He expresses a burning desire that all the world may know God and he suffers because he does not know the language well enough to preach Christ crucified to the Indians.[48]

The next month, April 1794, he still suffers from a sense of his limitations and wonders how he can convince others of God when he is not sure he has the grace of God himself. And yet he affirms that all his hope and comfort are from God without whom no one can be converted and with whom all can receive faith. He yearns for an earthly friend to whom he can bare these sufferings. When he left England, he writes, his hope for conversions were strong, but with all the obstacles of his first years it would die except that God upholds it.[49] In May of

[45] E. Carey, *ibid.*, pp. 73, 75.
[46] *Ibid.*, p. 95.
[47] *Ibid.*, p. 105.
[48] *Ibid.*, p. 111.
[49] *Ibid.*, pp. 112-14.

1794, he still is tormented by an awareness that he has done nothing for God, and, worse, he feels no desire to do anything.[50] But in July of that year he says that he has been much comforted by Job's fidelity and constancy and was able to pray well for the success of the gospel in India.[51] In August of 1794 and in January of 1795, he reflects again on the dryness and barrenness of his soul which makes him almost despair because he feels totally unfit for the ministry, not to mention the vocation of missionary.[52]

From these brief selections of Carey's Journal, the pattern of his spiritual life is clear and inspiring — he is a man with a burning desire to preach Christ, yet, at the same time, a man constantly beset with spiritual aridity and dryness. His only recourse is trust in God. To attain this he lives a life of persistent prayer and spiritual nourishment from Scripture and devotional reading.

Lest these be thought to be the sufferings of an unsettled missionary trying to regain his balance after the shock of arrival in India, it is worth taking note of a letter which Carey wrote in 1810 at the peak of his career after he had established his mission base at Serampore and had attained success as a missionary and a master and teacher of languages. In the latter he acknowledges his frequent discouragement because of the want of every natural and moral prerequisite for preaching the gospel. He says he is backward in spiritual conversation, barren of ideas, full of unsanctified affection, lacking in recollection to the extent that the gospel is not the work for which he feels fitted. For years, he confesses, he has had to drag himself on, subject himself to rules, impose the day's work upon himself, and constantly stir himself to the job at hand.[53] It is a humble confession and a perceptive insight into the life of faith and spirituality of a pioneer in missionary work, an acknowledgement of the extent to which his concern for Christ and obedience to his command led him, a living of the vision he had many years before that no hardship must stand in the way of the gospel. From his Journal

---

[50] *Ibid.*, p. 116.
[51] *Ibid.*, p. 125.
[52] *Ibid.*, pp. 133, 143.
[53] See John Clark Marshman, *The Life and Times of Carey, Marshman, and Ward: Embracing the History of the Serampore Mission*, I (London: Longman, Brown, Green, Longmans, and Roberts, 1859), 432-34.

and letters we know that Carey was a man who often found joy and consolation in his work on Scripture and preaching the gospel, but his writing also reveals the struggle which is often at the heart of missionary labor.

J. Hudson Taylor

The periods of greatest vigor in Christianity, Latourette states, have been times when the impulse within it has issued in fresh organizations.[54] Judged by this standard, it is clear why the nineteenth century is called the "Great Century" of Christian missions. In both the Catholic and Protestant churches, mission-sending societies and organizations multiplied greatly during this century. William Carey's Baptist Society, organized on the eve of the nineteenth century, was one of the first of the many denominational societies within Protestantism. The next figure I shall consider, J. Hudson Taylor (1832-1905), was the founder of the most numerous of the interdenominational organizations established for the evangelization of China during this century. Hudson Taylor's China Inland Mission is a prototype of the "faith missions" within Protestantism, and an early representative of the evangelical school of Protestant missionary work.

J. Hudson Taylor was born at Barnsley, Yorkshire, England, on May 21, 1832. At the age of seventeen, after experiencing a deep religious conversion, he felt personally called by God to go as a missionary to China. He was driven by compassion for the millions in China who were living in darkness without the gospel, and daily perishing without hope for eternity.[55] It was a motive he never lost sight of nor failed to instill in others during his missionary career. Most of the missionaries considered so far in this survey undertook their labors as mature men in their thirties and forties. Hudson Taylor is an exception to this pattern. After several years during which he studied medicine, read Scripture, prayed much, and practiced the self-discipline he felt would be necessary for a missionary, he left England at the age of twenty-one to

---

[54] Latourette, *Expansion,* VI, 26, 54.

[55] Dr. and Mrs. Howard Taylor, *Hudson Taylor in Early Years: The Growth of a Soul* (London: Morgan and Scott, 1912), pp. 110, 129-30, 140; see also J. Hudson Taylor, *China's Spiritual Needs and Claims* (6th ed., London: Morgan and Scott, 1884).

undertake mission work in China under the auspices of the Chinese Evangelization Society. Having arrived in Shanghai in March 1854, he began six years of missionary preaching, years which were the apprenticeship for his life of missionary work, and years during which he developed the theory and practice which he would later incorporate into the China Inland Mission. At the time of Taylor's arrival missionaries were confined to a few treaty ports along the coast of China. His dream was to get beyond these ports to the millions of people who lived inland.

He spent the greater part of these early years in China engaged in direct evangelization of the peoples in and around the areas of Shanghai and Ningpo. In 1855, he had the good fortune to work with William Burns of the English Presbyterian Mission, a kindred soul with whom he labored for several months. He has left a description of their mission methods:

> We were in the habit of leaving our boats, after prayer for blessing, at about nine o'clock in the morning, with a light bamboo stool in hand. Selecting a suitable station, one would mount the stool and speak for twenty minutes, while the other was pleading for blessing; and then changing places, the voice of the first speaker had a rest. After an hour or two thus occupied, we would move on to another point at some distance from the first, and speak again. Usually about midday we returned to our boats for dinner, fellowship, and prayer, and then resumed our outdoor work until dusk. After tea and further rest, we would go with our native helpers to some tea-shop, where several hours might be spent in free conversation with the people. Not infrequently before leaving a town we had good reason to believe that much truth had been grasped; and we placed many Scriptures and books in the hands of those interested.[56]

The content of his preaching at this time was Christ crucified. He warned men of their sinful state, but consoled them by telling them that God loved them greatly and that atonement had been made for them by Jesus Christ who died in their stead and paid the price of their guilt.[57] During these years, he made

---

[56] J. Hudson Taylor, *A Retrospect* (Toronto: China Inland Mission, 1898), p. 60.

[57] Taylor, *China's Spiritual Needs and Claims*, p. 66; H. Taylor, *Hudson Taylor in Early Years*, pp. 296, 369.

himself fluent in the Chinese language and further identified himself with the people by adopting Chinese dress, hair style, and dietary customs, something for which he was at first criticized, but which became characteristic of the missionaries of the China Inland Mission in the years to come. Taylor acknowledged that from William Burns he learned two important missionary principles which were "seed-thoughts" that bore fruit in the organization of the China Inland Mission: the value of evangelism as the great work of the Church, and the importance of the order of lay evangelists as a lost order that Scripture required to be restored.[58] In 1857, he resigned from the Chinese Evangelization Society because of a dispute over funds and was forced to fall back on prayer and faith to sustain himself. With this he put into practice another principle which was to characterize the future China Inland Mission: never making appeals for funds but depending upon God to arouse interest and raise support for what was ultimately his work.

In 1860 Hudson Taylor was forced to return to England because of ill health and he spent the next five years studying medicine, working on a translation of the New Testament into the Ningpo dialect, and seeking to arouse interest in missionary work in China. On June 25, 1865, unable to bear the sight of a congregation of a thousand Christian people rejoicing in their own security while millions were perishing, he walked on the beach at Brighton and experienced a great moment of faith during which he rededicated himself to God for mission service and asked him for twenty-four fellow workers, two for each of the eleven inland provinces of China and two for Mongolia.[59] Shortly thereafter, he organized the China Inland Mission and, together with his wife, wrote *China's Spiritual Needs and Claims,* a small book which rivals Carey's *Enquiry* in its importance for arousing mission interest in the nineteenth century. In May of 1866 the first group of China Island Missionaries, sixteen in number, sailed from England to join the few who were already at work in China. Hudson Taylor spent the rest of his life doing direct evangelization work in China, administering the mission he had founded, and making trips back to England, to Europe, North

[58] Taylor, *A Retrospect,* p. 59.
[59] *Ibid.,* pp. 119-20.

America, and Australia to organize branches and inspire others to join in the work.

Near the end of the century, China Inland Missionaries made up about half of the Protestant mission force at work in China — in 1898 there were over 780 missionaries, including wives and associates, together with 467 native helpers who labored in one hundred and fifty stations and about the same number of out-stations.[60] Hudson Taylor died in China in 1905, and, although the missionary accomplishments of the society he founded and inspired were enormous, the impact of the man upon Christian missions through his writings, his lectures, his personal character and example of faith, and his interest in promoting all evangelical missions was wider still.

Taylor's monograph, *China's Spiritual Need and Claims*, written after his first experiences as a missionary in China and close to the founding of the Inland Mission, develops the motives which underlay his mission spirituality. Throughout the book two themes are played against each other: the great spiritual need of the people of China, and the command of Christ to go to the nations. Through graphs, statistics, and comparisons with England, Taylor describes the situation of the millions of "poor benighted China" who are in "spiritual destitution," held in the thraldom of sin and Satan, and "destitute of all that can make man truly happy."[61] Confronted by this need, the Christian is challenged by the gospel to be the light of the world and preach to every creature.[62] A recurring scriptural theme used to reinforce his argument is from Proverbs (24:11-12):

> If thou forbear to deliver them that are drawn unto death,
> And those that are ready to be slain;
> If thou sayest, Behold, we knew it not;
> Doth not He that pondereth the heart consider it?
> And He that keepeth Thy soul, doth not He know it?
> And shall not He render to every man according to his works?[63]

Having confronted his reader with this double challenge — the needs of China and the command of Christ — Hudson Taylor

[60] *Ibid.*, pp. 128-29.
[61] Taylor, *China's Spiritual Needs and Claims*, pp. 3, 12-13, 48.
[62] *Ibid.*, pp. 2, 12, 37.
[63] *Ibid.*, p. 1.

hopes that his little book will result in fervent prayer and strenuous self-denying effort for the salvation of the benighted Chinese.[64] The response he is looking for is: Lord what would you have me do to make thy kingdom come in China.[65] Similar to William Carey, Taylor felt that no hardship was too much of an obstacle. If the Lord commands, it is not man's part to ask if that command can be obeyed.[66] Faith that God will be faithful to those who obey him is central to his spirituality and theology.[67] What is more, dangers and difficulties only cause men to realize their weakness and poverty and force them to draw more deeply, and rest more implicitly, on the richness and fullness of Christ.[68] Compassion for souls and obedience to the command of the Lord, therefore, are the fundamental motives in Taylor's theology and spirituality of mission. A third motive is also presented — to follow the example of the "Romish" missionaries, but this does not dominate his thought.[69] All of this is set in a context of faith, trust that God will remain faithful to those who serve him, and faith that he will perfect them in their weakness.

The type of mission which Hudson Taylor founded has been called a "faith mission" and at this point it is opportune to say something about the principles behind this kind of mission which marked the life style of Hudson Taylor and those who followed him. Early in his career Hudson Taylor was forced to rely upon trust in God once he had severed his dependence upon the Chinese Evangelization Society in 1867. This same deep faith was built into the China Inland Mission. His basic principle was "God Himself, God *alone,* is sufficient for God's own work."[70] Accordingly, no appeals for funds and no collections were taken by the Mission; nor were missionaries automatically guaranteed their support once they had departed. This should not be taken to mean that Hudson Taylor was naively disinterested in mission support. It seems, rather, to be a point of emphasis — money and material

---

[64] Taylor, *ibid.*
[65] *Ibid.*, p. 48.
[66] *Ibid.*, p. 62.
[67] *Ibid.*, p. 85.
[68] *Ibid.*, pp. 62-65.
[69] *Ibid.*, pp. 13-14.
[70] Dr. and Mrs. Howard Taylor, *Hudson Taylor and the China Inland Mission: The Growth of a Work of God* (London: Morgan and Scott, 1918), p. 52.

means were not to be considered as central concerns; what was essential was an increase of spiritual life in order to produce the missionary spirit.[71]

During his hidden years in England (1860-65), study of Scripture convinced him that prayer to God for laborers and deepening of the spiritual life of the Church so that men would be unable to stay home were what was needed, not elaborate appeals for help. He saw that the Apostolic plan was not to raise ways and means, but to go and do the work, trusting in God's Word, "Seek ye first the Kingdom of God and His righteousness, and all these things shall be added unto you."[72] In Taylor's mind, the missionary was one called and sent by God to do God's work at his command, and therefore one who must above all depend upon God for assistance and supplies.[73] The peril of the Chinese living in darkness without Christ and the Lord's command to assist them were the basis of mission. Once this mission and commission were made known to men and accepted with faith, Hudson Taylor was sure that God in his faithfulness would not fail to raise support for his own work. As the century progressed and the China Inland Mission developed, it seems that Taylor's emphasis proved fruitful — he was not left without assistance when he prayed for it and needed it.

In structure the China Inland Mission was non-denominational. Volunteers from many different churches of Protestantism were accepted as long as they adhered to broad evangelical theological patterns. Eventually the missionaries were grouped by denominations in China. The goal of mission, according to Taylor, was not conversions and not establishing churches, although members of the mission did both. The primary goal was to preach the gospel to every creature, to make Christ's finished work known to all the people of China.[74] His work, therefore, was primarily evangelistic and non-sectarian — to win souls for Christ, not to spread any particular views of Church government.[75] In some cases, when the gospel had been preached, the fruits were left to be gathered by others. The way in which the gospel was to be made known in China was through systematic and repeated itinerant preach-

---

[71] *Ibid.*, p. 53.
[72] Taylor, *A Retrospect*, pp. 117-18.
[73] H. Taylor, *Hudson Taylor and the China Inland Mission*, p. 54.
[74] See Taylor, *A Retrospect*, p. 131.
[75] Taylor, *China's Spiritual Needs and Claims*, p. 87.

ing and bookselling.[76] Taylor himself was trained in medicine, but it seems that he never let medical work or educational work take predominance over what he considered to be the primary means for mission — direct evangelization and preaching the Word.[77]

From what has been said so far, several qualities of the spirituality of Hudson Taylor are clear: the deep sense of personal call and vocation to be a missionary; the compelling force of compassion for those without Christ and obedience to the command of Christ to carry the gospel to them; the primacy of evangelization in the missionary's life; preaching of the atonement and finished work of Christ; identification with the people in language, dress and custom; the importance and role of the layman in missionary work. Above all and almost needless to say, Hudson Taylor was a man of prayer and self-abnegation, prayer which was deeply rooted in constant Scripture reading, and self-abnegation which accepted willingly the hardships of mission life.

John Pollock has called the official biography of Hudson Taylor by Dr. and Mrs. Howard Taylor a spiritual classic.[78] I have already made many references to this two-volume work; it is valuable for an understanding of the man not only because of the account of his life which it gives but also because of the numerous citations from his diaries and letters which it contains. From this source the spirituality of Hudson Taylor is characterized by two dominant themes: faith and trust in God and in his faithfulness, and a felt sense of the presence of God and union with Christ.

The faith foundation of Hudson Taylor's personal life was built on a realization that missionary work is God's work through men. The important element, therefore, was not human planning; rather, men should begin with God, seek his plans, offer themselves to him, and hold fast to his faithfulness to accomplish the mission.[79] Utter trust in God enabled Taylor to accept all the hardships he had to encounter in mission work and to bear his own weakness. He had no illusions about the immensity of the

---

[76] Taylor, *A Retrospect*, pp. 131-32.

[77] See H. Taylor, *Hudson Taylor and the China Inland Mission*, p. 407.

[78] John Pollock, "James Hudson Taylor," *Concise Dictionary of the Christian World Mission*, eds. Stephen Neill et al. (Nashville: Abingdon, 1971), p. 587.

[79] H. Taylor, *Hudson Taylor and the China Inland Mission*, pp. 278, 355.

work calling him and his own insufficiencies. Yet, he felt, this gave him a special claim to God's faithfulness. He was fond of quoting Paul's experience in this regard: "My grace is sufficient for you, for my power is made perfect in weakness" (2 Cor. 12:9).[80] Late in his career he observed that every important advance in the Mission had sprung from, or been connected with, times of sickness or suffiering which cast him in a special way upon the Lord.[81]

The second characteristic of Hudson Taylor's spirituality was his sensible experience of the presence of God. For him God was a living, bright Reality which caused him great joy and a desire for service.[82] He had a special appreciation for the Song of Solomon and felt that it expressed his personal relationship to the Lord.[83] In all stages of his missionary life, the sense of God's presence was with him. When he first arrived in China, he took strength in Christ's promises to be with his disciples.[84] Amid the hardships and sufferings of this first stay, he admitted that he did not know what he would do if he did not feel the sensible presence of God which gave him the strength he needed and constantly drew him to prayer and to rest in the Lord's promises.[85] The same sense of God's care and presence was still with him after his return to China in 1866.[86]

In 1869, this mystical awareness of God's presence was deepened further. In that year Hudson Taylor experienced a newness in his relationship with Christ, a spiritual phenomenon which his biographers have called "the exchanged life." He came to realize that the secret of the spiritual life was not merely to get sap out of the vine which is Christ, but to remember that Jesus is the vine and that we are in him—"The Lord Jesus tells me I *am* a branch. I am *part of Him.*" It was the same mystical insight which possessed Paul—no longer I, but Christ in me (Gal. 2:20). As a result, Hudson Taylor had a greater awareness of the presence of God and his oneness and identification

80 *Ibid.*, p. 65.
81 *Ibid.*, p. 253.
82 Taylor, *A Retrospect*, p. 13.
83 H. Taylor, *Hudson Taylor and the China Inland Mission*, p. 426.
84 H. Taylor, *Hudson Taylor in Early Years*, p. 201.
85 *Ibid.*, pp. 237, 242-43, 321.
86 H. Taylor, *Hudson Taylor and the China Inland Mission*, p. 166.

with Christ. This insight and experience overwhelmed him and gave him new energy to dedicate himself to the work of God.[87]

This consideration of Hudson Taylor's spirituality of mission can be concluded by the qualifications he lists as necessary for the missionary:

> A life surrendered to GOD and controlled by HIS SPIRIT.
> A restful trust in GOD for the supply of all needs, apart from human guarantees.
> A sympathetic spirit, and a willingness to take a lowly place.
> Tact in dealing with men, and adaptability to new circumstances.
> Zeal in service, and steadfastness under discouragement.
> Love for communion with GOD, and for the study of His Word.
> Some experience and blessing in the LORD'S work at home.
> A healthy body, and a vigorous mind.[88]

CHARLES DE FOUCAULD

Important as they are, William Carey and J. Hudson Taylor are not totally representative of the vast Protestant missionary enterprise which blossomed in the nineteenth century and continued into the twentieth. They were pioneers and leaders in Protestant mission work whose spirituality is worthy of consideration. Furthermore, their approach to missionary work is illustrative of the characteristics which Latourette sees in nineteenth-century Protestant missions: stress upon individual conversion, acceptance of the Bible as the standard of faith, organizational division with a tendency to cooperation, the employment of large numbers of lay missionaries, less use of the sacraments and less stress upon Church planting.[89]

During the latter part of the eighteenth century and the early nineteenth century, Roman Catholicism suffered a series of setbacks in its mission work. These were due to factors such as the decline of Spain and Portugal, the suppression of religious orders, especially the Jesuits, a growing religious skepticism and apathy in Europe, the political and social unrest caused by the

---

[87] *Ibid.*, pp. 171-210; Dr. and Mrs. Howard Taylor, *Hudson Taylor's Spiritual Secret* (London: China Inland Mission, 1950), pp. 110-16.
[88] Taylor, *A Retrospect*, p. 133.
[89] Latourette, *Expansion*, IV, 45.

French Revolution and the Napoleonic Wars in Europe, and a number of persecutions in mission lands.[90] Nevertheless, once Europe had settled down after the Age of Napoleon, Roman Catholic missions experienced a revival and no small measure of success. One manifestation of their rejuvenation was the large number of orders and congregations for missionary work founded during this century.[91] As it had been since the early Middle Ages, mission work in the Catholic Church was advanced mainly by the religious orders and congregations of men and women. In contrast with the characteristics of Protestant missions during the nineteenth century, Roman Catholic missions, according to Latourette, were marked by centralized authority and clerical control, with the thrust being not to broadcast the Christian message or to transform entire peoples but to build up the Church as an institution.[92]

In this chapter, I shall not consider any other figures in Protestant mission history, although a score of great men and women from the mission societies of the nineteenth and twentieth centuries could be mentioned. After considering Xavier and the Jesuit ideal, I have not discussed any other personalities in the Roman Catholic missionary movement, first because of reasons of economy, but secondly because I feel that Xavier and the Jesuit model, which dominates so much of modern Church's mission history, is fairly representative of the Catholic Church's mission work down to the present century. I shall close this chapter with the consideration of a man who in many ways represents a return to some very ancient patterns of mission spirituality and method, and in other ways might point the way for future work — Charles de Foucauld (1858-1916).

Charles de Foucauld was born into a well-to-do Catholic family in Strasbourg on September 15, 1858. Some men such as J. Hudson Taylor and Count Zinzendorf seem to be gifted with deeply religious lives from their youngest days; others like Augustine of Hippo and Ramon Lull come to deep personal faith and religious commitment only after years of struggle and searching. Foucauld falls in this latter class. He admits to having lost his faith at about the age of fourteen and his early life was marked by undisciplined pleasure seeking. He studied at the French military

[90] *Ibid.*, III, 454-56.
[91] *Ibid.*, IV, 26 ff.
[92] *Ibid.*, IV, 45.

academy of Saint-Cyr where his academic record was hardly outstanding and his personal life was play-boy in style. He was nicknamed "the Pig." After a brief career as an officer in North Africa, he was forced to resign his commission because of the incongruities between his life style and the requirements of military discipline.

Africa had captured Foucauld's imagination and in 1883 he returned there, more serious minded, to learn Arabic and to engage in an expedition of exploration into Morocco. The reports he published as a result of these explorations won him some fame and recognition. Becoming more and more serious and disenchanted with his past life, Foucauld began to search for faith. "Lord, if you exist," he prayed, "make yourself known to me."[93] In 1886 his path crossed with the man who was to be the catalyst towards his conversion and his spiritual director for many years, Abbé Huvelin. Foucauld was converted in October 1886, received his "second first Communion," and placed himself under the direction of Abbé Huvelin to determine what course his life should take next. From this time on, Foucauld was influenced by one conviction: "As soon as I believed there was a God, I knew I could not do otherwise than to live only for Him. God is so great!"[94]

Following his conversion, Foucauld's life can be divided into two periods: first, the period during which, under Abbé Huvelin's direction, he was a Trappist monk at Akbès in Syria (1890-1897) and then a hermit-handyman at the Convent of the Poor Clares in Nazareth (1897-1900); second, the time following his ordination in 1901 during which he worked in semi-solitude as a monk-missionary in the Sahara. During the first period, he developed the foundations of his spirituality in solitude, prayer, and works of humility. The second period saw him attempting to live his spirituality mainly among the Tuaregs, a nomadic people of the Sahara. During this time he witnessed to Christ by his life, worked on translating the Scripture into the Tuareg language, and attempted to organize a group of followers to carry on his mission. He made almost no conversions, but conversion was not his goal. On December 1, 1916, he was murdered at his hermitage at Tamanrasset.

---

93 Jean-Francois Six, *Witness in the Desert: The Life of Charles de Foucauld*, trans. Lucie Noel (New York: Macmillan, 1965), p. 27.

94 *Ibid.*, p. 28; Anne Fremantle, *Desert Calling* (New York: Henry Holt, 1949), p. 126.

During the first period after his conversion, one principle dominated Foucauld's spiritual life — the imitation of Christ. Like the great missionaries before him, he was captured by the love of Christ, a love which could only show itself in perfect imitation. The aspect of Christ's life he chose to imitate, however, was not Christ's public life of teaching and preaching, but the humble, poor, hidden life of the workman of Nazareth. In this spirit he entered an order where he thought humility, poverty, abandonment, and solitude would be most possible, the Trappists.[95] Early in this period, Foucauld seems to have had no desire to engage himself actively in the apostolate. He saw his vocation as one of preaching the gospel silently as Christ must have during his hidden life.[96] He was developing another principle which was later to dominate his missionary spirituality — total self-conversion must take place before any attempt is made to convert others.[97] Personal goodness was axiomatic in his mission spirituality so that men would come to conclusions such as these: since this man's life is so good, his religion must be good; or, if the servant is so good, how much more so must be the Master.[98] Because of this life style of poverty, abnegation, solitude, and humble work, it has been suggested that Foucauld does not follow the traditional patterns of Western spirituality; rather, his asceticism is of the more kenotic type found in the Greek and Russian traditions.[99]

After several years in the Trappists, Foucauld slowly came to the conclusion that even the severities of this strict monastic order offered him more security than he wished to enjoy as a perfect imitator of the humble Christ of Nazareth. He left the monastery to live as a solitary servant of the Poor Clares in the town of Nazareth. During this time of transition and solitude, he began to dream of founding a new order which would incorporate the spirituality he had been striving to attain. His desire was to form a band of followers who would live in small groups

---

[95] Jean-Francois Six (ed.), *Spiritual Autobiography of Charles de Foucauld*, trans. J. Holland Smith (New York: P.J. Kenedy and Sons, 1964), pp. 19, 55, 83; Fremantle, *Desert Calling*, p. 129; George Gorrée, *Memoirs of Charles de Foucauld Explorer and Hermit Seen in His Letters*, trans. Donald Attwater (London: Burns, Oates, and Washbourne, 1938), p. 36.

[96] Six, *Spiritual Autobiography of Charles de Foucauld*, p. 49.

[97] Fremantle, *Desert Calling*, p. 155.

[98] Six, *Spiritual Autobiography of Charles de Foucauld*, p. 22; Six, *Witness in the Desert*, p. 174.

[99] Fremantle, *Desert Calling*, p. 171.

stressing absolute fraternity with no hierarchy, support themselves and their charity by manual labor, and stress poverty, abjection, prayer, and silence. They would have a twofold orientation: to produce as faithfully as possible the life of Jesus of Nazareth, and to follow this life in both Christian and non-Christian lands with the hope that presence, example, prayers, and offering Mass would influence others for good.[100] During this time, the latter years of the nineteenth century, Foucauld's ideal was still more contemplative than active; later, after experience in the Sahara, he placed more stress on contact with the people, especially through works of charity.[101]

In 1901, the solitude of the Trappists and his sojourn at Nazareth behind him, Charles de Foucauld was ordained priest. The question now was how to exercise his ministry. Foucauld's earlier fascination with the French possessions in North Africa was still strong. Living at the peak of the colonial period at the end of the nineteenth century, Foucauld was a man of his times. He saw French North Africa, Algeria, Tunisia, Morocco, Sudan, and the Sahara as a trust given to France for a twofold purpose: to administer and civilize and to raise to the level of France, and to evangelize with Christianity.[102] Foucauld melded his spirituality with the latter purpose and went to the Sahara, where there were scarcely any priests, to exercise his ministry of Nazareth among the most poor and abandoned.[103]

During this period following his ordination, Foucauld began to show a greater concern for saving souls. This became a passionate desire with him, always, however, built upon the principle that any good one does in this regard is in direct proportion to one's personal holiness.[104] North Africa would be converted, he was convinced, only by those bent on making every sacrifice and who had but one desire: to glorify Jesus by following and obeying him perfectly.[105] Converts, however, were not his immediate aim. He felt that the Moslem peoples of North Africa were not ready

---

[100] Fremantle, *ibid.*, p. 160; Six, *Witness in the Desert*, pp. 51-53.

[101] Gorrée, *Memoirs of Charles de Foucauld*, p. 41.

[102] Fremantle, *Desert Calling*, pp. 256, 327-28; Gorrée, *Memoirs of Charles de Foucauld*, p. 111; Six, *Witness in the Desert*, pp. 208, 212.

[103] Fremantle, *Desert Calling*, p. 209; Six, *Spiritual Autobiography of Charles de Foucauld*, pp. 138-39.

[104] Six, *Spiritual Autobiography of Charles de Foucauld*, pp. 144, 168.

[105] Gorrée, *Memoirs of Charles de Foucauld*, p. 74.

for this step because of their lack of "civilization" and education. Their attachment to Islam was too firm, and their intellectual state kept them from seeing the falseness of their religion and the truth of Christianity.[106] He saw his role, and the projected role of those who would join him, as being an advance guard to plow the first furrow. This was to be done by prayer, abnegation, identification, and charity. The type of missionary he strove to be was not one who would preach the Word directly, but one who would identify and live with the people, offer the Mass and adore the Blessed Sacrament in their midst, and live an exemplary life on the model of Christ in Nazareth, exercising the evangelical virtues, especially charity.[107]

The missionary life style he attempted to develop and institutionalize in a new order, therefore, was based on three principles. First, prayer and adoration: Foucauld felt that offering Mass and adoring the presence of Christ in the Sacrament could not but have efficacious results among non-believers. Second, double identification: he sought identification with the example set by Christ poor and humble at Nazareth, and identification with the people by living a Christ-like life among them, mastering their language and culture, and thus building up trust. Third, example: he wished to cry the gospel not with words but with one's whole life by living a life of prayer, penance, and evangelical charity so that non-believers could not but be attracted to Christianity. In short, it was evangelization by presence, the presence of Christ in the Mass and Sacrament, and the presence of Christ in the life of the missionary. Only after the ground had been broken in this manner, and only when men's hearts had been properly prepared through these means, should the preaching and teaching orders, such as the Salesians, Jesuits, Dominicans, and Carmelites, begin the actual work of direct evangelization and conversion.[108]

Since the days of his seclusion in the East, Foucauld dreamed of forming religious congregations for men and women which would embody these principles and carry on his work. Before he died, he made several trips to France to advance these projects.

---

[106] Six, *Spiritual Autobiography of Charles de Foucauld,* pp. 180-81.

[107] Gorrée, *Memoirs of Charles de Foucauld,* pp. 56, 61, 74-75; Six, *Spiritual Autobiography of Charles de Foucauld,* p. 148; Six, *Witness in the Desert,* pp. 194-95.

[108] Gorrée, *Memoirs of Charles de Foucauld,* pp. 74-75.

His vision of the missionary dimension of Christian life also expanded gradually. After several years in the Sahara, he became convinced that the salvation of souls should be one's life work no matter what place he had in life.[109] The faithful in all lands were called to witness by their lives so that non-believers would be won for Christ.[110] Therefore, in addition to the orders he wished to found, Foucauld envisioned confraternities of lay men and women who would style their lives on the model he had developed. Specifically, he hoped to bring farmers, artisans, and landowners, men of all classes, to Africa to support missionary work by their example and goodness. These would be the nucleus to which the first converts could be aggregated once these had accepted the faith.[111] During his lifetime, Foucauld was unsuccessful in forming the type of religious order he envisioned. He died as he lived, alone, witnessing to Christ among the Tuareg people. His ideas were eventually institutionalized in the 1930's when the Little Brothers of Jesus and the Little Sisters of Jesus were founded following his inspiration.

I remarked in the beginning of this section that Foucauld's spirituality in some ways represents a return to very ancient approaches to mission spirituality and in other ways might point out future directions. Certainly his emphasis upon evangelization by presence and example is similar to the way Christianity spread during the first three centuries of the Church. Furthermore, the asceticism and self-abnegation he demanded fits into the monastic tradition first highlighted by the Celtic monks from Ireland. But Foucauld also sets directions for future mission spirituality. In a de-Christianized world, a world in which deeply convinced Christians in all countries are in the minority, a world of diaspora Christianity which has perhaps heard too much of direct preaching and evangelization, in this world, which is still a world looking for spiritual leadership and inspiration, a Christian missionary following the principles of Charles de Foucauld by living the gospel might be a very effective means for furthering the cause of Christ as a sign of the divinely inspired possibilities still realizable in fully Christian and fully human existence.

---

[109] Six, *Spiritual Autobiography of Charles de Foucauld*, p. 210.
[110] *Ibid.*, pp. 185, 190.
[111] Gorrée, *Memoirs of Charles de Foucauld*, p. 118.

Conclusion: Some Patterns of Mission Spirituality

It will now be helpful to summarize some of the qualities of mission spirituality seen in the last two chapters. Then we can raise the questions of the relevancy and value of these qualities for the present situation of Christian missionary work.

In Chapter II, I discussed tradition as one of the contributing factors in spirituality and listed some of the traditions of spirituality in the Church; for example, the tradition of martyrdom in the early centuries, the monastic-religious order traditions within Roman Catholicism, *devotio moderna* in the Late Middle Ages, and Pietism in Protestantism. It is not surprising that mission spirituality often coincides with these more general traditions of Christian spirituality. Columban and Charles de Foucauld fall within the monastic-religious order tradition, with great stress given to, and high motivation drawn from, personal asceticism. Boniface, Lull, and Xavier are within the more active branches of this same tradition. Zinzendorf came from the tradition of German Pietism. William Carey is one of the forerunners in the movement of denominational mission-sending societies within Protestantism. J. Hudson Taylor fits into the tradition of interdenominational faith missions which stress direct evangelization and individual conversion, one of the more flourishing traditions within Protestant mission work today.

Over and above these, there are two other great traditions concerning the approach to mission and therefore mission spirituality. These two traditions can be identified by the theological stance taken concerning the relation of Church and mission: the one stresses the identity of the two — the Church is mission and totally for mission; the other would not deny this identity but would see mission work as carried on not by the whole Church but rather as the responsibility of specifically organized groups within the Church — the Church has missions.

The first tradition predominated in the early Church to the extent that ordinary Christians, by their lives and personal witness, were the primary force in the spread of the faith. It appears in Zinzendorf's Moravian Church which made the whole community responsible for mission. There is a hint of it in the challenges raised by William Carey and Hudson Taylor when they asked whether all Christians should follow the command of Christ and engage themselves in spreading the knowledge of Christ. Finally,

Foucauld, in his later years, seems to have entered the same tradition when he saw the necessity for all Christians to witness to Christ by their lives.

The second tradition appears with the rise of the professional missionaries. Columban, Boniface, and Xavier all stand in this tradition. On the Protestant side, although Carey and Taylor saw mission as a challenge for all Christians, the fact that they founded societies specifically for the purpose of evangelization places them in the second tradition where the society or the order is responsible for mission within the Church.

The first set of questions which present themselves, therefore, concerns the relation of Church and mission. Is the Church mission and totally for mission, or does the Church have missions? Is mission at the heart of the Church or on its periphery? Is missionary spirituality, therefore, at the heart of all Christian spirituality, the focal point of all Christian spirituality, or is it but one of the many possible ways for Christians to determine their life styles? Granted that specialization is necessary, how is the Church to value the role of the specialist vis-à-vis her mission? Are missionary orders and societies the best and only way to approach mission today, or is a broader approach necessary?

Constants in Mission Spirituality

Categorizing the missionaries considered above into two broad traditions is a simplification. It might seem to smooth over their differences a little too much and take the heart out of their individual genius and spirituality. After all, can the Moravian Zinzendorf justly be classed with the ex-Trappist Foucauld, or can Xavier the Jesuit be categorized along with Hudson Taylor the faith missionary? The answer to these questions is both *yes* and *no*. In some very important ways, the spirituality of these men and all the men considered here is very similar. If there is one conclusion which stands out in these two chapters it is this: deep spirituality, faith, and holiness are not limited by denominations and traditions. There are remarkable consistencies in the missionary spirituality found in all the men considered in these chapters. I will first consider these similarities, and, in a later section, turn to the differences found in mission spirituality. The constants which appear from this study can be summarized under four categories.

1. *Fascination with the Love of God and Christ.* In every person and period considered in these chapters, this element, expressed in one manner or another, has existed. It consists in a consuming love for God and Christ, the conviction that men need Christ, and an impelling drive to tell others of him. The main mission motivation in the early Church was a sense of gratitude, devotion, and dedication to the Lord who had rescued men and given them a new life. Columban's passion was to love Christ by imitation of his pilgrimage upon earth. Once converted, Foucauld could not but love God, and the manifestation of his love became the imitation of the hidden life of Nazareth. Boniface and Xavier were driven to make conversions so that God might be glorified more. Lull was enraptured by a vision of Christ's love on the cross. Xavier worked for the glory of God by accepting the challenge of Christ the King to bring others into the kingdom. Christ as the Lamb of God was central to the spirituality of Zinzendorf and his followers. Carey and Hudson Taylor were driven to tell others of the expiatory death of Jesus for sinners. In a variety of ways and under a variety of images, then, the love of God and Christ dominated the spirituality of all the great missionaries considered here.

Closely connected with this is the need which men have for Christ because of the human condition, especially sinfulness. Expressed in one form or another, the need which men have for Christ and the Church has permeated mission theology and spirituality throughout the centuries. In the early Church, the situation of men without Christ was seen to be perilous. Boniface labored to bring the German peoples into the Church as the Ark of Salvation. Despite his openness to Islam, Lull was convinced of the impossibility of salvation without Christ. Xavier was driven passionately by the conviction that the peoples of the East were lost without baptism in Christ. Zinzendorf's constant desire was to win souls for the Lamb. Carey and Taylor spread the gospel and preached the expiatory death of Christ as the only hope for sinful non-believers.

The first constant for mission spirituality, then, is this consuming love for Christ which impels one to spread the knowledge of him to others. It is impossible to question the relevancy of this attitude for missionaries in any period of the Church. What can be questioned and approached from many directions is the stance which Christians take with regard to non-believers. Granted the universality of sin, how does this square with the universality of Christ's redemptive death? And, is explicit knowledge and acceptance of Christ absolutely necessary for salvation? Is the state of non-believers as perilous as missionaries over the centuries believed? Are they condemned to eternal damnation? In other words, what is the situation of the non-believer with regard to salvation? Finally, how does this affect the missionary's drive to tell others of Christ. These are the most important issues confronting mission theology and spirituality today.

2. *Union with God, Personal Holiness, and the Witness of Christian Living.* The missionaries considered in these two chapters have been men of outstanding holiness. As Xavier saw clearly, this is the *sine qua non* for mission. Foucauld placed great stress upon total personal conversion before one could approach others concerning Christ. In some cases, such as Columban and Foucauld, the asceticism of striving for personal holiness took precedence over evangelistic work in their life styles. All the missionaries considered, however, were men of personal sanctity which was developed through prayer, reading of the Scripture, and self-sacrifice. Hudson Taylor is an example of strict self-denial and an awareness of the presence of God which seems to have had mystical qualities in its sensible manifestations. The witness value of such a life of personal holiness is one of the primary means for mission which has remained constant in history. In the case of the early Church, historians agree that it was the example of the lives of Christians which drew others to Christ. Boniface labored to shore up the lives of the clergy in Germany to make them effective ministers of Christ. Zinzendorf saw personal example as central to mission work. Lull, Carey, and Xavier stressed a life of love as the means to conquer for Christ. Finally, Foucauld's whole emphasis was upon witness as the way to prepare men for acceptance of Christ.

It can be said, therefore, that personal holiness and union with God have been constant and necessary for mission spirituality, and, secondly, that the witness which comes from such a life has remained one of the primary means for bringing others to faith. Holiness, however, has had a variety of manifestations over the centuries, ranging from the withdrawal and seclusion of the monk to the involvement and commitment of the man of action. The question now is this: How are men called to be holy today; that is, what forms of self-denial, charity, and commitment to Christ will have most credibility for our times? What forms of sanctity are most appealing and most authentic in this age?

3. *Trust in God.* A third constant which appears in missionary spirituality throughout the centuries is deep faith and trust in God. Because of the great challenge and difficulty which is inherent in the effort to bring other men to accept Christ, missionaries have been forced to place all their reliance and trust in God. Boniface had complete confidence that it was God's will that he labor for the Church in Germany. Xavier, the first modern missionary to be confronted with the millions of the Far East, was forced to acknowledge that God was the source of any success he had laboring for souls. Xavier and Carey realized that it was God who changes hearts, not men. Carey's trust in God sustained him in the desolation and discouragement of his early years in India. Taylor's missions were called faith missions; he possessed a living sense of the faithfulness of God to those who have trust in him.

Intimately linked with such a stance of trust in God are three other qualities which appear regularly in mission spirituality. First, a certain boldness and strength which results in the conviction that no difficulty is too great and no hardship too severe to keep one from witnessing to Christ. Xavier, Carey, and Taylor all possessed this attitude. Second, great courage and perseverance. Zinzendorf insisted that there be no faintheartedness among his followers. Lull, Xavier, Carey, Taylor, and Foucauld labored despite failures because of the convictions flowing from their trust in God. Finally, joy. A sense that one is called to work for Christ and that one is doing the work of Christ issues in a great sense of joy and consolation. The early Christians witnessed joyfully to Christ by their lives and in death. Xavier stated that, despite the hardships and difficulties, he had never had greater joy than when doing God's work in the Indies. Zinzendorf and Spangenberg sent their missionaries around the world in happiness and joy. Carey's joy centered on an impelling desire to preach Christ crucified.

The missionary is a man thrust upon God for his sustenance at its deepest level. This raises the question whether the missionary is his own man, or whether he is a man of the Church, or, ultimately, whether he is the man of God. In other words, whose mission is it — ours or God's? Has this fact been obscured in the history of Christianity? How can it become clearer today? How can confidence and trust be built up in an age when much of the missionary movement seems to have lost its heart?

4. *Loving Service and Humility.* Service and humility are but two of the qualities and virtues which have marked the lives of great missionaries of the past. They flow naturally from a life of personal holiness. Christian charity and the fellowship of love in the Christian community drew men to the early Church and have continued to draw men to Christ through the centuries. Lull, Carey, and Foucauld, each in different ways, stressed the primacy of love in bringing men to Christ. Xavier insisted that his co-worker, Mansilhas, deal with non-believers with great kindness. Loving service has marked the life styles of missionaries over the centuries. Although it has not been stressed in these chapters, this has been the underlying motive behind the vast works of education (the monasteries of the Middle Ages, the Jesuits, men like Carey and Alexander Duff), work for social welfare (the reductions, Bartolomé de las Casas, anti-slavery campaigns), and the work of hospitals and dispensaries which have appeared over the centuries under the sponsorship of Christian missions.

Personal humility is a second quality which is necessary and constant in the missionary life style. Although not all missionaries have pushed this stance of humility to its furthest extent, mostly because they were men of their times who could not overcome the prejudices and cultural blocks of their age, in one way or another it has been present over the centuries. Lull begged the Catholic Church of the Middle Ages to study and learn the religious traditions of Islam. Xavier insisted upon personal humility and a sense of one's limitations as essential for the missionary. Zinzendorf called his followers to be men of humble faith and servants of others to bring them to Christ. Carey and Taylor came to India and China to learn the languages and present the Word of God to the people in their own tongues. Carey counseled others never to think of themselves haughtily nor to despise the people of India. Foucauld stressed complete identification with the people of the Sahara in order to win their confidence and witness Christ to them.

The questions for present-day mission spirituality are these: In what should loving service consist today? And, what is demanded by humility in the present situation of the world-wide phenomenon of rising self-consciousness and pride on the part of the different peoples and nations?

Relative Differences in Mission Spirituality

Having considered some of the constant elements in mission spirituality, I now wish to turn to elements which have differed among the missionaries considered. I shall approach this from the viewpoint of theology and then from culture. I use the term *relative* to describe them because they have differed over the centuries as theology itself, the science of faith, has differed and developed, according to the Church's reflection upon Scripture, in the culture and circumstances of history.

1. The Nature and Role of the Church. The missionary's life style will be fundamentally affected according to the theological understanding he has of the nature and role of the Church. Is the Church to be considered as the Ark of Salvation (Boniface) outside of which there is only extreme peril and danger of damnation (Xavier)? Or is it a less rigid reality, with the gospel being the important message, not the establishment of the Church (J. Hudson Taylor)? Is the Church to be totally identified with the Roman Catholic Church (Xavier)? Or is it a much less clearly defined reality with both visible and, more importantly, invisible dimensions (Zinzendorf)?

Secondly, what is the role of the Church? Is it to bring all men into itself as the only hope for their salvation (Xavier)? Or is it more an open, witnessing fellowship of believers whose role is service (Zinzendorf), abiding the times in witness and prayer, and silently drawing men to Christ and itself (Foucauld)? These differing positions regarding the nature and role of the Church are most important for the spirituality of mission. The life style of the missionary will be different depending on the positions he holds regarding them. Xavier was compelled to baptize almost indiscriminately because of the ecclesiology he held. For J. Hudson Taylor, the gospel and direct evangelization towards conversion were the main concerns. Foucauld opted for the role of prayerful presence.

2. *The Object of Mission.* Intimately a part of the ecclesiological problem is the question of the purpose of missions. What is it that the missionary goes out to achieve? Again, over the course of history different objectives have been present. Boniface would be an example of those who saw their role to be one of planting the Church, in his case the Roman Church in Germany. The establishment of the Church has been a prevailing goal in Catholic mission history down into the twentieth century.[112] Another approach, with a slightly different emphasis, sees the role of the missionary as one who must make converts (Xavier), or one who must preach the gospel of Christ (Carey and Taylor). Are conversions and the spreading of the knowledge of Christ to be given the emphasis in mission work? Finally, how is evangelization to be carried out — by directly preaching Christ and distributing Scripture (Carey and Taylor), or more indirectly by the witness of Christ-like living and charity (Foucauld)? Again, missionary life styles have differed depending on how the missionary saw his objective.

3. *Salvation and the Church.* Most of the missionaries of the past centuries took an extremely negative stance regarding the possibility of salvation outside the Church. Compassion for lost souls drove them to superhuman efforts to tell others of Christ and to baptize millions. The state of non-believers with regard to salvation and the soteriological status of non-Christian religious traditions must be reckoned as an all-important factor in determining the missionary's life style. For our times it is the most important factor. If the Christian engaged in mission is convinced that all non-believers are damned, or if he is convinced of the great peril and sinful condition of non-Christians, he will spend every effort to preach the gospel and baptize. On the other hand, if he has a more positive view of the non-Christian's relation with God and the revelatory and redemptive possibilities of non-Christian traditions, his life style as a witness to the gospel will take a different course.

4. *The Role of the Missionary vis-à-vis the World.* Under this heading comes the tension which has always existed in Christianity between the here and the hereafter, between life now and

---

112 See Francis X. Clark, S.J., *The Purpose of the Missions: A Study of Mission Documents of the Holy See, 1909-1946* (New York: Mission Union of the Clergy, 1948).

eternal life. Ultimately the issue comes down to the meaning and interpretation of salvation and eschatology. Is salvation to be thought of as solely a matter of saving souls, a phrase which appears so frequently in mission history? Or does it have a this-worldly dimension to it as well? Coming out of the ascetic tradition of Celtic monasticism, Columban saw human life in terms of transition and pilgrimage to eternal life, but the stress was heavily upon the hereafter as man's true state of being. Over the centuries this view of man's ultimate destiny has tended to dominate Christianity, ultimately because of the difficulties in handling the dualism so hard to escape if man is seen as embodied spirit. Some have tended to shun this world entirely and look only to the life hereafter; for example, early monastic traditions; others have gone to the opposite extreme and identified man's salvation with historical progress; for example, certain tendencies in the nineteenth century which extolled progress and saw a direct line between Christian civilization and the gospel.

Concretely and practically, however, missionaries have more often than not witnessed to the value of earthly life by their work in education, social reform, and health. The value one places upon this-worldly existence, therefore, has been an important determinant in the missionary life style. How are man's being in this world and his future being in the final era to be balanced? Finally, what can be said about the theme of man as pilgrim upon the earth? This predominated in the Irish tradition, but it is a theme which has recurred again in the history of missions. Does it have a relevance for today, and, if so, in what sense?

5. *The Agents for Mission.* In the periods and persons presented in these chapters, a variety of positions have been seen concerning those who have engaged in missionary work. In the early Church, the ordinary Christians carried the burden in the expansion of the faith. With the development of the monastic traditions, monks and members of religious orders were almost the sole agents in the expansion of Roman Catholicism. With the awakening of missionary interest in the Protestant traditions, a greater share in mission work was given to laymen by men like Zinzendorf, Carey, and Taylor. The next important question, then, is who are best suited to engage in mission today?

6. *Ecumenism and Mission.* From earliest centuries, Christianity has been split into different groups or denominations. These

chapters have considered missionaries from the Roman Catholic and Protestant traditions; little reference has been made to mission work done by other Christian churches. Ecumenical concerns are rather recent in the history of Christianity, despite the pioneering ideas of Zinzendorf. The Jesuits were renowned for being the shock troops of the Catholic Counter-Reformation in the sixteenth century. In the eighteenth century, the Jesuit missionary Constantine Beschi (1680-1746) clashed with Bartholomäus Ziegenbalg and the other early Lutheran missionaries in India. Although William Carey and Hudson Taylor were openminded towards other Protestant missionary enterprises, both of them were partially driven by a desire to emulate and offset the efforts of "'Romish" missionaries.

The modern ecumenical movement, however, is one of the proud results of the missionary movement within Protestantism.[113] The scandal which Christian disunity offered in the nineteenth and twentieth centuries impelled the Protestant churches to work towards greater cooperation and unity. The Roman Catholic Church has shown a positive interest in this concern only late in the present century. One thing is certain, however: no one, whether Protestant, Catholic, or from the Eastern churches, can engage in mission work without taking a stance regarding the ecumenical movement and the strides being made to unify the different branches of Christianity. His attitude to this will definitely affect his life style and spirituality, making it more or less open or closed to the value of the witness given by all the different Christian churches.

Some Cultural Concerns

In Chapter II the relation between culture and spirituality was discussed. It was seen that Christian spirituality is both formed by and in turn helps to form culture. This relationship has also been evident in the spiritualities of mission outlined in the last two chapters. These are some of the factors which stand out in this area.

---

[113] See William Richey Hogg, *Ecumenical Foundations: A History of the International Missionary Council and Its Nineteenth-Century Background* (New York: Harper and Brothers, 1952).

1. *The Relationship between the Culture of the Missionary and that of the People to Whom He is Sent.* In the sixth and seventh centuries, missionaries from Ireland brought the Celtic monastic traditions from their homeland to Europe and had no small influence upon the development of Christian culture on the Continent. Boniface worked within the political framework of his times to develop the Roman model of Christianity in Germany. Ramon Lull saw the value of mastering Islamic language and religious thought before he could attempt to convince its people of Christianity; but, living at the height of the Middle Ages, he was a man of his times when he advocated the use of crusading methods to convert the Moslems. Xavier labored under the aegis of Portugal in the Far East to introduce Christianity there. He had a very shallow appreciation of the religions of the East, but his outstanding successors in China, India, and Japan spent lifetimes striving to enculturate Christian theology and practice in the East. Each in his own way, William Carey, J. Hudson Taylor, and Charles de Foucauld, held the European culture of the West in higher esteem than the cultures into which they went, and saw the gospel as a civilizing factor for other peoples, or, in the case of Foucauld, saw the necessity of civilizing peoples according to European patterns before the gospel could gain acceptance.

An important issue in missionary life style, therefore, will be the relationship the missionary sees between his culture and the culture of peoples different from himself, and between the gospel as accepted and lived in his own culture and its possibilities for realization in a new cultural situation.

2. *The Development of Peoples.* Intimately connected with the cultural problem, and closely related to the form of evangelistic witness, is the question of the development of peoples. Objectively speaking, it would be a mistake to believe that the patterns of every culture are of equal value. A culture which flourishes on slavery, or one which relegates women to a role of servitude, or which suppresses large numbers of people for the advantage of a few, cannot, in the objective order, be rendered completely compatible with Christianity today. In one manner or another, the missionary has always been an agent of cultural change. Columban and the monks from Ireland nurtured learning in Europe. Jesuits have consistently stressed education in mission

lands. Like Carey, thousands of missionaries have labored to master new languages and translate the gospel into them. Missionaries, like the followers of Zinzendorf, have introduced agricultural and technological skills; they have established medical centers; and they have worked to eradicate social injustices.

The next question which must have an influence upon the missionary's life style is his relationship to the social and material development of peoples. This presupposes, of course, that he sees his role not only as a preacher of the gospel but as an agent for the betterment of peoples' whole lives.

3. *Pre-Christendom, Christendom, and Post-Christendom.* It was remarked early in Chapter III that the situation of the Church in the pre-Constantinian period differed greatly from the Church in the following ages inasmuch as Christianity before Constantine was a minority religion with more opposition than approval from the state. In the ages that followed, the relationship between Christianity and the ruling powers in Europe changed radically — Christianity became the official religion. Boniface worked with the blessings of the rulers of his times. Lull sought to get the influence of the leaders of Church and state to sponsor his missionary program. Xavier and the Jesuits in the Portuguese and Spanish colonies worked under royal patronage with support from the rulers of those countries. The larger portion of missionary expansion in the past has followed the pattern of movement from Christian countries to those not Christian. Christendom was the powerhouse from which missionaries went out to non-Christendom. As mentioned in Chapter I, the situation has changed with the gradual demise of Christendom. This ultimately will affect mission, both how a missionary lives and, more importantly, where he works.

4. *The Milieu of the New Christian.* Another factor which distinguishes the missions of the Middle Ages and part of the modern period from those of the early Church and those of more recent times is the phenomenon of group conversion. Mass movements of this type have been characteristic of areas where religion is integrally an affair of the people or the tribe. Although more prevalent in previous ages, it has continued into our own times; for example, most recently in Indonesia. One of the important questions raised by this phenomenon is the relation of a new Christian to his environment. Missionaries over the centuries have realized the importance of the milieu in which the faith is lived.

A most dramatic example of this is the case of the Jesuit reductions in Latin America. When mass conversion is no longer possible, and where there is a well accepted tradition of religious pluralism in a society, how does the missionary form his life style and the life styles of new Christians in order to make Christianity possible?

Motivation

The last area which remains to be discussed in this chapter is missionary motivation. Motive is the impelling force behind the life style of the missionary. The missionary's aim, goal, or objective is related to his motivation, but the two do not necessarily coincide. For example, a missionary's goal may be to plant the Church or to convert souls; this might also be his motive in mission, but more often than not he will have other motives which rest deeper; for example, all his work of Church planting and evangelization is but for the glory and service of God. Often a missionary will have many motives arranged hierarchically or parallel to each other. At times, however, one motive stands out more than the others. In this final section, I shall list some of the missionary motives which have occurred in the periods and persons considered in the last two chapters. In my enumeration, I am indebted to the categories of mission motivation presented in literature written on this topic in recent years.[114]

1. *Theocentric and Christocentric Motives.* The glory of God and the love and service of Christ are perhaps the most fundamental and omnipresent motives in mission spirituality. The theo-

[114] See R. Pierce Beaver, "American Missionary Motivation before the Revolution," *Church History*, 31 (1962), 216-226; *idem*, "Missionary Motivation Through Three Centuries," *Reinterpretation in American Church History*, ed. Jerald C. Brauer (Chicago: University of Chicago, 1968), pp. 113-51; *idem*, *Pioneers in Mission: The Early Missionary Ordination Sermons, Charges, and Instructions* (Grand Rapids, Mich.: William B. Eerdmans, 1966), pp. 17-23; Johannes van den Berg, *Constrained by Jesus' Love: An Inquiry into the Motives of the Missionary Awakening in Great Britain in the Period Between 1698 and 1815* (Kampen: J.H. Kok, 1956); Sidney H. Rooy, *The Theology of Missions in the Puritan Tradition: A Study of Representative Puritans: Richard Sibbes, Richard Baxter, John Eliot, Cotton Mather, and Jonathan Edwards* (Grand Rapids, Mich.: William B. Eerdmans, 1965); Paul A. Varg, "Motives in Protestant Missions, 1890-1917," *Church History*, 23 (1954), 68-82; Max Warren, *The Missionary Movement from Britain in Modern History* (London: SCM Press, 1965).

centric motive, the glory of God, was seen in Boniface, Xavier and the Jesuits, and Carey. It marked the mission efforts of the Puritans in America. The Christocentric expression of this motive, the love and service of Christ, was illustrated in the life of Ramon Lull, Zinzendorf, and in Jesuit spirituality.

2. *Soteriological.* Pity and compassion for those outside the Church or without the knowledge of Christ and the gospel has been another almost constant motive in mission spirituality. In one form or another, it has been found in all the missionaries seen in the last two chapters, perhaps most strongly in Xavier, Carey, and Hudson Taylor.

3. *Ecclesiological.* This motive, like the one above, often coincides with the aim of mission. Its central focus is the establishment and nurturing of the Church. Boniface, Xavier, and modern Roman Catholic missions have been characterized by this motivation.

4. *Ascetic.* According to this, missionary work is a type of spiritual discipline pleasing to God and helpful towards one's own sanctification and salvation. Boniface was reminded that he would work out his personal salvation through mission. Columban viewed mission more in terms of self-perfection through pilgrimage than in terms of the salvation of others. In modern times, Foucauld approaches this motive with his life of extreme asceticism and stress upon personal conversion before conversion of others.

5. *The Command of Christ.* Over the centuries, the "Great Commission" (Matt. 28:18-20; Mark 16:15-16; Luke 24:46-49; Acts 1:8) has had differing degrees of prominence in mission motivation. Christ's command was rarely cited in the early Church as a motive for mission. It appears in Boniface, but it is less pronounced in Roman Catholic mission history than in Protestantism. It was one of the primary motives appealed to by William Carey and Hudson Taylor.

6. *Corpus Christianum.* The supposition behind this form of motivation is that religion and state or religion and culture form a unity. The missionary, therefore, is not only engaged in spreading the gospel but also in building Christendom. Boniface worked closely with the rulers of Germany. Lull was motivated in this manner when he advocated crusades as a way to spread the Catholic Church. Xavier and the Jesuits worked under the patronage of the kings of Spain and Portugal. Modern missionaries, both Protestant and Catholic, have by and large been less closely tied

to governments, and in some cases they have opposed colonial practices. Nevertheless, the cultural presuppositions of the colonial era, especially with regard to Western supremacy, have dominated many missionaries. In the twentieth century, Foucauld offers an example of thinking which still reflects the *corpus Christianum* mentality — he saw the role of France in North Africa to be one of civilization through French culture and evangelization.

7. *Humanitarianism.* With this form of motivation, pity and compassion are had not only for the "lost souls" of non-believers, but also because of their temporal condition. It has been closely associated with the preceding motive — the benefits of Western civilization are to be spread to less fortunate peoples in order to render them more civilized. The Irish monks with their monastic centers had something of this motive. It appears in differing degrees over the centuries and rather explicitly in men like William Carey and Hudson Taylor for whom the gospel was a means towards civilization.

8. *Gratitude.* Michael Green mentions that this was a prevailing motive in the early centuries of the Church. It does not seem to appear too frequently over the centuries, but it is intimately connected with the theocentric and Christocentric motives of love and service.

9. *Called by God.* Most missionaries feel an inner call towards mission. This motive would also have to be ranked in any listing of missionary motives. It appears in Columban, the call to pilgrimage; in Boniface, the will of God to be a missionary; and clearly in J. Hudson Taylor. Another form of this would be the call by God through the Church; for example, the Jesuit idea of superiors expressing the will of God in assigning a man to mission work.

10. *Counteracting the Missionary Efforts of other Churches.* In the post-Reformation age, anti-Protestant feelings and anti-Catholic feelings were part and parcel of being Catholic or Protestant. Not all missionaries possessed Zinzendorf's ecumenical open-mindedness. Occasionally missionaries have been motivated by a desire to offset the accomplishments of other Christians. This motive was seen in the writings of William Carey and Hudson Taylor, although it is far from the predominant motive for these great men.

The motives listed above have all appeared, in one expression or another, in the lives of the men considered in these two chapters. However, they do not exhaust the possibilities of mission motivation. Throughout the centuries, other motives have occurred; for example, the eschatological motive of mission as a form of hastening the coming of the kingdom of God, mission as introducing the millennium, or mission as one of the signs of the kingdom; the motive of debt and reparation for past evils inflicted upon a people; romantic motives connected with the desire to visit and work among primitive peoples in picturesque places; and, finally, the motive of martyrdom.

As I mentioned in the beginning of this section, there is no sealing these motives off from each other, for most missionaries have been inspired by several of them. Ruth Rouse, in an article written some years ago, maintained that all missionary motivation could be reduced to one basic motive: "Belief that God has a purpose for the life of each one of us, and a purpose for the whole world: conviction that He works out His purpose through our acceptance of His plan for the life of each one of us — such is the supreme missionary motive. A five-word phrase sums it up — 'Saved: to serve: the world.' "[115] As suggested earlier, there is a great similarity in some of the fundamentals of mission spirituality. If all the motives which historians have dissected from the lives of missionaries over the centuries can be reduced to this one, as Ruth Rouse maintained, there is greater reason to affirm a basic unity in all mission spirituality. The question which must be asked as we move from the motive or motives of the past into present-day and future motivation is which motives or which expression of the one basic motive will be most appropriate for our times.

---

[115] Ruth Rouse, "The Missionary Motive," *International Review of Missions,* 25 (1936), 250-58.

V

THE FOUNDATION OF MISSION AND THE NATURE OF THE CHURCH

The examples of missionary spirituality given in the previous two chapters have shown that during the course of mission history there have been both constant and relative characteristics in mission theology and spirituality. The thesis suggested in this book is this: because the context of mission work has changed in our times, and because the theology of mission is being reassessed, the mission spirituality which has come to us from the past may likewise have to be reassessed or differently expressed in the present-day situation.

The purpose of the next three chapters is to present one approach to contemporary mission theology. From this, guidelines for a spirituality of mission will be suggested. But first, it is important to note that the present theological situation is problematic inasmuch as the theology which forms the basis of mission spirituality is in a state of development. That is, theological doctrines concerning such important areas as grace, revelation, sin, the nature of the Church, the goal of mission, the relation of the Church and the churches, and the stance of the Church towards other religious traditions — all of which are central for mission — are being discussed, examined, and restated among Christians. Therefore, at this point it is important to set down an important methodological principle; the purpose here is not to resolve theological problems which are at the root of mission theology. This would be impossible in the present context. Nevertheless, because the Church must engage in mission, those who dedicate themselves to this cannot wait for the theological problems to be solved before they develop a personal spirituality. Therefore, what will be done in the present situation is to propose one approach to the theology of mission and develop corresponding options and conclusions for mission spirituality.

As I stated in Chapter I, the stance taken here is from within the Roman Catholic tradition. My intention, then, is to take positions which are consistent with this tradition while at the same time taking account of the wealth of theological insight available from a study of other Christian churches and theologians. In truth, many of the theological issues concerning mission today are identical for both Protestant and Catholic theology, and if there is any great division in mission theology, it often does not arise from the fact that one is a Protestant or a Catholic, but rather from conservative and liberal trends which crosscut both traditions.[1]

This chapter will discuss the trinitarian foundation of mission and the nature of the Church as the agent of God's Mission. Chapter VI will be concerned with the goal of missionary work and offer an identification of the missionary for today. Chapter VII will discuss the relationship between Christianity and the other religious traditions of the world. In each chapter the implications for mission spirituality which flow from the theological positions taken will be developed.

The Trinitarian Foundation

The triune God is the origin, chief agent, and the end of Mission. This proposition, which has been elaborated in both Protestant and Roman Catholic mission theology in recent years, is the dogmatic foundation of both mission theology and mission spirituality. It has been expressed and developed by the Roman Catholic Church in the documents of Vatican II. God, out of his wisdom, goodness, and love, created the world for his own glory and with a plan to glorify man by enabling him to participate in divine life. Refusing to abandon man to sin, and in order to establish his peace and communion between men and himself and to fashion men into a fraternal community of adopted sons, the Father sent his Son, clothed in our flesh, as the Mediator who might reconcile the world to himself. When the Son's work was accomplished, the Holy Spirit was sent to carry out God's

[1] See, for example, Gerald H. Anderson, "Some Theological Issues in World Mission Today," *Mission in the '70s — What Direction?* eds. John T. Boberg, S.V.D. and James A. Scherer (Chicago: Chicago Cluster of Theological Schools, 1972), pp. 109-10.

saving work by sanctifying his people, the Church, and impelling it to expand so that what was preached and wrought by the Son for the salvation of the human race might be proclaimed and spread abroad. Sent by Christ and impelled by the Spirit, the apostles and their successors have preached the good news of God's plan to all the world. This mission is a continuing one. Initiated by the Father, unfolding in Christ, and prompted by the Spirit, the Church walks the same road which Christ walked, a road of poverty and obedience, of service and self-sacrifice to death and from death to resurrection, announcing in hope to the world and to the ages the gospel, the plan and purpose of God's Mission.

Missionary activity is the manifestation or epiphany of God's will inasmuch as God works out the history of salvation by means of Mission. The will of God, then, is the final reason for missionary activity, for God wants all men to be saved. God's people, the members of the Church, are impelled to carry on God's Mission by reason of the love with which they love God and by which they desire to share with all men in the spiritual gifts of both this life and the life to come. Finally, the context of Mission is history, the time between the first coming of the Lord and the second; missionary work tends toward the fulfillment which will come at the end time when the Church will be gathered into the kingdom of God.[2]

This summary of Vatican II condenses much of the theological basis of missions which will be developed in the following chapters. Mission is rooted in the life of the Trinity. Ultimately, the theology of Mission is trinitarian. God himself is the initiator and prime agent of Mission. The people of God have a participatory role in this trinitarian work. The goal of Mission is likewise God himself — ultimately salvation consists in all creation's sharing in God's life of glory. This goal is not totally other worldly — God desires not only that men share in his peace and communion but also that men be fashioned into a fraternal community here and now. The object of God's love and concern is the world and all men. The ultimate motive for Mission on God's part is love; on our part, the part of those who participate in the

[2] "Dogmatic Constitution on the Church," Sections 1-4; "Decree on the Missionary Activity of the Church," Sections 2-9.

Mission of the Trinity, the motive is love and obedience. The manner of Mission is founded in the self-giving and self-emptying model of the Trinity — those who participate in God's Mission walk the same road which Christ walked, a road of poverty and obedience, of service and self-sacrifice. Finally, the time of Mission is the time during which the kingdom of God is being realized between its initial proclamation with Christ's first coming and its final consummation at his last coming. Mission, therefore, is an ongoing process which is trinitarian in its initiation, trinitarian in its realization, and trinitarian in its fulfillment. As Greek theology expressed it, Mission is from the Father, by the Son, in the Holy Spirit — in the Holy Spirit, by the Son, back to the Father.[3]

Because of its trinitarian origin, direction, and end, Mission is not primarily an affair of men, the mission of the Church, or the mission of the Christian community, but rather the Mission of God. *Missio Dei* is the term which has been used in ecumenical circles during recent years to express this insight. The mission of the Church and the missions of men in the churches are participations in the Mission of God.[4] God's Mission works through the Church's mission, but at the same time it is wider than the Church's mission. Historically, the Mission of God antedated the mission of the Church and it continues today to work for men and the world beyond the boundaries of the Church. This point of emphasis is important — Mission is not a Church-centered activity but rather a God-centered action. If Mission is centered and based on the Church, then missions become a matter of propagation of the Church, or more concretely, of the churches, and the historical and cultural peculiarities of particular churches.[5] Although it is not possible to separate the historical Church from the peculiarities of cultures and civilizations, when Mission is seen to be primarily

[3] Quoted from Marie-Joseph Le Guillou, O.P., "Mission as an Ecclesiological Theme," *Re-thinking the Church's Mission*, ed. Karl Rahner, Concilium 13 (New York: Paulist, 1966), p. 119.

[4] See George F. Vicedom, *The Mission of God: An Introduction to a Theology of Mission*, trans. Gilbert A. Thiele and Dennis Hilgendorf (St. Louis: Concordia Publishing House, 1965); J.G. Davies, *Worship and Mission* (New York: Association Press, 1955), p. 32; Walter J. Hollenweger (ed.), *The Church for Others and the Church for the World: A Quest for Missionary Congregations* (Geneva: World Council of Churches, 1969), p. 14.

[5] Hans J. Margull, *Hope in Action: The Church's Task in the World*, trans. Eugene Peters (Philadelphia: Muhlenberg, 1962), p. 66.

an affair of God and not only of the churches, the tendency to absolutize particular historical participations in the Mission of God can be more effectively countered.

If the theology of Mission is founded on the theology of the Trinity, missionary spirituality must rest on the same foundation. In the first place, it can be said that the theology of the *missio Dei* offers a foundation for those constant elements which have occurred in the history of missionary spirituality. As pointed out in the two historical chapters, the love of God and fascination with Christ have been recurring themes in mission spirituality. The realization that the mission of the Church is a participation in God's Mission gives this love a trinitarian base. Out of love the Father sent the Son, and out of love the Spirit was sent to continue the Mission of God. Those who participate in God's saving Mission ground their missionary love in the same love which is part of the inner life of the Trinity and at the heart of the Trinity's Mission.

Two other recurring themes in mission spirituality were confidence and trust. A realization of the participatory and instrumental nature of human missionary effort, that Mission is not ours nor the Church's but God's, grounds confidence and trust not in any human work or institution but in the life and work of the Trinity. Furthermore, a knowledge that it is not our mission but God's Mission is the source of boldness, strength, and joy as we participate in the *missio Dei*. It is also the basis for hope — hope not in human work but in God's work unfolding through the human.

Finally, because the Mission of God is not something which occurred once in history but is rather a process which continues in history under the direction of the Holy Spirit to its ultimate fulfillment when men shall be united with God and the kingdom fully established, mission spirituality founded on the Mission of God avoids excessive otherworldliness or a vertical split between the transcendent God "above" and the world process "below." God's Mission in history was introduced in Israel, it was realized in Christ, and in an analogous fashion it continues in the world through God's people, the Church, which is guided by the Spirit, and it exists beyond the Church in a mysterious fashion not fully known by men. God's presence and activity in the process of history, especially through the Mission of the Spirit, gives further grounds for missionary confidence, trust, and hope; and offers the opening for greater awareness of the divine presence on the part of those who participate under the guidance of the Spirit and in imitation of Christ in the *missio Dei*. Because God's Mission is historical and takes the process of human history and development seriously, a spirituality of mission must be adapted to history and to the times and ages. The Church's work of mission must correlate itself to the times; and the spirituality of mission must be attuned to the different ages and cultures. This is another way of underlining the importance of cultural and historical factors for mission spirituality.

The Church and Mission

Missionary theology and spirituality have the Trinity for their foundation. However, although the primary truth in salvation history is the *missio Dei*, and although it cannot be denied that God's Mission is wider than the mission of the Church, nevertheless the role of the Church in God's Mission is not to be considered unimportant. God is not only the Sender but also the One Sent in Mission — the Second Person of the Trinity was enfleshed in time and walked our roads. In turn, the community gathered by Christ was sent, under the direction of the Holy Spirit, to announce and continue the Mission of God. Even though it is possible that God could have achieved his Mission in another fashion, and that God works his Mission even where Christ is unknown, the Mission of Jesus Christ is central to God's plan, and the community commissioned by Christ is the primary participant in the *missio Dei*. Within the perspective of Mission, therefore, the Church can be described as the visible, historical community whose task is to participate in, and carry on, the Mission of God through the times and the ages. Although God's Mission is realized in ways and manners which are beyond the Church, the Church has a primacy in the historical, visible realization and continuation of that Mission.

The notion of visibility is important. Theories of the Church which opt for an invisible form of its existence are neither meaningful nor functional. To speak of an invisible Church is as difficult as speaking of an invisible incarnation. The Church's participation in God's Mission demands that God's plan be made visible and present to the nations and ages. This is done by word, announcing the good news of the plan of God revealed by Christ (*kerygma*), by deed, service towards fulfilling this plan (*diakonia*), and in the community (*koinonia*) which performs and lives these tasks. To speak of an invisible Church and invisible Christians, or of anonymous or latent Christians — valuable though these constructs may seem to be for soothing Christian consciences — tends at best to be ambiguous, confusing, and open to misinterpretation, and, at worst, rather condescending to non-Christians. While it must be maintained that God's will and work are being achieved beyond Christianity, it would be a mistake to say that an invisible Church or anonymous Christians are doing that work. As it was done by Cyrus in biblical times, it is being done today by non-Christians and non-theists who, in a mysterious fashion, are guided by the favor of God.

Because the Church, after Christ, is the primary, visible participant in the *missio Dei,* it is missionary by definition and nature. As seen in Chapter III, the unity of Church and mission was a position taken for granted in the early centuries of Christianity. Throughout the centuries, however, save for a few key examples, the Church and theology lost sight of this essential unity. Only in recent decades has the oneness of the two been restated.[6] Because the Church and mission are one, because the Church is mission and for mission, and because the Church enjoys the primacy for continuing the *missio Dei,* the whole Church and all Christians are called, according to their various gifts and roles, to participate in mission. In the Catholic tradition, this position has been endorsed by Vatican II. According to the Council, the Church is missionary by its very nature and the work of evangelization is a basic duty of all the people of God; therefore, all should

---

[6] See Le Guillou, "Mission as an Ecclesiological Theme," *Re-thinking the Church's Mission,* ed. Rahner, pp. 81-82; Wilhelm Andersen, *Towards a Theology of Mission: A Study of the Encounter between the Missionary Enterprise and the Church and Its Theology,* I.M.C. Research Pamphlet 2 (London: SCM Press, 1955), pp. 13-14; Lesslie Newbigin, *A Faith for this One World* (New York: Harper and Brothers, 1961), pp. 109-10; *idem,* "Mission to Six Continents," *The Ecumenical Advance: A History of the Ecumenical Movement, Volume II, 1948-1968,* ed. Harold E. Fey (Philadelphia: Westminster, 1970), p. 179.

"spread and defend the faith by work and deed as true witnesses of Christ."[7]

In recent years the point has been made in Protestant ecumenical circles that God is primarily related to the world and not, as an older model would have it, to the world through the Church. Expressed schematically, this relationship would be God-world-Church, not God-Church-World.[8] The position taken here regarding the primacy of the Church in mission and the essential unity of Church and mission does not intend to deny the insight contained in this model; namely, that God's plan is for the world and is worked out in the world and not only through the Church. However, the model God-world-Church is open to the danger of relativizing the role of the Church to the extent that it becomes mere event, existing wherever there are men who are for their fellow men doing God's worldly work. Such a position seems to underplay the fact that in the divine plan there has been a chosen and appointed community whose role is to announce the plan of God, witness to it, and work to achieve it in the world. On the other hand, the model God-Church-world runs the danger of making the Church seem to have a monopoly over the Mission of God to the extent that it becomes the Ark of Salvation and a sanctuary to which men are gathered from the world.

The truths expressed in both models must be maintained in tension. The action of God cannot be limited to the Church alone; on the other hand, the primacy of the Church as participant in God's Mission is to be maintained. To deny this latter point would seem to go counter to the pattern of the Incarnation; that is, God's Mission is worked through Christ and might be expressed as God-Christ-world. Therefore, in order to avoid excessive separation of the Church from the world and to avoid making the Church into a type of sanctuary into which men are gathered from the world, the nature of the Church must be elaborated in open rather than in closed terms. Current Roman Catholic ec-

---

[7] "Dogmatic Constitution on the Church," Section 11; see also "Decree on the Missionary Activity of the Church," Sections 2, 35; "Pastoral Constitution on the Church in the Modern World," Sections 33, 35, 36; "Decree on the apostolate of the Laity," Sections 2, 3; Paul VI, *Evangelization in the Modern World [Evangelii Nuntiandi]* (Pasay City, Philippines: St. Paul, 1976), Sections 15, 59-73.

[8] See Hollenweger (ed.), *The Church for Others,* pp. 16-17.

clesiology does this by representing the Church as sign, sacrament, and the pilgrim people of God dedicated to a role of service of God and to the world. I shall develop these notions below, but first it is necessary to suggest some of the implications of what has been said so far for spirituality.

When the Church is seen to be a visible continuation and locus of the *missio Dei,* and when the Church is defined as missionary by its very nature, two implications follow for spirituality. First, on the broadest level, every Christian is missionary by vocation, and therefore the spirituality of every Christian must have a missionary dimension and recognize and take account of participation in the Mission of God. Second, more limitedly, this means that those who have been engaged in missionary work, as it has been understood in recent centuries, are engaged in an activity which closely conforms to, and takes part in, the very life and work of God himself. If, as mentioned in Chapter II, the imitation of Christ is one of the focal points of Christian spirituality, then the lives of missionaries take on great meaning inasmuch as they conform closely to the life of Christ and the work of Christ fulfilling God's Mission.

The call of the whole Church to mission can also be linked today in the Roman Catholic tradition to the call of all Christians to holiness. It was seen in Chapters III and IV that personal holiness has been considered a necessary requirement for mission work over the centuries. Mentioned above also was the fact that in the Catholic tradition the life of holiness and perfection has often been too exclusively identified with the religious or monastic life. Vatican II, however, offsets this tendency. The Council affirms a fundamental unity and equality among the people of God and refuses to limit the pursuit of holiness to any one class in the fellowship of believers. While not failing to praise the charism of religious life, the Council affirms that all the people of God are called to the fullness of Christ and to the perfection of charity.[9] It thus counteracts the imbalance which for centuries tended to make the monastic and religious traditions the mainstream of Christian perfection and holiness. But, more significantly, Vatican II offers an important contribution to mission spirituality when

[9] "All the faithful of Christ of whatever rank or status are called to the fullness of the Christian life and to the perfection of charity." ("Dogmatic Constitution on the Church," Section 40.)

it makes an essential spiritual requisite for mission, the call to holiness, coextensive with the theological foundation for mission, the duty of all the people of God to participate in God's Mission. In practice, at least in recent centuries, the Catholic Church would not deny this; what Vatican II did was officially to bring its theory of mission and spirituality in line with practice. Mission is the duty of all Christians and the example of their profoundly holy Christian lives is the primary means towards this task.[10]

Finally, the balance maintained by being open to the truths contained in the formulas God-Church-world and God-world-Church has implications for the spirituality of mission. Although the Church holds a primary place in the Mission of God, a realization that God's Mission is wider than the mission of the Church offers a check against triumphalism on the part of the Church and the missionary in approaching non-Christians, and an underpinning for humility and openness, two other constantly recurring missionary qualities. Furthermore, it serves as the theological basis for inculturation, accommodation, and indigenization both of theology and of spirituality. That God's Mission is at work beyond the range of the Church and Christians is the theological spur which urges the Church and Christians to approach the world with openness and humility, to look for the signs of God whose Spirit has gone before (see Acts 10:45-48), and to explicitate them in symbols not foreign to, but in conformity with, the indigenous culture.

The Church as the Pilgrim People of God

The Church has already been described in a preliminary fashion as the visible, historical community whose task it is to carry on the Mission of God through the centuries. Although God's Mission works itself out beyond the limits of Christianity,

---

[10] "As members of the living Christ, all the faithful have been incorporated into Him and made like unto Him through baptism, confirmation, and the Eucharist. Hence all are duty-bound to cooperate in the expansion and growth of His Body, so that they can bring it to fullness as swiftly as possible (Eph. 4:13)....

"Yet, let all realize that their first and most important obligation toward the spread of the faith is this: to lead a profoundly Christian life. For their fervor in the service of God and their charity toward others will cause new spiritual inspiration to sweep over the whole Church." ("Decree on the Missionary Activity of the Church," Section 36); see also Paul VI, *Evangelization in the Modern World,* Sections 41 and 76.

the Church has a primacy with regard to that Mission. In other words, the Church formally explicitates what God is doing through his Mission in the world. But more than this must be said concerning the nature of the Church.

It is fortunate within the Roman Catholic tradition that Vatican II explicitates the nature of the Church in terms of mystery, that is, a reality which cannot be fully captured by human thought and language.[11] Since the Church is mystery in this sense, it can be approached and defined from a variety of directions and in a number of ways. Because the Church is a mystery by nature, a plurality of ecclesiologies is rendered possible, for no one approach can fully fathom the mystery of the Church. It can be shown that Vatican II, a Council which focused upon the Church, contains differing ecclesiologies. For example, Richard McBrien believes that the Council documents contain three distinct ecclesiologies which he refers to as the scholastic, the kerygmatic or biblical, and the eschatological. McBrien ascribes these differing ecclesiologies to a difference in theological methods: the first two positions coming from positivistic methods which assume that theology is essentially a matter of reflecting upon, explaining, criticizing, and defending what is contained in a primary source, be it Scripture or doctrine; the third option, the eschatological, coming from what he calls a broad application of Tillich's method of correlation which makes an analysis of the human situation out of which the existential questions arise and demonstrates that the symbols used in the Christian message are the answer to these questions. McBrien feels that the Council makes no serious attempt to reconcile these different ecclesiologies.[12]

Ecclesiological pluralism is one of the reasons for the current crisis in missions, for the model one uses to define or describe the Church affects the way the Church participates in God's Mission. Thus, a model which sees the Church in scholastic terms as an institution into which all must be gathered in order to attain salvation in the hereafter will have a different concept of mission than models which stress the nature of the Church as a kerygmatic community which announces the good news of

---

[11] See "Dogmatic Constitution on the Church," Section 1.

[12] Richard P. McBrien, *Church: The Continuing Quest* (New York: Newman, 1970), pp. 5-13; for the method of correlation, see Paul Tillich, *Systematic Theology*, Vol. I, *Reason and Revelation, Being and God* (Chicago: University of Chicago, 1955), pp. 59-66.

salvation, or a diaconal community which devotes itself to service in the world in order to hasten and prepare for the arrival of God's kingdom. Of course, no model will remain pure in itself; each will contain elements from the others. The determining factor is the point of emphasis. Although the institutional-hierarchical model finds support in the documents of the Council, it is balanced by several other approaches to the Church which, in the long run, cannot but make the future institution of the Roman Catholic Church different from the past. First of all, a basic unity and equality is seen in the Church according to which all members participate in Christ's priestly, prophetic, and kingly offices.[13] Therefore, the hierarchy of the Church is defined not primarily in terms of power and domination, but rather in terms of a ministry of service to the brethren.[14] Secondly, the mystery of the Church is elaborated in terms of sign and sacrament and as a community of the pilgrim people of God. These latter notions have great import for mission theology and spirituality.

The theme of pilgrimage is no stranger in the history of mission theology. As seen above, it dominated the theology and spirituality of Columban and the Irish monk-missionaries. The ancient theme of the Church as pilgrim and of mission as a pilgrimage has been given new forcefulness in the Catholic Church by Vatican II. Without denying the more traditional approach to the Church as institution and hierarchy, the Council views the mystery of the Church in a more biblical framework by elaborating its nature in terms of community and the people of God. It is described as the new people of God which includes in various fashions all of those who are reborn through the Word and from water and the Holy Spirit. Despite their different gifts and calls, the people of God possess a common unity inasmuch as all participate in Christ's threefold role of priest, prophet, and king. They form a fellowship of life, charity, and truth which is God's instrument for the redemption of men, for the unity, hope, and salvation of the human race. This community is dynamic in nature, moving through the world, transcending the limits of time and race, and extending to all regions of the earth. Thus the people of God, the Church, is a wayfaring fellowship and a pilgrim Church which takes on the appearance of the passing

---

[13] "Dogmatic Constitution on the Church," Chapter II.
[14] *Ibid.*, Section 18.

world and dwells among creatures who await the revelation of the sons of God.[15]

At this point it is worth reflecting upon the implications of what has been said in this section for mission spirituality. The first point concerns ecclesiological pluralism. Because of the close link which exists between theology and spirituality, different theologies of the Church will result in different mission spiritualities. A plurality of theologies necessitates a plurality of spiritualities. Thus, for example, it is possible today to find some who hold the more traditional hierarchical, institutional notion of the Roman Catholic Church, similar to Boniface; and as a result their mission work and spirituality is totally concerned with bringing non-members into the Church. The intention here is not to deny the possibility of different theologies of the Church. Pluralism is a fact which must be accepted on the level of theology and spirituality. In this situation of pluralism, however, the intent of this chapter is to suggest the implications of newer approaches to the Church which will by necessity affect missionary spirituality today.

The emphasis which the Second Vatican Council has given to the Church as the community of the people of God is another element. By stressing the nature of the Church more in terms of fellowship than in terms of hierarchy, Vatican II underscores the importance of Christian community (*koinonia*) for today's situation. Excessive tendencies towards individualism and interest in one's personal salvation and the salvation of individuals can thus be questioned. Christian spirituality and mission spirituality, therefore, will be seen in communitarian rather than in individualistic terms since the whole Church sees itself as a priestly and prophetic community, a brotherhood and fellowship where all share in the mission of God by being a worshiping community of service to the world.[16]

The revival of the theme of pilgrimage likewise has important repercussions for mission spirituality. Christian spirituality as pilgrim spirituality is a theme which has been common in both

---

[15] *Ibid.*, Chapters II, VII.

[16] Joseph A. Grassi, M.M., "Blueprint for a Missionary Church: Scriptural Reflections on the Church as the People of God," *The Church as Sign*, ed. William J. Richardson, M.M. (Maryknoll, N.Y.: Maryknoll Publications, 1968), p. 26.

Protestant and Catholic traditions.[17] However, the pilgrim theme has a special meaning for mission spirituality. The image of the Church as a fellowship of the road and a community on the march is one of the most relevant for the present situation and an image offering great challenge.[18] The man who participates in the Mission of God is one who leaves the values of home and goes out — "Now the Lord said to Abram, 'Go from your country and your kindred and your father's house to the land that I will show you'" (Gen. 12:1). The "Great Commission," long seen to be one of the foundations of mission motivation, enjoins the disciples of Christ to go and make disciples of all nations (Mt. 28:19).

Since the people of God are sent as a community through the times and nations with the good news of God's plan for man, what might be called wayfaring virtues have an important place in the spirituality of mission. Mission is carried out in hope; the people of God travel the road with confidence in the guidance of the Spirit, both looking towards and working for the promises of God. The spirit of adaptation, accommodation, and enculturation is also grounded in the wayfaring approach to mission. Since missionary work is a God-directed project and process through time, and since God's mission is subject to the variations of history and people, missionary work demands flexibility and a willingness to adjust both thought and structure to new periods and peoples where the *missio Dei* is at work and is being consciously worked out by the fellowship of God's people. Flexibility is required both in thought and structure: the former gives ground for taking seriously the rich religious and cultural values of other peoples; the latter makes impossible what have been termed heretical structures and morphological fundamentalism, tendencies to return to structures of the past or to retain those of the present in a rigid manner instead of allowing the times, places, and needs of a locality to be creative in producing new structures.[19]

---

17 See Edward Farley, *Requiem for a Lost Piety: The Contemporary Search for the Christian Life* (Philadelphia: Westminster, 1966), Chapter X.

18 John A. Mackay, *Ecumenics: The Science of the Church Universal* (Englewood Cliffs, N.J.: Prentice-Hall, 1964), p. 92.

19 See J.C. Hoekendijk, "Morphological Fundamentalism," *Planning for Mission: Working Papers on the Quest for Missionary Communities,* ed. Thomas Wieser (New York: U.S. Conference for the World Council of Churches, 1966), p. 134.

Finally, it should be said that mission undertaken in the spirit of pilgrimage will demand suffering. One of the classic presentations of the missionary's life is that given in the Second Letter to the Corinthians by Paul when he describes the sufferings he encountered (see 2 Cor. 11-12). It reflects Jesus' own experience of having no place to rest his head (Luke 9:58). The spirituality of mission will be a spirituality and prayer rooted in faith in the Mission of God, open to newness and the possibility of suffering on the part of the Christian, and sustained by zeal, a zeal supported by confidence, trust, and joy because the Christian is pilgrimaging with the Lord.[20]

It should be added, however, that there is one important difference between the pilgrim spirituality of the twentieth-century Church and that which was common in the sixth-century Church. This is expressed, for example, by Vatican II's awareness of history, the positive role it assigns to human development, and its sensitivity to the signs of the times. This attitude is in marked contrast to the negative views taken of the world in the sixth century. Earthly values and progress, although they are to be distinguished from the kingdom of God, are of vital concern to the building of that kingdom.[21] According to the earlier view, the pilgrimage is through a world which is seen as dangerous and threatening to man's eternal destiny; the newer view of pilgrim theology acknowledges the ambiguity of the world, but prefers to look toward its goodness as something to be developed and perfected for the kingdom of God.

The Sacramental and Semiological Aspects of the Church

It is not sufficient to describe the mystery of the Church solely in terms of community, fellowship, or as the people of God who participate under the guidance of the Spirit in the *missio Dei*. To do so leaves out the Christological element essential

---

[20] See Adrian Hastings, *Mission and Ministry* (London: Sheed and Ward, 1971), Chapter VI.

[21] "Therefore, while we are warned that it profits a man nothing if he gain the whole world and lose himself, the expectation of a new earth must not weaken but rather stimulate our concern for cultivating this one. For here grows the body of a new human family, a body which even now is able to give some kind of foreshadowing of the new age.

to the nature of the Church. This element is introduced when the Church is elaborated in terms of "sign and sacrament," and as the Body of Christ. Roman Catholic theology places great importance on the sacramental principle according to which God's self-communication in grace and love is mediated to men by means of material symbols. The sacraments are the face of redemption turned visibly towards men so that through material symbols we are able to encounter Christ.[22]

In addition to discussing the Church in terms of the people of God, Vatican II also elaborates the nature of the Church in sacramental terms. In what Karl Rahner has termed the most timely as well as the most original statement of Vatican II,[23] the Church is described as the universal sacrament of salvation. It is the sacrament or the sign and instrument of the intimate union of men with God and with each other.[24] The Council also restates the Catholic tradition by describing the Church according to the Pauline image of the Body of Christ.[25] There is a connection between the Church's sacramental nature and the Church as seen as the Body of Christ; if a sacrament is said to be God's grace and love made present through material form and symbol, then Christ is the primordial sacrament or channel of this grace, and the Church and the sacraments of the Church may be considered as secondary or separated sacraments, prolongations into

---

"Earthly progress must be carefully distinguished from the growth of Christ's kingdom. Nevertheless, to the extent that the former can contribute to the better ordering of human society, it is of vital concern to the kingdom of God." ("Pastoral Constitution on the Church in the Modern World," Section 39); see also Section 57.

[22] See Edward Schillebeeckx, O.P., *Christ the Sacrament of the Encounter with God* (New York: Sheed and Ward, 1963), pp. 43-44.

[23] Karl Rahner, S.J., "How to Receive a Sacrament and Mean It," *Theology Digest*, 19 (Autumn, 1971), 232.

[24] "By her relationship with Christ, the Church is a kind of sacrament or sign of intimate union with God, and of the unity of all mankind. She is also an instrument for the achievement of such union and unity. For this reason, following in the path laid out by its predecessors, this Council wishes to set forth more precisely to the faithful and to the entire world the nature and encompassing mission of the Church."

The English translation of this is defective; the Latin text reads this way: "Cum autem Ecclesia sit in Christo veluti sacramentum seu signum et instrumentum intimae cum Deo unionis totiusque generis humani unitatis, naturam missionemque suam universalem, praecedentium Conciliorum argumento instans, pressius fidelibus suis et mundo universo declarare intendit." ("Dogmatic Constitution on the Church," Section 1); see also "Decree on the Missionary Activity of the Church," Section 1.

[25] "Dogmatic Constitution on the Church," Section 7.

time of the presence of Christ with men. Thus, sacramentally considered, the Church can be described as the earthly extension of the body of the Lord.[26]

A sacrament is essentially a result-producing sign. That is, sacraments are by nature material realities which point beyond themselves to divine realities, and in their materiality serve as channels for divine grace and love. Thus, Christ, the Church, and the sacraments of the Church, each in differing ways and each analogously, are signs of God's self-communication. As sacrament, the Church is an effective, result-producing sign. In the words of Vatican II, the Church, because of her relationship with Christ, is a sacrament or sign and instrument of the union of mankind with God and with each other.[27] Both Vatican I and Vatican II describe the Church in Isaian terms as a standard lifted up for men to see (Isaiah 11:10-12).[28] The Christian community is to be the sign of God's presence in the world.[29] The mission of the Church is a sign of brotherhood among the nations through its sharing of the gospel message with all men.[30]

It is of special importance to note that the Church as sign points in a twofold direction — to God and to men. Through its sacramental instrumentality, the Church signifies and works to achieve peace and unity between man and God and between man and man. Once more, in the words of Vatican II, the purpose of God's Mission is to establish peace or communion between sinful human beings and himself and to fashion mankind into a fraternal community.[31] Since the Church by nature participates in the *missio Dei*, it is the sacrament, sign, and instrument for

---

[26] See Schillebeeckx, *Christ the Sacrament of the Encounter with God*, p. 41; Karl Rahner, *Theology of Pastoral Action*, trans. W.J. O'Hara (New York: Herder and Herder, 1968), pp. 44-49.

[27] "Dogmatic Constitution on the Church," Section 1.

[28] "Decree on Ecumenism," Section 2; for Vatican I, see Henricus Denzinger and Adolfus Schönmetzer, S.J., *Enchiridion Symbolorum* (New York: Herder, 1963), Number 3014.

[29] "Decree on the Missionary Activity of the Church," Section 15.

[30] "Pastoral Constitution on the Church in the Modern World," Section 92.

[31] "In order to establish peace or communion between sinful human beings and Himself, as well as to fashion them into a fraternal community, God determined to intervene in human history in a way both new and definitive. For He sent His Son, clothed in our flesh, in order that through this Son He might snatch men from the power of drakness and of Satan (cf. Col. 1:13; Acts 10:38) and that in this Son He might reconcile the world to Himself (cf. 2 Cor. 5:19)." ("Decree on the Missionary Activity of the Church," Section 3.)

achieving these ends. Expressed in another manner and more biblically with an Old Testament concept, the Church is the sign and instrument of God's *shalom* being worked out in history. The term *shalom* means peace, integrity, community, harmony, and justice as expressed in the messianic promises of Psalm 85:10-11: "Steadfast love and faithfulness will meet; righteousness and peace will kiss each other. Faithfulness will spring up from the ground, and righteousness will look down from the sky."[32] The Church is God's sign and sacrament for realizing his messianic promises partially now and fully at the end times.

This brings up the relationship between the *Church* and the *kingdom of God.* The Church is a sign pointing to the kingdom of God and a sign which realizes and makes partially present the *shalom* of the kingdom. The kingdom of God is a central concept in ecclesiology and missiology. Jesus came announcing the good news of the kingdom (Mk 1:14-15). It is both the goal and purpose of the *missio Dei* and the goal and final meaning of history.[33] It is also the goal of God's people, the Church.[34] The kingdom of God is the symbol used to describe that eschatological reality which will fully come about as a result of divine action at the end times but which has been announced and rendered partially present by the mission of Jesus Christ.[35] In Oscar Cullmann's terms, the kingdom of God possesses "already" and "not yet" qualities — it has already been announced and proleptically introduced with the life, death, and resurrection of Jesus, but it is not yet here in its fullness. This will only occur by an act of God at the end of time.[36]

---

[32] See J.C. Hoekendijk, *The Church Inside Out,* trans. Isaac C. Rottenberg (Philadelphia: Westminster, 1966), p. 21.

[33] See Paul Tillich, "Missions and World History," and Wilhelm Andersen, "Further Toward a Theology of Mission," *The Theology of the Christian Mission,* ed., Gerald H. Anderson (Nashville: Abingdon, 1961), pp. 281, 304; Vicedom, *The Mission of God,* p. 14.

[34] "Dogmatic Constitution on the Church," Section 9.

[35] The view of eschatology presented here is obviously following the salvation history theory of eschatology as espoused by theologians such as Oscar Cullman. It stands in opposition to theories such as Albert Schweitzer's consistent eschatology, C.S. Dodd's realized eschatology, and R. Bultmann's existential eschatology.

[36] Oscar Cullmann, *Christ and Time: The Primitive Christian Conception of Time and History,* trans. Floyd V. Filson (Philadelphia: Westminster, 1964), Chapter V; Alan Richardson, *An Introduction to the Theology of the New Testament* (New York: Harper and Row, 1958), Chapter IV; Rudolf Schnackenburg, *God's Rule and Kingdom,* trans. John Murray (New York: Herder and Herder, 1963), p. 350.

The Church and the kingdom of God are related, but in no way should they be identified with each other. Catholic theology has had a tendency to make this identification in the past. Rather, participating in the *missio Dei,* the Church is a sign partially realizing the kingdom and at the same time pointing to its final realization at the *eschaton*. The Church, therefore, is the means to the *eschaton,* the final times.[37] It is the agent, anticipation, and partial realization of the kingdom of God.[38] The mission of the Church is the dynamic action of the Church as sign with regard to the kingdom. The time of the Church and the time of mission is the time between times—between Jesus' announcement of the kingdom and its partial revelation, and the time when it will be fully revealed by the Father in the end. The Church, therefore, is a pilgrim between the times on its way to, pointing towards, and partially realizing the end of God's Mission, the kingdom. The Church takes its total meaning from this mission which is to further the Mission of God by proclaiming the initial manifestation of the kingdom in Jesus (*kerygma*), by being itself a Spirit-transformed community (*koinonia*) of faith, hope and love, and thereby a sign and anticipation of the *shalom* of the kingdom, and by working in service (*diakonia*) to announce and realize the kingdom.[39]

Speaking of the mystery of the Church in the images used so far—pilgrim people, sacrament and sign, Body of Christ—is open to the danger of speaking too abstractly. It might be asked: Where are the people of God? or, where and in what form is the sacramental sign of the Church made concrete? In present-day Roman Catholic theology, the answer to these questions is being worked out by some in terms of the *local Church*.

The theology of the local Church is one of the most fertile and important areas under investigation in Catholic ecclesiology and missiology today. In answer to the question, Where is the Church of Christ totally and fully present?, contemporary Catholic theology is thinking not only in terms of the Church universal with its centralized bureaucracy in Rome but also in terms of the local Church. One of the achievements of the Council

---

[37] "Decree on the Missionary Activity of the Church," Section 9.

[38] Tillich, "Missions and World History," *The Theology of the Christian Mission,* ed. Anderson, p. 282.

[39] McBrien, *Church: The Continuing Quest,* p. 73.

was the rediscovery of the universal Church as the sum and communion of the local Churches, understood as fully themselves, and the rediscovery of the universal Church in the local Church.[40] In the words of the Council, "This Church of Christ is truly present in all legitimate local congregations of the faithful which, united with their pastors, are themselves called churches in the New Testament."[41] The Church exists fully where Christ is effectively present unifying man with man and men with God; spiritually in the interior communion of faith, hope, and love; visibly in the external communion of profession of faith in God's Word in Christ, of adhesion to God's will in obedience to Christ's representatives, of participation in the life of grace through the sacraments, especially baptism and the Eucharist.

In terms of Catholic polity, these conditions are met in the diocese. This is the concrete unit of the local Church where the nature of the Church is fully realized, although smaller units which participate in the triple unifying presence of Christ, the parish, sub-parish units, and the family, participate in a similar degree in the ecclesial quality of the local Church. It should be noted that dioceses, therefore, are not just administrative units. Rather, because Christ is effectively present in them, they are *the* Church of Christ, not only *part* of the Church of Christ, not only *a* Church of Christ. They are served by the bishop in the name of Christ, not in the name of the pope; they have their own traditions and independent functions within the Church as a whole. The Church, therefore, is not to be conceived in political or managerial terms as a super-state or organization in which different regions and groups are solely administrative units with no independence and life of their own. Rather, the Church is wholly present in each local Church, and the Church universal might be described as a catholic communion of local churches. Its unity, therefore, is a unity with pluriformity.[42]

---

[40] Aloys Grillmeier, "The People of God," *Commentary on the Documents of Vatican II*, ed. Herbert Vorgrimler, I (New York: Herder and Herder, 1967), 167; Hastings, *Mission and Ministry*, p. 7.

[41] "Dogmatic Constitution on the Church," Section 26.

[42] See Joseph J. Blomjous, "Ecclesial Dimensions of Mission Responsibility," *The Word in the Third World*, ed. James P. Cotter (Washington: Corpus Books, 1968), pp. 223-57; *idem*, "Missionary Societies and the Mission of the Local Church," *The Church as Sign*, ed. Richardson, pp. 76-132; Hans Küng, *The Church*, trans. Ray and Rosaleen Ockenden (New York: Sheed and Ward, 1967), pp. 85-86; Karl Rahner, "Church," *Sacramentum Mundi*,

The theology of the local Church has important repercussions for mission. It has been said that in the past, at least in the Roman Catholic tradition, mission responsibility has been conceived too much in terms of the Church universal with the result that it became something a little too far removed from particular dioceses and parishes, and resulted in too facile a distinction between the pastoral function of the Church and its missionary function.[43] When the local Church is seen to be the full expression of the Church of Christ, mission responsibility falls directly upon it. It is not, therefore, a task belonging primarily to the Church universal, nor to international mission-sending societies and orders, although this pattern has predominated in the past. The subject of mission is the local Church gathered around its pastor, the bishop; and missionary outreach is directed both to those in the area of the local Church who do not acknowledge the name of Christ, and to those in the areas of other local churches which have need. Mission, therefore, takes place between local churches, and, in the case which involves members from one local Church going abroad to another Church, it is, if possible, always under the care and direction of the local Church to which they are invited and sent.

Under the topic of the local Church it is appropriate to introduce *ecumenism.* In the Protestant world the ecumenical movement is the grandchild of the missionary movement. As Protestant missions became more numerous during the nineteenth century, the scandal of Christian disunity was realized as one of the greatest difficulties in mission work. The International Missionary Council, which grew out of the seminal World Missionary Conference held in Edinburgh in 1910, prepared the ground for the World Council of Churches and eventually merged with it in 1961.

The Roman Catholic Church was fifty years slower than the Protestant churches to recognize officially the ecumenical mandate towards Christian unity. By the time of Vatican II, however, the theological reflection which had been going on among Catho-

---

eds. Karl Rahner et al., I (New York: Herder and Herder, 1968), 328; Rahner, *Theology of Pastoral Action,* p. 95; Lesslie Newbigin, *One Body, One Gospel, One World: The Christian Mission Today* (New York: International Missionary Council, 1959), p. 49; Paul VI, *Evangelization in the Modern World,* Sections 61-64.

[43] See Blomjous, "Missionary Societies and the Mission of the Local Church," *The Church as Sign,* ed. Richardson, p. 93.

lics during the previous decades bore fruit. The Catholic Church moved from a position of narrow exclusivism with regard to other Christian churches towards a position of openness and dialogue. The new estimation of the mystery of the Church which views it more in terms of the community of God's pilgrim people and less in terms of a rigid, hierarchical society with fixed and clearly defined limits made this stance of openness possible. The Council was careful not to make a complete identification between the Church of Christ and the Roman Catholic Church.[44] The Catholic Church at Vatican II stressed the importance of the common elements which are shared by all Christians — Scripture, the sacraments, especially baptism and the Eucharist, the gifts and graces of the Holy Spirit, Christian prayer, and other spiritual benefits.[45] Because of this, the Catholic Church, while cautious against certain defects which it still considered present in other Christian churches, recognized that other Christian churches as such are means of salvation for their members.[46] In terms of the future, this position seems hardly to go far enough; however, in terms of the past, when this stance of openness and acceptance of other Christian churches is compared with the exclusivity, self-righteousness, and triumphalism which characterized post-Reformation Catholicism, it represents a true *volte-face* on the part of the Catholic Church.

An ecumenical attitude is important for all Christians today, and it is of special importance for missionary work since it was and is in the area of mission that the scandal of divided Christianity has been most damaging. The essentials of such an attitude are outlined by Vatican II's "Decree on Ecumenism." Negatively it demands an elimination of words, judgements, and actions which might be prejudicial to truth, mutual respect, and dialogue between Christians.[47] While avoiding the pitfall of uncritical religious indifference, it demands a rejection of proselytism and quarrelsome rivalries among Christians.[48] Positively, Christians are called to give common witness to their faith and hope in

---

[44] See Johannes Feiner, "Catholic Principles of Ecumenism," *Commentary on the Documents of Vatican II,* ed. Vorgrimler, II, 69.

[45] "Dogmatic Constitution on the Church," Section 15.

[46] "Decree on Ecumenism," Section 3.

[47] *Ibid.,* Section 4.

[48] See "Decree on the Missionary Activity of the Church," Section 15; "Declaration on Religious Freedom," Section 4.

God and in Christ.[49] In imitation of Christ who came to serve, they are urged to cooperate in whatever projects Christian conscience sees as necessary for the common good of mankind.[50] This cooperation between Christians is especially necessary in view of the grave social concerns and needs experienced by modern men.[51] The Uppsala meeting of the World Council of Churches in 1968 expressed similar views on cooperation between Christians for joint planning and action upon local and international situations.[52] Thus there is an official desire among Protestants and Catholics for a truly ecumenical mission among Christians. The specifics of this will only be developed in the years to come.

Finally, it is most appropriate to include this brief consideration of the ecumenical attitude within the discussion on the theology of the local Church. For, if it is at the level of the local Christian community that the sacramental and sign nature and function of the Church become concrete and effective, it seems that the development of the theology of the local Church will have great importance for the ecumenical movement. When conceived in terms of the community of the pilgrim people of God, the Church will only possess unity amid legitimate local diversity. This diversity will allow for differences in Church polity, in liturgy and spirituality, and in theological expression. In fact, one of the most pregnant statements in the "Decree on Ecumenism" concerns the possibility of a variety of theological expressions with various theological formulations to be considered often as complementary rather than conflicting.[53] When such local diversity of theological expression is allowed, there can develop a true

[49] See "Decree on Ecumenism," Sections 4, 12.

[50] *Ibid.*, Section 4.

[51] *Ibid.*, Section 12; "Decree on the Missionary Activity of the Church," Section 15; "Pastoral Constitution on the Church in the Modern World," Sections 88, 90.

[52] Norman Goodall (ed.), *The Uppsala Report 1968: Official Report of the Fourth Assembly of the World Council of Churches, Uppsala, July 4-20, 1968* (Geneva: World Council of Churches, 1968), pp. 35-36.

[53] "What has already been said about legitimate variety we are pleased to apply to differences in theological expressions of doctrine. In the investigation of revealed truth, East and West have used different methods and approaches in understanding and proclaiming divine things. It is hardly surprising, then, if sometimes one tradition has come nearer than the other to an apt appreciation of certain aspects of a revealed mystery, or has expressed them in a clearer manner. As a result, these various theological formulations are often to be considered as complementary rather than conflicting." ("Decree on Ecumenism," Section 17.)

catholic community of local Churches which will preserve the unity of the Church of Christ and differing expressions of the gospel. It seems that it is toward this goal that the ecumenical movement, especially within the Roman Catholic tradition, must aim in years to come.

For the Church not to be separated from the world, its nature must be elaborated in open rather than in closed terms. Considering the *Church as sign and sacrament* renders this possible. A sign is nothing other than a reality which serves a mediating function by pointing to something else beyond itself. Signs show where the road will end, where danger is present, where information and help are available. The Church as sign can be conceived in a similar manner.[54] It is a visible, earthly reality whose essential role is to point beyond itself. To what? To God's Mission and saving purpose for all men, to the unity of man with man and man with God, to the blessings of *shalom,* to the kingdom. The role of the Christian and, more specifically, the role of the missionary is to realize and make this sign in the world.

Where spirituality is concerned, the challenge confronting the missionary is that the visibility of the sign be not obscured and its purity not contaminated. This is Charles de Foucauld's idea that self-perfection is necessary before evangelizing others. Negatively, this calls for constant, ongoing *metanoia* and evaluation of life and work — the area of self-discipline, self-criticism, and asceticism. Positively, it can be expressed according to the biblical images of being the light of the world and the salt of the earth.

The Church is not merely a sign which points to something else. It is also an efficacious, fulfilling sign, a reality which makes present the reality to which it points. This is because of its sacramental nature. The challenge for Christian spirituality, then, is that the Church, that is, all the people of God, be efficacious signs which render present, always through the action of Christ in them as in a body, what they point to and speak of. If the Church is the sign and sacrament of union and peace between

---

[54] William B. Frazier contrasts the Vatican II image of the Church as sign with a more traditional image of the Church as sanctuary. As Frazier develops the two images, a sign points beyond itself while a sanctuary is a place of refuge; a sign is a disclosure whereas a sanctuary is an enclosure; a sign is humble, a sanctuary haughty; a sign is for service, a sanctuary for separation; a sign is cooperative, a sanctuary competitive. See William B. Frazier, M.M., "The Church as Sign," *The Church as Sign,* ed. Richardson, pp. 1-15.

man and God and between men, if the Church is the sacrament of *shalom*, if the Church is the partial realization of the kingdom of God, Christian spirituality and mission spirituality must be centered on reconciliation, unity, peace, the blessings of *shalom* and of the kingdom. It should be noted that the Church as sign points in a double direction — to man and to God. Its goal is to unify men with each other and with God. It is important for spirituality not to lose sight of either dimension. In other words, the reality the sign points to and makes present, reconciliation, unity, peace, *shalom* — in short, salvation — is something which is both here and hereafter.

One last but all-important implication for mission spirituality can be drawn from this consideration of the Church as sign. A sign is not self-serving but for the service of others — that to which or to whom it points, that for which or for whom it points. Service, therefore, is of the essence of sign. As indicated above humble, loving service has been one of the constants in mission spirituality over the centuries. A spirituality of service is based on Christ, the one who emptied himself to serve (see Phil. 2:5-8; John 13). Jesus challenged his followers to be like salt, fire, light, and leaven — all images of service, of losing self for the kingdom.[55] Vatican II speaks of the Church as a leaven for human society, and the people of God as having a servant function.[56] When ecclesiology is developed in terms of sign and sacrament, the service element of traditional mission and Christian spirituality is well grounded. Humble, loving service as the manner of mission is, perhaps, the overarching and all-important virtue demanded for mission spirituality in our times. No matter what motives and attitudes were operative in the past, the present and future manner of one engaged in mission must be one of humble service.[57]

---

[55] See Elton Trueblood, *The Validity of the Christian Mission* (New York: Harper and Row, 1972), pp. 92-93.

[56] See "Pastoral Constitution on the Church in the Modern World," Sections 11, 40.

[57] See R. Pierce Beaver, *The Missionary Between the Times* (Garden City, N.Y.: Doubleday, 1968), pp. 36-37; *idem*. "The Missionary Image Today." *Mission in the 70s — What Direction?* eds. Boberg and Scherer, pp. 29-30; Theodore Eastman, *Chosen and Sent: Calling the Church to Mission* (Grand Rapids, Mich.: Eerdmans, 1971), pp. 42 ff.; Gabriel Fackre, *Humiliation and Celebration: Post-Radical Themes in Doctrine, Morals, and Mission* (New York: Sheed and Ward, 1969), pp. 257-58; Hoekendijk, *The Church Inside Out*, pp. 71-72; John Power, S.M.A., *Mission Theology Today* (Maryknoll, N.Y.: Orbis Books, 1971), p. 151.

The people of God serve each other and the world by signifying and realizing as far as possible reconciliation, unity, peace, and the *shalom* of the kingdom. Expressed in another fashion, it can be said that the missionary serves the world and the nations by announcing the message and good news of Christ and the kingdom (*kerygma*), by living in, and helping to form, a community (*koinonia*) which embodies and is a proleptic realization of the *shalom* and blessings of the kingdom, and by working in the world in a humble, self-giving manner (*diakonia*) for the reconciliation, peace, and unity which are at the heart of God's Mission and at the core of salvation.

The servant form which mission life style will have to take is also demanded by the theology of the local Church. Since the basic unit of the Church is the local Church which represents the whole Church of Christ, mission is the task and responsibility of the local Church. Missionary outreach, accordingly, is a service rendered by one local Church to another. Since each local Church is totally the Church of Christ and responsible for its own traditions, customs, and government, those who come to it come in the role of service to place themselves at the disposal of the local Church. The missionary flow, then, is primarily in the form of service from one local Church to another. The Church universal is served inasmuch as its unity in plurality will only be preserved if missionary service follows a twofold pattern — from older churches to younger churches and from younger churches to established churches. Disinterested and imaginative service from local Church to local Church is one of the main changes in the image of the missionary vocation in recent years.[58] The key phrases are "to be of service to," "at the disposal of," and "by the invitation of." This attitude will have to be at the heart of mission spirituality in the coming years.

This view which sees the local Church as the locus of mission responsibility gives added emphasis to a fact which has already been suggested; namely, that mission spirituality and Christian spirituality are intimately connected. It has been said that after Constantine mission and Church were effectively separated, and mission was no longer considered the task of the local congre-

[58] See Blomjous, "Ecclesial Dimensions of Mission Responsibility," *The Word in the Third World*, ed. Cotter, pp. 236-37; Hastings, *Mission and Ministry*, p. 16.

gation.[59] In a recent series of lectures, Cardinal Josef Suenens remarked that it is difficult to convince the average lay person that the Church is missionary by essence.[60] It must be admitted that what has been said about the local Church in these pages has been more by way of hoped-for direction than by way of actual fact. However, if this notion is developed, and if the implications of the theology of the local Church are fully thought out, the locus for responsibility and interest in mission will once more be placed where it was in the early centuries of the Church. The congregation will become missionary by definition and all Christian spirituality will have a missionary dimension to it.

Finally, it can be said that if the local Church has an essential role to play in mission, it has a correspondingly important role to play in ecumenism. The judgement has been made that, despite the accomplishments of the ecumenical movement in the past half century, the most painful gap in the whole framework is that it is inadequately rooted in the local churches.[61] The ecumenical attitude, like the missionary attitude, can have no permanent and deep effects unless it is firmly established in the local Church. The ecumenical attitude which is necessary for all Christians is most fundamentally a matter of spirituality. It was seen in Chapter II that *metanoia* is one of the essential features of all Christian spirituality. The point was made in this chapter that concern for the purity of the Christian sign and witness gives one area for continual Christian *metanoia.* It can be said here that ecumenism furnishes another area.

The elements required for this spiritual conversion are outlined in the "Decree on Ecumenism" of Vatican II. Insofar as it is a human institution, the Church is summoned by Christ to continual reformation as she goes on her pilgrim way. Therefore, essential to work towards Christian unity is a change of heart which involves a revision of attitudes, mutual love, and humble self-denial in the service of others. Christians are reminded by the Council that the more purely they strive to live according

---

[59] See, for example, James A. Scherer, *Missionary, Go Home: A Reappraisal of the Christian World Mission* (Englewood Cliffs, N.J.: Prentice-Hall, 1964), p. 46.

[60] Michael Ramsey and Leon-Joseph Cardinal Suenens, *The Future of the Christian Church* (New York: Morehouse-Barlow, 1970), pp. 80-81.

[61] See H. Krüger, "The Life and Activities of the World Council of Churches," *The Ecumenical Advance,* ed. Fey, pp. 61-62.

to the gospel, the more they are fostering ecumenism, for mutual brotherhood can only be achieved through profound communion with God. Change of heart and personal holiness will by necessity issue in public and private prayer for unity on the part of all Christians.[62] This is a program which has been called spiritual ecumenism. It is the spirituality which is the only possible foundation for the common witness and cooperation called for by Protestant and Catholic churches. It cannot be effective unless it is lived and expressed on the level of the local Church.

---

62 "Decree on Ecumenism," Sections 4, 6, 7, 8.

VI

THE GOAL OF MISSIONS AND THE IDENTIFICATION OF THE MISSIONARY

By way of transition, two statements can be made at this point: First, the Mission of God determines the mission of the Church. For the Church has no other function than to participate in, and be a bearer of, God's Mission, the Mission of the Trinity. Secondly, the mission of the Church determines the nature of the Church. The Church must be that kind of sacrament which efficaciously realizes the Mission of God for men and for the world.

God's Mission and the Church's Mission

The Mission of God determines the mission of the Church. The goal of the *missio Dei* is the establishment of God's *shalom* in the kingdom. For the Christian this is the final meaning of history. In Pauline language, God's plan and Mission is to unify all things in himself through Christ (Col. 1:19-20; Eph. 1:9-10). According to this plan, the human race and the entire world will be reestablished in Christ. God's plan is to make all men adopted sons in the kingdom and to dignify all men with participation in divine life.[1] Stated in another way, God's plan is concerned with salvation, the salvation of men and of the world. According to the New Testament, the expected great act of salvation and new creation has taken place in the death and resurrection of Christ and its final consummation will be revealed at the *parousia* of Christ.[2] The Church is the eschatological community of salvation whose mission it is to participate in God's Mission to bring this plan to fulfillment. Her mission can only take its thrust from God's plan and Mission.

It is important that the mystery of salvation be expressed as broadly and as clearly as possible, since this is the purpose

[1] See "Dogmatic Constitution on the Church," Sections 2, 3, 48.

[2] Alan Richardson, *An Introduction to the Theology of the New Testament* (New York: Harper and Row, 1958), p. 80.

of God's Mission and therefore of the mission of the Church. For breadth of expression, the symbol of the kingdom of God and the Pauline notion of recapitulation in Christ as found in Colossians and Ephesians are helpful. For the sake of clarity, it is important to distinguish some of the strands which are included in the notion of salvation. This can be done with a series of contrasts. Positively considered, salvation has to do with restoring men and all things in Christ and the unification of all things in God's kingdom; negatively considered, it is concerned with liberating men and the world from sin, death, and the powers of evil. Salvation has both a personal and a cosmic dimension. It concerns the personal fate of individuals, their justification, liberation from sin and death, and their reconciliation and sanctification in Christ; but it also concerns the world and the achievement of its final goal and meaning in Christ.

Salvation, therefore, has both a material as well as a spiritual dimension to it. The *shalom* of the Old Testament (Ps. 85) has an unmistakable material content. The Christian mystery of the resurrection of the body underscores the same truth. Salvation is concerned with both the present and the future, with here and what is to come. Although the kingdom of God is an eschatological reality referring to the final times, God's reign has been introduced with Christ and is present with its fruits partially and in mystery now. Salvation, therefore, is not purely otherworldly nor purely this-worldly. It includes the completing of God's purpose for his whole creation, the healing of all that is broken, and the destruction of all that enslaves, although we do not understand fully how these blessings of the kingdom are related to what lies beyond this life.[3]

Finally, salvation is from God — it is only God who saves, not man. The final stage of salvation, the establishment of the kingdom, is totally God's work and doing. Therefore, earthly progress must be distinguished from the growth of Christ's kingdom. The Church has a saving and eschatological purpose which will only be fully attained in the future, but, because it can contribute better to ordering human society, earthly progress is of vital concern to the kingdom of God.[4] Although the world does not contain in

[3] Lesslie Newbigin, "Salvation," *Concise Dictionary of the Christian World Mission*, ed. Stephen Neill et al. (Nashville: Abingdon, 1971), p. 538.

[4] See "Pastoral Constitution on the Church in the Modern World," Sections 39-40.

itself the total secret of its own redemption, and although the establishment of the kingdom is an act of God's power, the position described here with regard to worldly progress and salvation is similar to that of Teilhard de Chardin, and it finds support in the documents of Vatican II. It sees continuity rather than discontinuity between temporal development and final fulfillment, or, in other terms, between nature and grace.[5]

Salvation. therefore, pertains to the establishment of God's kingdom and the restoration of all things in Christ. It is an event which is both personal, social, and cosmic; it has material and spiritual dimensions; it is concerned with the present and the future; it is both worldly and otherworldly; and, lastly, although the final state of the kingdom is totally the work of God, God's kingdom has some continuity with human and worldly history. This description of salvation does not intend to imply that all of the opposing terms are of equal weight. In considering the meaning of salvation, however, it is important to strike a balance among these characteristics. If God's plan and Mission are concerned with all of these dimensions, the mission of the Church must be attentive to all of them. If the Church ignores one or several of these elements, it runs the danger of rendering itself unsuitable for achieving the Mission of God. Thus a theory of salvation which stresses only hamartiology and individual salvation leads the Church to adopt an individualistic approach to mission and the gospel, and to overlook the cosmic dimensions of salvation. Again, a soteriology which tends to be excessively otherworldly will result in the mission of the Church being oblivious to the material needs of men and of the times.

If God's Mission determines the mission of the Church, it can be said that the mission of the Church must determine the nature of the Church. This is why the Church is essentially instrumental in character, that is, sacramental. The Church is a function of the Mission of God. It was instituted to be an efficacious instrument for Mission, that is, for salvation. By nature the Church must be such as to realize the goals of God's Mission. It must be concerned with the personal and the cosmic, with the present and the future, with the material as well as the spiritual. The nature of the Church

---

[5] For a discussion of the theory of continuity versus discontinuity, see René Laurentin, *Liberation, Development, and Salvation*, trans. Charles Underhill Quinn (Maryknoll, N.Y.: Orbis Books, 1972), pp. 54-60.

must be conceived, structured, and function so that it can fulfill all of the dimensions of God's Mission.

Stated in a slightly different manner, the Church is a messenger and herald of the gospel, but not just a herald; the Church is a healing agent working for a community of peace, freedom, and brotherly friendship, but she has an otherworldly mission besides this; the Church is a sacrament incarnating its message of peace and justice in its life, but its sacramental nature must not take undue precedence over the Word and its mission as herald and speaker of the Word.[6] When the Church is presented in terms of a divine-human mystery, and when the mystery of the Church is elaborated according to flexible models and images, then its nature is fluid and open, not fixed, and the Church can be an apt instrument for different times and cultures in working out the Mission of God. This is possible when the Church is presented in terms of community and the pilgrim people of God, in terms of the sign and sacrament of salvation, in terms of the body of Christ, as a stable organization or institution whose basic unit, the local Church, allows for diversity and pluralism.

The Aim and Purpose of Mission

The nature of the Church, therefore, does not directly determine the Church's mission. Rather the Mission of God determines the mission of the Church which, in turn, affects the nature of the Church. When one asks about the purpose of missions, or, in more traditional terms, about the aim of the Church's missionary work, it is important to express the question properly. The heart of the matter is not so much what the Church should do, or what the Church should aim for, in its mission. The question is this: Is the Church faithful to its role in the Mission of God? How does God see salvation, and does the Church approach the mystery of salvation in the same way? Stated simply, *How* is the Church fulfilling God's Mission? The answer to this *how* question has in the past been given as the purpose and goal of missions. Thus, if the purpose of God's Mission was seen as essentially related to personal conversion and acceptance of Christ, the Church answered the

[6] These ideas are suggested by Avery Dulles, S.J., "The Theology of Hans Küng: A Comment," *Union Seminary Quarterly Review*, 27 (Spring, 1972), 138.

how question by preaching the gospel and converting individuals. This was the goal of mission work. Or, if salvation was seen as being possible only within the institutional Church, the Church answered the *how* question by baptizing as many as possible and establishing the institution wherever and as soon as possible. Establishment of the Church was set down as the goal of mission.

These two examples are presented in their most extreme form. However, these two goals, evangelization towards conversion and Church planting, have predominated in the history of missions. In recent years, Catholics have tended to stress the latter; conservative Protestants the former. Both goals appear in all traditions, however, for they are really inseparable. In the Roman Catholic tradition, Vatican II has not settled exclusively for either one.[7] The "Decree on Missionary Activity" states that the specific purpose of missionary activity is evangelization and the planting of the Church among those peoples and groups where she has not yet taken root.[8] It might be thought that this definition attempts to walk midway between the Christocentric and personal goal which stresses proclamation and conversion, and the ecclesiocentric goal which emphasizes Church planting and the organization of young churches.[9] From another point of view, however, Vatican II's statement of aim might be seen as a reflection of the complexity and variability of the situation in which the Church sees its mission today. Protestant theologians of recent years have set down still other goals for missions. R. Pierce Beaver, for example, states that the aim of mission is presence, not conversion or Church planting. He feels that genuine presence must first be achieved before real communication of the faith is possible.[10] His position recalls that of Charles de Foucauld. Others would say that the goal of missionary effort for our times must be concerned with humanization,

---

[7] See Suso Brechter, "Decree on the Church's Missionary Activity," *Commentary on the Documents of Vatican* II, ed. Herbert Vorgrimler, IV (New York: Herder and Herder, 1969), 118.

[8] " 'Missions' is the term usually given to those particular undertakings by which the heralds of the gospel are sent out by the Church and go forth into the whole world to carry out the task of preaching the gospel and planting the Church among peoples or groups who do not yet believe in Christ." ("Decree on the Church's Missionary Activity," Section 6.)

[9] See Samuel Rayan, S.J., "Mission after Vatican II: Problems and Positions," *International Review of Mission,* 59 (October, 1970), 425-26.

[10] R. Pierce Beaver, "The Missionary Image Today. Internal Pressures for Change: Self-Understanding of Church and Mission," *Mission in the '70's—What Direction?*, eds. John T. Boberg, S.V.D. and James A. Scherer (Chicago, Ill.: Chicago Cluster of Theological Schools, 1972), p. 34.

with creating a new humanity in Christ in the midst of the secular world.[11]

All of these specific aims — conversion, Church planting, presence, and humanization — answer the question *how* the Church works for salvation, or, more properly, how the Church participates in the Mission of God. Rather than opt for any one of these, I would express my position in the following manner. First, all of these aims for missions are, and can be, means used by the Church for the working out of God's Mission provided they are not set up as exclusive objectives. If this happens, the multidimensional nature of salvation and the Mission of God will be neglected. Secondly, it is important not to conceive and express the Mission of God and the Church's mission too abstractly. Except for the most general objectives — for example, to establish the kingdom, to glorify God, to save men, to unite men with God and each other — no one specific goal or objective should be set up for the whole Church throughout the world. This means, thirdly, that it will be the local Church and the local situation which will determine the specific goal and aim of mission for that area.[12] In this sense, the world should write the agenda for the Church;[13] that is, the world of the local Church and the local situation should determine the approach to mission and the goal for mission.

By way of example, several situations can be presented. First of all, there is the situation where no local Church and no indigenous Christian community exists. Traditionally this has been the context of Christian missions. It seems, however, that for our times it would not be wise even in this situation to settle too hastily upon any one goal for mission beforehand. Perhaps it will be possible to engage in direct evangelization and preaching of the gospel. But, on the other hand, perhaps it would be better to take the approach of Charles de Foucauld among the Tuaregs and devote onself to the quality of Christian living, presence, and service

---

[11] See, for example, Walter J. Hollenweger (ed.), *The Church for Others and the Church for the World: A Quest for Structures for Missionary Congregations* (Geneva: World Council of Churches, 1968), pp. 77-78; M. Richard Shaull, "Towards a Reformation of Objectives," *Protestant Crosscurrents in Mission: The Ecumenical-Conservative Encounter,* ed. Norman A. Horner (Nashville: Abingdon, 1968), pp. 101-07.

[12] See Adrian Hastings, *Mission and Ministry* (London: Sheed and Ward, 1971), p. 1.

[13] See Hollenweger (ed.), *The Church for Others,* p. 20.

towards humanization. One can wonder how Francis Xavier or J. Hudson Taylor would have approached the Tuaregs, and one can question whether their methods today would have met with any more success. Much depends upon the locality and the character of the person engaged in mission. It seems, however, that legitimate diversity must be allowed until it be clearly proven that one method of approach and goal is definitely better than another.

Secondly, in the case of a recently established young church, it might be necessary to concentrate upon Church planting and the formation of the Christian community. This situation might occur where there is a definite "people movement" in progress, with numbers of people and families turning to Christianity.[14] Or, as might be the case in extremely underdeveloped areas, the situation of the young church might demand all-out efforts towards development, liberation, justice, and reconciliation. These different approaches — presence and service aimed at humanization and development, evangelization and proclamation, establishing the Church and strengthening Christian community — may follow each other in time or may be mixed with each other and interpenetrate each other, with stress now being given to one and later to another. All of this is difficult to determine apart from the local situation and the gifts of the Christians who enter and live in the situation.

Thirdly, in the case of a long-established church, mission work is still essential and necessary. The distinction often and justly made between the missionary apostolate which is directed to non-believers and the pastoral apostolate which is exercised among the faithful has validity only if both are seen in the context of God's wider Mission, and if pastoral work does not exclude missionary work. It would be a rare established church in our times which does not have numerous non-believers around itself or which is not confronted with the necessity of striving for peace, justice, and reconciliation. Because the Church is missionary by nature, there is no member of a local congregation who can be fully a Christian without a missionary dimension to his life. Christians by vocation share in the Mission of the Trinity and must go out to others — by directly speaking the Word if necessary and if possible, or by living lives of presence and service towards humanization. There-

[14] For a discussion of "people movements" see Donald A. McGavran, *Understanding Church Growth* (Grand Rapids, Mich.: William B. Eerdmans, 1970), pp. 296 ff.

fore, missionary work on one level and on all levels is necessary for all churches in all areas of the world.

By way of summary it can be said that the aim of the Church's mission is the aim of God's Mission. God's Mission is a complex and multidimensional goal for the world which in most general terms can be described by using the symbol of the kingdom of God. It is concerned with the personal, the social, and the cosmic; and it has present and future, material and spiritual dimensions. The traditional question which asks the aim or purpose of mission work can be transposed to a question of *how* the Church is to participate in God's Mission. The answer is determined by the context of the local area to which the faith comes. Therefore, activities which, depending on the situation, are directed towards Church planting, or conversion, or presence, or humanization, all have validity as aims and purposes of mission work. The ultimate objective is to fulfill God's plan and to work towards the kingdom. All other goals and aims are intermediate and relative to different times and places.

Evangelization versus Development

Because the plan of God's Mission of salvation is multidimensional, and because the local situation will affect the specific goal of mission, no clear-cut and simple answer can be given to one of the most debated and divisive issues of present-day mission theology — the discussion of proclamation versus development as the purpose of mission. This debate has caused no little doubt and confusion concerning the identity and goals of mission work. These issues are being discussed within Roman Catholicism, but they have been more keenly felt within the churches of the Protestant world. What seemed for some to be an apparent opposition between the gospel of personal conversion and the gospel of social responsibility was one of the central theological issues of the 1968 Uppsala meeting of the World Council of Churches. No one would deny the value of social work in mission. Work of this kind has always been closely associated with the Church's missions from earliest times. However, some have seen the Uppsala statement on mission as a betrayal of the traditional missionary practice of the Church, almost a sell-out to the confused spirit of our age because of its stress upon the horizontal (that is, the social) dimension to the detriment of the vertical (that is, the God-to-man relationship) dimension of the Church's work.[15] This is one of the issues at the heart of the rift between the Ecumenical churches and the Evangelical churches within Protestantism.

The question is important and cannot be passed over in silence. Must the first goal of mission always be the explicit glorification of God and the proclamation of the lordship of Christ throughout the world so that work for humanization and development cannot be considered on the same level?[16] Must social action always include a verbal witness to Jesus Christ?[17] In short, what is the relationship between evangelization and proclamation of the Word towards conversion and the establishment of the Church, and works of humanization and development? Or what is the relationship between proclamation (*kerygma*) and service (*diakonia*)? Few Christians would deny that both of these are part of Christian witness. The question is whether or not work towards building the human and developing the world can be called missionary work, and whether this type of work is possible as mission work without some explicit effort being made at the same time to proclaim the gospel.

If, as we suggested above, God's plan is considered in all its complexity, and if a balance is kept between all the elements involved in salvation, man's present as well as his future well-being, man's human as well as his spiritual development, then it seems that both goals, proclamation and humanization, are acceptable for mission. However, this answer seems to be overly facile and to miss the very heart of the problem — can man be totally fulfilled and humanized without being made explicitly aware of Jesus Christ? Speaking in broad terms, in terms of the Church's mission as it must be carried on over centuries, the answer is *no*. However, it might be necessary and desirable to work for human development in a specific area and

---

[15] See, for example, Peter Beyerhaus, *Missions: Which Way? — Humanization or Redemption,* trans. Margaret Clarkson (Grand Rapids, Mich.: Zondervan Publishing House, 1971), pp. 20, 46.

[16] See "The Frankfurt Declaration," in Beyerhaus, *Missions: Which Way? — Humanization or Redemption,* p. 114.

[17] See "The Wheaton Declaration," in Harold Lindsell (ed.), *The Church's Worldwide Mission: An Analysis of the Current State of Evangelical Missions, and a Strategy for Future Activity* (Waco, Texas: Word Books, 1966), p. 235.

at a specific time without introducing the gospel of Christ in an explicit fashion. Furthermore, one can be engaged in this without betraying his Christian responsibility, without being unfaithful to the Mission of God.

What underlies this possibility is an estimation of man and the world which sees nature and grace, humanization and divinization, and God, the world, and the kingdom not in terms of dualism or opposition, but in terms of complementarity and continuity. God's Mission incorporated itself in history and concerned itself with the sufferings and blessings of the world; Christ became fully human in order that man might become godlike. Therefore, it might be said that man and his world will only be divinized to the extent that they are fully humanized. If God's Mission is seen to be creation of the world which is good, in an analogous fashion man's mission can be regarded as co-creation working toward building the good world with God. Man's co-creativity focuses upon himself (humanization) and upon the world (development). Human activity is a partnership with the divine action of perfecting the world through history.[18] There is continuity, therefore, between the goal of God's Mission, the establishment of the kingdom, and man's work towards the kingdom. The kingdom is not here, nor will it be achieved by human means alone; but what is done here for man and the world contributes to the kingdom.[19]

Therefore, the solution to the problem of evangelization versus development can only be found from an eschatological stance which is based upon an integral humanism and a positive evaluation of man and the world which reflects a continuity between man's humanization and development here and the final establishment of the kingdom at the end time. If opposition and discontinuity are seen between man's profane life and his religious fulfillment in the kingdom, then the goals of proclamation and humanization cannot be easily reconciled. However, if man and his world, in their secularity and profaneness, contain the religious dimension within themselves and as such are to be brought to

[18] See "Pastoral Constitution on the Church in the Modern World," Sections 34-36; Alfons Auer, "Man's Activity throughout the World," *Commentary on the Documents of Vatican II*, ed. Vorgrimler, V, 194-95.

[19] See "Pastoral Constitution on the Church in the Modern World," Section 39.

fulfillment, not overcome or negated by the kingdom, then these two approaches to mission do not stand in stark opposition.

Hence the Uppsala meeting could speak of mission in terms of a new man and a new humanity which will be summed up in Christ. There can be no turning to God which does not at the same time bring man face to face with his fellow men.[20] Hence the Roman Catholic Church can speak of a transcendent humanism, or, in the words of *Populorum Progressio,* integral humanism — the full development of the whole man and every man.[21] This is called transcendent humanism because men know their true nature only if they see themselves as sons of God,[22] and because it is not a humanism closed upon itself but open to the values of the spirit and to God who gives all human life its true meaning.[23]

The position taken here, based upon the multi-dimensional nature of God's Mission and salvation, and upon integral, transcendent humanism, sees no opposition between evangelization and development. Both are half truths — evangelization and proclamation are both part of, but not the whole of, the Church's mission. Neither can be separated from the other. The connection between the two is ontological — both come out of the new being of man in Christ.[24] The total mission of the Church and the Mission of God are concerned with both.[25]

But the problem still remains: Must evangelization and proclamation always be considered as the primary work of the Church? or must any work for social development and humanization always be accompanied with explicit reference to Jesus Christ? As mentioned above, when the mission of the Church is considered abstractly and broadly in its relation to the nations and the ages, an affirmative answer must be given to these questions — the Church

---

[20] Norman Goodall (ed.), *The Uppsala Report 1968: Official Report of the Fourth Assembly of the World Council of Churches, Uppsala, July 4-20, 1968* (Geneva: World Council of Churches, 1968), p. 25.

[21] Paul VI, *On the Development of Peoples* (Paterson, N.J.: Association for International Development, 1967), Sections 14, 42.

[22] Goodall (ed.), *The Uppsala Report*, p. 38.

[23] Paul VI, *On the Development of Peoples,* Section 42.

[24] See Lesslie Newbigin, *One Body, One Gospel, One World: The Christian Mission Today* (New York: International Missionary Council, 1959), p. 22.

[25] Yves Congar, "The Role of the Church in the Modern World," *Commentary on the Documents of Vatican II,* ed. Vorgrimler, V, 203-04; see also Paul VI, *Evangelization in the Modern World,* Sections 29-35.

must name the Name, speak of the lordship of Christ, and challenge men to accept Christ in faith. However, once more the caution must be introduced of not speaking of the mission of the Church and the mission of Christians too abstractly. It is here that the theology of the local Church and the situation of the local Church and the people to whom the local Church addresses itself must be considered. It has been stated that the way the good news of salvation comes alive cannot be determined a priori.[26] In a situation which is completely dehumanized because of factors such as hunger, oppression, despair, and injustice, it may be necessary to work for humanization and development without any explicit proclamation of the gospel. In this situation the work itself speaks more eloquently and possibly more successfully of God's plan for man than any explicit efforts at proclamation could. Therefore, Christians can give themselves totally to this mission and it can validly be called the mission of the Church and a participation in God's Mission for men.

The danger of such an approach is that those engaged in mission work of this type might become totally secularized and have no desire to speak of God and Christ. In this regard, the demands of what has been termed transcendent humanism must be kept in mind. Man is incomplete if he is not open to the transcendent. Although the Christian engaged in mission may not be able to speak of this basic orientation of man, it must never fail to animate his personal life. Hence the intention is important for mission spirituality — the missionary is a man who intends to bring others to faith in Christ; he is one who intends to work for the fulfillment of God's kingdom, a project which he acknowledges to be radically beyond his own power to achieve. This orientation and intention cannot be absent from his spirituality. His prayer and his sacramental life must be directed towards deepening this stance of openness to God. It will be both the source of his power and accomplishments as well as the source of his humility, his trust, and his basic awareness of the ambiguity of development and humanization if these actions are accepted without reference to Christ and the kingdom.

---

[26] See Lesslie Newbigin, "The Call to Mission — A Call to Unity?" *The Church Crossing Frontiers: Essays on the Nature of Mission in Honor of Bengt Sundkler*, eds. Peter Beyerhaus and Carl F. Hallencreutz, Studia Missionalia Upsaliensia 11 (Uppsala: Gleerup, 1969), p. 260.

MISSION SPIRITUALITY: THE MISSIONARY—THE PLACE—THE MOTIVE

With the aim of the mission of the Church developed in such a broad and multidimensional fashion, the question naturally arises concerning the identification of the missionary. On this theory, who is the missionary? In answer to this question, I would suggest that the missionary for our times should not be defined primarily by his role or function in the Church, that is, by what he does. The missionary should be identified in the first instance by who he is. He is a Christian, a member of God's pilgrim people, one who has received the privilege of being called into the community of the people of God, and one who has the privilege of participation in the Mission of the Trinity. As already proposed in Chapter V, all Christians are missionaries and all Christian spirituality must have a missionary dimension. This is the case before one engages in any activity or role in the Church or the world. For this reason I have chosen first to describe the missionary in terms of what he is before entering into what he does, in terms of being rather than of action.

Distinctions of the past between Church and mission and mission and pastoral work must take account of this basic, natural orientation of the Christian. The key word used in this most broad description of the missionary is the word *privilege*. The Christian is one who has been privileged, gifted by being a member of God's pilgrim people and a bearer of God's Mission. The response of one who has been gifted and privileged by another is loving gratitude. Gratitude and love, two elements of missionary motivation and spirituality found from the earliest times, remain foundational in missionary spirituality and Christian spirituality. The anthropology of Karl Barth offers a good example of this view of the Christian and, in Barth's terms, of man himself. Man is a being who is summoned and chosen by God, and because of this he is a being who lives in gratitude.[27]

Karl Barth is also of assistance in understanding who is a missionary from the point of view of role and function. In his anthropology, the second key word for understanding man is *responsibility*. Man is, and is human, as he performs an act of respon-

[27] Karl Barth, *Church Dogmatics*, Vol. III, *The Doctrine of Creation*, Part 2, trans. Harold Knight, et al. (Edinburgh: T. and T. Clark, 1960), Section 44.3, especially pp. 150, 166.

sibility, that is, of offering himself as the response to the Word of God.[28] In a missiological context, the missionary is one who responds to the privilege of participating in the Mission of God by offering himself to work for, and give witness to, the salvation of the kingdom on one or on all of the levels where God's Mission is being achieved in history. Because the Church is essentially instrumental and sacramental in nature, the missionary is one who is the responsive and effective sacrament of God's Mission.

At this point, two important characteristics for mission spirituality can be mentioned — *discernment* and *fidelity*. Discernment is part of the process of ongoing conversion and *metanoia* which are required of all Christians. It involves listening to discover and decide, under the direction of the Spirit, where and how God's Mission and will are best achieved in the present. Discernment comes into action on the personal level with the question of vocation, that is, the attempt to decide how one is to participate in God's Mission so that the meaning of one's own life, one's own salvation, is fulfilled. Discernment becomes communal on the level of the local Church which must always check itself to be sure that God's Mission is being fulfilled in all its dimensions, and which must decide which elements of salvation — for example, work for development, or church planting — must be stressed at a particular time and place. This is similar to what Vatican II calls scrutinizing the signs of the times.[29] Finally, discernment takes place on the level of the Church universal, the catholic communion of local churches. Here it must be decided whether the whole Church is being faithful to the Mission of God, whether any one church needs special help and in what form, whether any one church or group of churches has become locked in the past and untrue to God's work in the present. Fidelity is the quality of response required for mission. On the personal level, it is being true to one's self and one's vocation within the context of the Mission of God. On the broader level, it is faithfulness of the whole Church to the whole gospel and to all the elements of the Mission of God. In sum, the man of mission, the missionary, is a man of discernment with fidelity

[28] Barth, *ibid.*, pp. 174-75

[29] "Pastoral Constitution on the Church in the Modern World," Section 4.

and knowledge of his role in the Mission of God and readiness to offer himself as a responsive instrument for the *missio Dei.*

Because God's Mission is multidimensional, and because salvation must be worked out on many levels, those who might be called missionaries can perform a variety of functions and roles in the world.[30] *Missionary work is multiform,* and no one task or role can be set down as *the* work of Mission. God's Mission concerns itself with the present and the future, with the temporal and the spiritual, with signs of the kingdom now and the arrival of the kingdom when God sees fit. It includes pastoral work, evangelization, and Church planting, but it is broader and wider in extension than all of these. Although all Christians participate in the Mission of God, the ways in which they participate differ. All have the privilege and responsibility to speak the gospel and name the Name of Jesus, all have the privilege and responsibility to do God's worldly work and devote themselves to humanization and social welfare.

But specialization is inevitable. It is here that personal discernment enters. Some will be full-time preachers of the Word; others will be tent-maker missionaries whose time is divided between worldly work and proclaiming the gospel; others still will be totally devoted to God's worldly work with perhaps little opportunity or even no possibility of speaking of the fullness of God's plan. In addition to the needs of the place, the norm for discernment will be the gifts, or in Pauline terms the charisms which one possesses (see 1 Cor. 12-13). The gifts of the Spirit are diverse — some are called to give clear witness to the desire for a heavenly home and to keep that desire green among the human family; others are called to dedicate themselves to the earthly service of men and to make ready the material and celestial realm by this ministry.[31]

There is another problem with this description of the missionary. To identify the missionary and the Christian and to refuse to specify the role of the missionary by a definite task, such as Church planting or conversion, seems to rob missionary activity of its meaning and endanger the outreach and expansion of the Church. In the Catholic tradition, Eugene Hillman has raised this

---

[30] Yves Raguin, "Y a-t-il une spiritualité missionnaire?" *Spiritus,* 11 (August-September, 1970), 248-49.

[31] "Pastoral Constitution on the Church in the Modern World," Section 38.

problem with great concern largely because of the tendencies in post-war Europe to place work among the de-Christianized peoples of Europe on the same footing as more traditional missionary work among non-Christian peoples and nations.[32] The result of this confusion of roles, Hillman contends, is a tendency for a church to turn in upon itself and never to reach out to those peoples who have not heard the gospel.

Several responses can be made to such criticism. First of all, if there is a temptation for the Church in a locality to turn in upon itself, to concentrate on its own affairs, and not to reach out with the gospel, the necessity for the discernment mentioned above becomes all-important. If a local Church is true to the constant demand for conversion and self-evaluation in the light of the Mission of God, then members of that Church will be forced to evaluate their relation to God's Mission in world-wide terms and not only in local terms. And if the universal Church is sensitive to the needs of all areas of the world, then such a discerning process should make it impossible for a particular church to turn in upon itself, or an area of the world in need of the gospel to have no one to come to it.[33]

Secondly, it might justly be asked whether or not the identification of the vocation of the Christian with the missionary vocation will not, in the long run, result in a greater desire to reach out than in the past. When all Christians become educated to the reality of their role in God's Mission, the structures of the past will have to give way to new missionary structures which will make it possible for all to exercise their missionary role. In the Roman Catholic Church, for example, missionary work has been juridically reserved to the pope.[34] Missions have been carried out by international missionary orders responsible to the Holy See. Pope Pius XII in 1957 and Vatican II underscored the fact that the bishops of the Church have an obligation to be solicitous for the whole Church, not just their own dioceses.[35]

---

[32] Eugene Hillman, C.S.Sp., *The Church as Mission* (New York: Herder and Herder, 1965), Chapter I.

[33] See A.M. Fiolet, "Toward a Theology of Development," *Foundations of Mission Theology,* ed. SEDOS, trans. John Drury (Maryknoll, N.Y.: Orbis Books, 1972), p. 121.

[34] *Codex Juris Canonici,* Canon 1350, Number 2.

[35] Pius XII, *On Expanded Missionary Activity Especially in Africa [Fidei Donum], Catholic Missions: Four Great Encyclicals,* ed. Thomas J.M. Burke,

Vatican II has likewise stressed the importance of the laity in the mission of the Church.[36] This expansion of responsibility for mission stands in contrast to Canon Law's restriction of responsibility to the Holy See, and to the position of the Catholic missiologist, Joseph Schmidlin, who held that it is necessary to be a priest to exercise the missionary office in its full extent.[37] The point is that the present structures for realizing a missionary calling were formed in the past and have not been adapted to the present theological position which sees mission as the duty of all.

Thirdly, the position taken here of defining the missionary in terms of who he is and his intention, rather than in terms of his function within the people of God, might offer even more motives and reasons for reaching out to men around the world. The Christian participates in the *missio Dei* not only by going out to evangelize and plant churches, but by working for the kingdom and salvation on all the levels where this is possible and necessary. He thus has a number of options and reasons for going out compared with the more narrow options of the past. Perhaps the best way for him to participate in God's Mission will be by direct evangelization; or perhaps it will be something radically different, a role which will require him to stay home and work for another local Church from where he is. This latter missionary role has been suggested by Joseph Alemán who advises American Jesuits that they might best aid Latin America by working in the United States to change the policies of the United States government which are having dehumanizing effects in Latin America.[38]

If the mission of the Church cannot be defined simply in terms of what the Church does or what Christians do, neither can it be defined in terms of where the Church exercises its mission. As mentioned in Chapter I, the world of Christendom is no more. What Keith Bridston has referred to as the "salt water myth" has been invalidated by the modern world. No longer does mis-

S.J. (New York: Fordham University Press, 1957), Section 59, p. 71; "Dogmatic Constitution on the Church," Section 23.

[36] "Dogmatic Constitution on the Church," Section 32.

[37] Joseph Schmidlin, *Catholic Mission Theory,* trans. Matthias Braun, S.V.D. (Techny, Ill.: Mission Press S.V.D., 1931), p. 172.

[38] Joseph A. Alemán, S.J., "The Role of the North American Jesuit in the Latin American Apostolate," *Studies in the International Apostolate of Jesuits,* 1 (1972), 11.

sion involve crossing great water barriers which separate Christian countries from non-Christian lands.[39] Protestant ecumenical thinkers in recent years have referred to the present situation as the six-continent theory of mission. There is but one mission for the Church and it is on all six continents. The missionary movement now involves Christians in all six continents; it is the common witness of the whole Church bringing the whole gospel to the whole world, wherever and however Christ needs to be proclaimed and men are open to the message of the kingdom of God.[40] Stephen Neill expresses a concern, not unsimilar to that of Eugene Hillman, that this theory of mission can run the danger of blurring and overlooking the differences which exist between what were considered Christian countries and places which have been totally without any Christian presence and influence. Yet this way of looking at mission does have the advantage of making it clear that no longer is mission a one-way movement from Christian to non-Christian lands.[41]

Geographic Christendom today has been replaced by what R. Pierce Beaver has called diffused Christendom and what Karl Rahner calls diaspora Christianity. According to Beaver's theory, the frontiers of mission are not geographical but exist wherever there are men unreconciled with God and with each other.[42] The Church, therefore, and the Church's mission would consist in its sign role as an effective witness of double reconciliation. According to Rahner, the diaspora situation means that Christianity exists, with varying proportions, everywhere in the world and everywhere in diaspora. Effectively in terms of numbers it is a minority everywhere; and nowhere does it fill such a role of effective leadership as would permit it to set upon the age, with any force of clarity, the stamp of Christian ideas. The future will only see an increase in this diaspora character of Christianity.

---

39 Keith R. Bridston, *Mission Myth and Reality* (New York: Friendship Press, 1965), pp. 21-40.

40 Stephen Neill, *The Unfinished Task* (London: Lutterworth, 1957), p. 146; Newbigin, *One Body, One Gospel, One World,* p. 12; Ronald K. Orchard (ed.), *Witness in Six Continents; Records of the Meeting of the Commission on World Mission and Evangelism of the World Council of Churches Held in Mexico City, December 8-19, 1963* (London: Edinburgh House Press, 1964), p. 175; Goodall (ed.), *The Uppsala Report,* p. 35.

41 Stephen Neill, *Call to Mission* (Philadelphia: Fortress, 1970), pp. 95-96.

42 See R. Pierce Beaver, *From Missions to Mission: Protestant World Mission Today and Tomorrow* (New York: Association Press, 1964), pp. 61, 108.

In the diaspora, the faith of the Christian is consistently threatened from without. Christianity will receive very little or no support from institutional morality, custom, civil law, tradition, public opinion, and normal conformism. Christianity ceases to be a religion one is born into and becomes a matter of personal choice amid indifferent or even perilous surroundings.[43]

Viewing mission in terms of the six-continent concept and in the cultural context of diffused or diaspora Christianity allows one to identify more than one important implication for a spirituality of mission. First of all, when Christianity is seen as a matter of free choice for all men in all parts of the world, the Church in mission must be a Church with great respect for human freedom.[44] All forms of coercion towards conformity, be they political or cultural, are rendered impossible. Secondly, once more the Church in mission is challenged to be true to its nature as sign of what God is planning for all men. The purity of its witness becomes all-important. This means, thirdly, that the prophetic role of the Church in mission in the diaspora becomes essential. Amid a plurality of values and life styles, the mission of the Church must witness to those values both temporal and eternal which are the *shalom* values of the kingdom. Fourthly, Christian community becomes absolutely decisive for the support and strength of those who work in mission in the diaspora. One caution is in order, however; in no manner should this community be allowed to become a ghetto, closed in upon itself and in retreat from the world.[45] This would be to return to conceptions of the Church as sanctuary of safety from encroachments and challenges of the modern world — a position which would be ruinous for mission and a position which would negate the sign value and nature of the Church. Finally, in diaspora the Church must be an active Church, a Church whose mission is not reserved to one class, the set-apart class of the clergy, but a Church of the laity.[46] This latter class will enter intimately into the mission of the Church. The diaspora situation, therefore, offers another reason and foundation for affirming that all

---

[43] Karl Rahner, S.J., *The Christian Commitment: Essays in Pastoral Theology*. trans. Cecily Hastings (New York: Sheed and Ward, 1963), pp. 17, 23.

[44] See Vatican II's "Declaration on Religious Freedom."

[45] See Rahner, *The Christian Commitment*, p. 28.

[46] *Ibid.*, p. 24.

Christians are for mission and all Christian spirituality must have a missionary dimension. Some would say, in fact, that the ministerial clergy are unequipped for mission in the post-Christian age and that it is the laity who must assume the prime role.[47]

In summary, then, the missionary is not to be described in terms of his role or function in the people of God, nor is he to be defined in terms of where he exercises his function or charism. The missionary is defined in terms of who he is — a Christian privileged by God to participate in the *missio Dei.* If this position is accepted, are there any particular differences among Christians which can help one to identify the man of mission more clearly? I suggested above that the context and intention of a Christian's life style were important. He is a man of the kingdom, concerned with the blessings of the kingdom, and above all with the Lord of the kingdom, Christ.

Expressing this in a slightly different way, I would agree with Lesslie Newbigin that the special *differentia* of the man of mission is the intention he has of bringing others to cross the frontier between faith in Christ as Lord and unbelief. Newbigin states that this is the case whether or not the missionary's journey is long or short.[48] It might be added that this is the special difference whether the missionary is dedicated solely to evangelization, Church planting, or a spiritual ministry, or whether he is dedicated to worldly development. Furthermore, it is the case whether or not the missionary has any success at, or even possibility of, helping to bring others to belief in Christ. Mission spirituality is a spirituality which lives on this frontier. Its intention is this. The interior life of the missionary and his life style are oriented to non-believers. In one set of circumstances he may have success and celebrate with new Christians in community the paschal mystery of Christ; in another set of circumstances — and perhaps this will be the most common situation in today's world — his orientation towards non-Christians will consist of service and witness in patient advent hope and waiting for God to work his plan in his own time.[49]

---

[47] See J.C. Hoekendijk, *The Church Inside Out,* trans. Isaac C. Rottenberg (Philadelphia: Westminster Press, 1966), pp. 54, 86; Hollenweger (ed.), *The Church for Others,* p. 24.

[48] Newbigin, *One Body, One Gospel, One World,* p. 29.

[49] See Raguin, "Y a-t-il une spiritualité missionnaire?" p. 253.

The last topic to be discussed in this section is *missionary motivation*. At the end of Chapter IV, an enumeration of the classic motives for mission was given. In this and the preceding chapter, it was said that the overarching aim of mission work was that God's kingdom might come and that the first signs of that kingdom might be made present by reconciling men with each other and with God. Aside from this general orientation and context, it was also said that a variety of other motives for mission more appropriately answer the question *how* this is to be achieved. Thus the ecclesiological (Church planting), soteriological (preaching the Word for conversions), humanitarian (development), and ascetic (self-perfection) motives all tell how the Church and Christians participate in God's Mission of bringing about the kingdom.

The question of missionary motivation is more appropriately a *why* question. Why mission or missions, or why the Church? The only answer to this question is the traditional theocentric motive — the glory of God. This is the *why* of God's Mission; it remains the basic motive for the Church's participation in the *missio Dei*. At the heart of the matter is the privilege men have of participating in the *missio Dei*. This privilege of participation in the trinitarian Mission for the glory of God and of intending to bring others to live for this same end is done in a context of gratitude, love, and service on the part of the Christian. The traditional motive of obedience stands in second place. If the "Great Commission" had not been given in so many words, the motive it expresses would still hold.

Ruth Rouse's basic motive for mission, therefore, is only strengthened by the view of mission presented here — belief that God has a purpose for the life of each one of us, and a purpose for the whole world; conviction that he works out his purpose through our acceptance of his plan for the life of each one of us. In sum, we are saved to serve the world.[50] Finally, in the context of the theology and spirituality of mission presented here, the question can never be asked, why are there missions, or why should one be a missionary? The only possible way of expressing this question is this: Why should we not go out to others for Christ?[51]

---

[50] Ruth Rouse, "The Missionary Motive," *International Review of Missions*, 25 (1936), 250-68.

[51] See Bridston, *Mission Myth and Reality*, p. 118.

VII

THE CHURCH AND THE RELIGIOUS TRADITIONS OF THE WORLD

In Chapters III and IV, it was shown that for the most part the missionaries of the past held a rather dim view concerning the possibility of salvation apart from the gospel or the Church. Xavier was not the only missionary who thought that the peoples of India were engaged in nothing other than devil worship. Carey and Taylor were concerned with the extremely dangerous condition of men without the gospel. From the Catholic point of view, this attitude was due in some extent to a rigorous interpretation of the axiom *extra ecclesiam nulla salus,* outside the church no salvation. On the Protestant side, the focus, with exceptions of course, was less upon the Church and more upon the absolute necessity of the gospel and faith in Christ for salvation. There is no doubt that when the situation of non-believers was viewed in this fashion the missionary movement of Christianity had an extremely powerful motive and reason for existence.

During the last century, however, the Christian estimation of non-Christians and non-Christian religious traditions has been forced to change. One reason for the change has been wider contact with, and deeper theological understanding and therefore appreciation of, the depths and riches of the non-Christian religious traditions. Another reason arose from the need Christians felt to reconcile God's universal salvific will and Christ's all-embracing redemptive death with the knowledge that the greater part of men who have lived and who are living now are not Christians. It came to be acknowledged, therefore, that salvation must be possible without explicit knowledge of the gospel or membership in the visible Church. Obviously such a position seems to weaken the foundation supporting the missionary expansion of the Church, for it neutralizes one of the traditional and long-standing motives for missionary work. If every man can be saved, what reason is there for the Church? Some have contended that membership in the Church makes salvation less difficult.[1] But if salvation is a question of what is more or less difficult depending on whether one is outside or inside the Church, why should what is less difficult be required?[2]

The conflict between the traditional policy of conversion and the accessibility of salvation outside of the visible Church has been described as the hinge of the contemporary crisis in mission work.[3] Catholics and Protestants alike would probably agree with R. Pierce Beaver's estimation that the most crucial question in world mission today is the relation of Christian faith to other faiths and what the answer implies for missionary aims and means.[4] More conservative theologians, both Catholic and Protestant, have viewed what they see to be overly optimistic positions with regard to men without the gospel or the Church as the erosion of the missionary vocation and the death of the mission of the Church.[5] Missionary bishops at the Second Vatican Council saw the problem clearly and asked for a statement concerning non-Christians and salvation because of a fear that the missionary spirit would be weakened in the Church.[6] Therefore, the theology of mission, mission spirituality, and missionary motivation must come to terms with the problem of salvation outside the Church.

---

[1] See Bernard J. Kelly, *Missionary Spirituality* (Dublin: M.H. Gill and Sons, 1960), Chapter II.

[2] Henri de Lubac, S.J., *Catholicism: A Study of Dogma in Relation to the Corporate Destiny of Mankind,* trans. Lancelot C. Sheppard (New York: Longmans, Green, and Co., 1950), pp. 108-09.

[3] John Power, S.M.A., *Mission Theology Today* (Maryknoll, N.Y.: Orbis Books, 1971), p. 9.

[4] R. Pierce Beaver, "The Missionary Image Today. Internal Pressures for Change: Self-Understanding of Church and Mission," *Mission in the 70's — What Direction?*, eds. John T. Boberg, S.V.D. and James A. Scherer (Chicago: Chicago Cluster of Theological Schools, 1972), p. 36.

[5] See, for example, Prudencio Damboriena, S.J., "Aspects of the Missionary Crisis in Roman Catholicism," *The Future of the Christian World Mission: Studies in Honor of R. Pierce Beaver*, eds. William J. Danker and Wi Jo Kang (Grand Rapids, Mich.: Eerdmans, 1971), p. 78; Harold Lindsell, "Missionary Imperatives: A Conservative Evangelical Exposition," *Protestant Crosscurrents in Mission: The Ecumenical-Conservative Encounter* (Nashville: Abingdon, 1968), p. 69.

[6] Suso Brechter, "Decree on the Church's Missionary Activity," *Commentary on the Documents of Vatican II*, ed. Herbert Vorgrimler, IV (New York: Herder and Herder, 1969), 122.

SALVATION OUTSIDE THE CHURCH

Two realities must be reconciled with regard to the Church and non-believers. The first is God's universal salvific will. The second is the centrality which belongs to Christ and the Church in mediating salvation to all mankind. The problem arises from the fact that the greater part of mankind has never had, nor does it have, the opportunity to know and accept Christ and the Church.

The doctrine that God's Mission is concerned with the salvation of all men, and not just a portion of the human race or a chosen community, has roots in Scripture. Although universalism is not the only strand which is found in the Old Testament, it has support in the priestly tradition, which sees God's covenant of election made with the whole race, and in strands of the prophetic tradition, which recognize the possibility of God's grace and justice being present beyond Israel.[7] Although Jesus performed his works in Israel and did not carry on a mission to the Gentiles, he accepted individual Gentiles (Mark 7:24-30), denied that Israel would have any priority for final salvation (Matt. 8:11-12), and proclaimed that the coming kingdom of God would comprehend all mankind (Matt. 25:31-46). By proclaiming to Israel the kingdom of God, Jesus' message and works became a witness for all to hear.[8] God's will to save all men is well attested in the early Church (2 Cor. 5:19; Eph. 1:10; 1 Tim. 2:3-5; Titus 2:11). When the theological truth that God's Mission intends to save all men is coupled with the statistical fact that at the present time — to say nothing of past ages or the future — Christians make up perhaps only a third of the world's population, it is difficult to hold the position that there is no salvation without explicit knowledge of the gospel or membership in the visible Church.

Accordingly, Vatican II summarized the Catholic tradition of recent times by reaffirming the possibility of salvation for those outside the Church:

---

[7] See, for example, Hans Küng, "The World Religions in God's Plan of Salvation," *Christian Revelation and World Religions*, ed. Joseph Neuner, S.J. (London: Burns and Oates, 1967), pp. 38-41. For instances of universalism, cf. Gen 9; Is. 2:2-4; 61:5, 6, 9; Ps. 96:10; 97:1-2; and the book of Jonah.

[8] Ferdinand Hahn, *Mission in the New Testament*, trans. Frank Clarke, Studies in Biblical Theology 47 (Naperville, Ill.: Alec R. Allenson, 1965), pp. 31-32, 34, 38-39.

> Those also can attain to everlasting salvation who through no fault of their own do not know the gospel of Christ or His Church, yet sincerely seek God and, moved by grace, strive by their deeds to do His will as it is known to them through the dictates of conscience. Nor does divine Providence deny the help necessary for salvation to those who, without blame on their part, have not yet arrived at an explicit knowledge of God, but who strive to live a good life thanks to His grace.[9]

As the Catholic position stands, therefore, it is impossible to maintain that salvation and therefore grace are not to be found outside the Church. For this reason, as Hans Küng advises, extreme care must be taken to make sure that the ancient theological dictum *extra ecclesiam nulla salus* is understood in the proper context and manner. When this axiom in its negative formulation is interpreted absolutely and literally it leads to a rigorism which is heretical.[10] One present tendency in Roman Catholicism is to interpret this formula in a positive rather than in a negative sense. It should not be regarded as answering the question, Who will be saved? but as answering the question, What is commissioned to discharge the ministry of salvation?[11] It is through the Church that salvation comes to all mankind.[12]

In this sense, the axiom could be rephrased *sine ecclesia nulla salus*, without the Church no salvation. Or, in view of the intimate link that exists between Christ and the Church, and the fact that Christ in God's plan is the mediator of grace and salvation for all men (see Eph. 1), it is better still to interpret

---

[9] "Dogmatic Constitution on the Church," Section 16; see also "Pastoral Constitution on the Church in the Modern World," Section 22; "Decree on the Missionary Activity of the Church," Section 7.

[10] See Küng, "The World Religions in God's Plan of Salvation," *Christian Revelation and World Religions,* ed. Neuner, pp. 31, 37; the classic case in modern Roman Catholicism is the Boston heresy, Henricus Denzinger and Adolfus Schönmetzer, S.J., *Enchiridion Symbolorum* (New York: Herder and Herder, 1963) Numbers 3866-73; for a brief history of the axiom *extra ecclesiam nulla salus,* see: Karl Rahner, S.J., "Membership of the Church According to the Teaching of Pius XII's Encyclical *Mystici Corporis Christi,*" *Theological Investigations,* trans. Karl-H. Kruger, II (Baltimore: Helicon, 1964), 36 ff.

[11] See Yves Congar, *The Wide World My Parish: Salvation and Its Problems,* trans. Donald Attwater (Baltimore: Helicon Press, 1961), pp. 98-113; Heinz Robert Schlette, *Towards a Theology of Religions,* trans. W.J. O'Hara, Quaestiones Disputatae 14 (New York: Herder and Herder, 1966), p. 17.

[12] See H. de Lubac, *Catholicism,* pp. 117-18.

the axiom in a Christological rather than in an ecclesiological manner — *extra Christum nulla salus.* Christ is the source of salvation for the whole world and anyone who reaches salvation achieves it through Christ and the grace of Christ which is made knowable and accessible through the Church.[13]

Therefore, two questions must be kept in mind with regard to the salvation of men of other faiths: the first is *whether or not* they can be saved; the second is *how* they are saved. With regard to the first question, an affirmative position is held because God's plan is for all men and his universal salvific will is to save all men, and because of the unity of the human race and its history and Christ's oneness with the human race in virtue of the incarnation and redemption. Concerning the second question, *how* salvation is possible for non-believers, it can be stated, first, that it is by the grace of God which is mediated through Christ and the Church to the human race. This, however, only advances the discussion to the heart of the problem: how is this possible for one who has never heard of Christ, the gospel, or the Church, or for one who belongs to a non-Christian religious tradition? With regard to this question, Vatican II has taken a position of openness before a mystery — God does this in ways known to himself.[14] Precisely how God does this is a mystery.[15] It is a matter which must be left to theological speculation.[16]

---

[13] "For the Church is compelled by the Holy Spirit to do her part towards the full realization of the will of God, who has established Christ as the source of salvation for the whole world. By the proclamation of the gospel, she prepares her hearers to receive and profess the faith, disposes them for baptism, snatches them from the slavery of error, and incorporates them into Christ so that through charity they may grow up into full maturity in Christ." ("Dogmatic Constitution on the Church," Section 17); see also Brechter, "Decree on the Church's Missionary Activity," *Commentary on the Documents of Vatican II,* ed. Vorgrimler, IV, 123; Küng, "The World Religions in God's Plan of Salvation," *Christian Revelation and World Religions,* ed. Neuner, p. 37.

[14] "Therefore, though God in ways known to Himself can lead those inculpably ignorant of the gospel to that faith without which it is impossible to please Him (Heb. 11:6), yet a necessity lies upon the Church (cf. 1 Cor. 9:16), and at the same time a sacred duty, to preach the gospel. Hence missionary activity today as always retains its power and necessity." ("Decree on the Missionary Activity of the Church," Section 7).

[15] Jean Daniélou, "Non-Christian Religions and Salvation," *Foundations of Mission Theology,* ed. SEDOS, trans. John Drury (Maryknoll, N.Y.: Orbis Books, 1972), p. 59.

[16] Brechter, "Decree on the Church's Missionary Activity," *Commentary on the Documents of Vatican II,* ed. Vorgrimler, IV, 122.

In recent times there has been no dearth of speculation on this point. No attempt will be made here to summarize all the theories which have been advanced concerning this mystery. The question remains open to much yet-to-be-done theological reflection. Furthermore, as we said in the beginning of Chapter V, the intention here is not to resolve the theological questions which lie at the heart of present-day mission theology. The most basic of these questions, are the way non-believers attain salvation and the salvational status of the non-Christian religious traditions. Nevertheless, one engaged in mission must have a basic openness to the speculation which is taking place, for the theories being advanced, whether he considers them advantageous or not, will affect his spirituality, life style, and motivation. Accordingly, the following pages will summarize some of the more common theories concerning salvation outside the Church and offer some of the implications which they have for mission spirituality.

Implicit Desire

In official Catholic teaching before Vatican II, the doctrine of the *votum ecclesiae* formed the bridge between the reality that most men are not members of the Church and the universal salvific will of God.[17] The principle underlying the possibility of baptism of fire or baptism of the Holy Spirit in the early Church, and the principle behind the Council of Trent's (1547) statement about baptism of desire[18] was applied to the Church in the nineteenth and twentieth centuries. Non-members who lived according to their consciences in invincible ignorance of the Church could attain the grace of salvation through an implicit desire for the Church, *votum implicitum ecclesiae*.[19]

Theological speculation attempted to work out the content of this implicit desire. Thus, for example, Jean Daniélou proposed the thesis of cosmic revelation whereby men (he was speaking specifically of those before Christ) received the revelation and grace of Christ through the positive values of their own religions and thus "believed in Christ without knowing Him and belonged

---

[17] Aloys Grillmeier, "The People of God," *Commentary on the Documents of Vatican II,* ed. Vorgrimler, I, 171.

[18] Denzinger and Schönmetzer, *Enchiridion Symbolorum,* Number 1524.

[19] *Ibid.,* Numbers 3869-70.

invisibly to the visible Church."[20] Yves Congar speculated that the meeting of non-believers with God could take place under the form of one of the master-words that stand for a transcendent absolute to which men give their love — Duty, Peace, Justice, Brotherhood, Humanity, Progress, Welfare, and, above all, what he refers to as the sacrament of our neighbor. Congar's reference with regard to this last concept is obviously to Matt. 25:31-46 — as you did it to one of the least of these my brethren, you did it to me. Congar, therefore, can speak of faith before faith, grace before grace, and a Church before the Church.[21] Other theories centered around special divine intervention, or choices made at the dawn of the first human act, a fundamental option to love, or decisions made possible at the hour of death. Each has been advanced in an attempt to explain how the mystery of God's saving grace is rendered possible for those who do not believe in God or who have had no contact with the Church or the gospel.[22]

Perhaps the most profound and most influential present-day theological attempt to explicitate the *votum ecclesiae* is Karl Rahner's theory of *anonymous Christianity*. It is profound and far-reaching because it is based upon a philosophical and theological anthropology, and involves a theory of grace, revelation, and Christology as well as a theory of the Church. Rahner's thesis has had significant influence on contemporary ecclesiology and missiology, and it cannot be overlooked by those interested in mission work either on the theoretical or practical level. Its optimism concerning the salvational status of non-Christians has provoked more than one strong response.

Rahner maintains that in order to reconcile God's salvific will and the necessity of Christian faith and the Church, somehow or other, historically and concretely, there must be degrees of membership in the Church. These must range in ascending stages, from baptism to confession of the full Christian faith, to

[20] Jean Daniélou, *Holy Pagans of the Old Testament*, trans. Felix Faber (London: Longmans, Green, and Co., 1957), p. 10.

[21] Congar, *The Wide World My Parish*, pp. 104-10.

[22] See, for example, Maurice Eminyan, S.J., *The Theology of Salvation* (Boston: St. Paul Publications, 1960), pp. 27-95; Piet Fransen, S.J., "How Can Non-Christians Find Salvation in Their Own Religions," *Christian Revelation and World Religions*, ed. Neuner, pp. 67-122; Anita Röper, *The Anonymous Christian*, trans. Joseph Donceel, S.J., (New York: Sheed and Ward, 1966), pp. 83-91.

recognition of the visible government of the Church, full fellowship of eucharistic life, and finally attainment of blessedness. However, there must also be descending stages going from the explicitness of baptism down to a non-official and implicit Christianity, which, Rahner maintains, "can and should be called Christianity in a valid sense, even though it cannot call itself such or refuses to do so."[23] In this "more and less" theory of Church membership Rahner seems to have Vatican II on his side inasmuch as the Council affirmed an open position with regard to membership in the Church by explicitating the various ways in which non-Catholics and non-Christians are linked with, and related to, the people of God.[24]

According to Rahner, non-believers and members of other religious traditions would belong to a "non-official and anonymous Christianity which can and should yet be called Christianity in a meaningful sense."[25] It is Rahner's philosophical and theological anthropology and his theory of grace and revelation which enable him to come to this conclusion. Being, God himself, is the a priori possibility and ground for all that man as embodied spirit can know. By what Anita Röper, interpreting Rahner, describes as transcendental implication, God is co-known in all human knowing in an unthematic and unconceptualized manner.[26] Man, therefore, is existentially determined to be open to transcendence and God himself, and accordingly to God's gift of himself, that is, grace. When man experiences his transcendence, his limitless openness, he experiences God's gratuitous bestowal of grace and revelation, although without explicit consciousness of

---

[23] Karl Rahner, S.J., "Salvation of the Non-Evangelized," *Sacramentum Mundi,* ed. Karl Rahner et al., IV (New York: Herder and Herder, 1968), 80; see also Karl Rahner, S.J., "Anonymous Christians," *Theological Investigations,* trans. Karl-H. and Boniface Kruger, VI (Baltimore: Helicon, 1969), 391.

[24] "The Church recognizes that in many ways she is linked with those who, being baptized, are honored with the name of Christian, though they do not profess the faith in its entirety or do not preserve unity of communion with the successor of Peter . . . .

"Likewise, we can say that in some real way they are joined with us in the Holy Spirit, for to them also He gives His gifts and graces, and is thereby operative among them with His sanctifying power . . . .

"Finally, those who have not yet received the gospel are related in various ways to the People of God." ("Dogmatic Constitution on the Church," Sections 15-16).

[25] Rahner, "Anonymous Christians," *Theological Investigations,* VI, 391.

[26] Röper, *The Anonymous Christian,* Chapter III.

grace as grace or a distinctly supernatural call, but in its meaningful reality.[27]

Grace, that is, God's gratuitous bestowal of himself, is the a priori horizon of all man's spiritual acts and accompanies man's consciousness subjectively, even though it is not known objectively.[28] Whenever man experiences and accepts his transcendence, for example, in infinite longing, radical optimism, unquenchable discontent, in the torment of the insufficiency of everything attainable, the radical protest against death, the absolute desire for love, and in his moral activity to do what is good, he experiences God's grace and revelation, which, however, are not necessarily known as such.[29] In saying *yes* to himself as openness, man makes an act of supernatural faith. This faith is not the work of man alone but the work of the grace of God, which is the grace of Christ and, in turn, the grace of the Church which is the prolongation of the mystery of Christ.[30]

Thus, Rahner can maintain that all non-Christians who accept themselves in this manner are linked to the Church in a minimal yet real fashion. They are anonymous Christians. Rahner admits that this theory is theological speculation and not the official position of the Catholic Church, but he feels that the thesis is present materially in Vatican II's "Dogmatic Constitution on the Church," Section 16, part of which was quoted above.[31]

The implications of this theory for mission work are revolutionary. Its opponents argue that it stands in marked opposition to the theological tradition of the Church and that it cuts the ground from under missionary outreach.[32] Rahner believes that

---

[27] See the following writings of Karl Rahner: "Anonymous Christians," *Theological Investigations,* VI, 392-94; "Concerning the Relationship between Nature and Grace," *Theological Investigations,* I, 311 ff.; "Nature and Grace," *Theological Investigations,* IV, 165-88; "Salvation of the Non-Evangelized," *Sacramentum Mundi,* ed. Rahner et al., IV, 80.

[28] Karl Rahner, S.J., "Christianity and the Non-Christian Religions," *Theological Investigations,* V, 313.

[29] Karl Rahner, S.J., *The Christian of the Future,* trans. W.J. O'Hara, Quaestiones Disputatae 18 (New York: Herder and Herder, 1967), p. 86; Karl Rahner, S.J., "Existence," *Sacramentum Mundi,* eds. Rahner et al., II, 306; Rahner, "Nature and Grace," *Theological Investigations,* IV, 183-84.

[30] Rahner, "Salvation of the Non-Evangelized," *Sacramentum Mundi,* ed. Rahner, IV, 80.

[31] *Ibid.*; Rahner, "Anonymous Christians," *Theological Investigations,* VI, 397; Rahner, "Christianity and the Non-Christian Religions," *Theological Investigations,* V, 117.

[32] See Paul Hacker, "The Religions of the Gentiles as Viewed by Fathers of the Church," and "The Christian Attitude Toward Non-Christian

this is not necessarily the case. Christians engaged in mission do not encounter a member of an extra-Christian religion as a mere non-Christian but as one who has been touched by God's grace and truth, that is, as an anonymous Christian. But the implicit thrust of anonymous Christianity towards God seeks explicitation and fulfillment. It has a dynamism not to remain anonymous but to arrive at its true identity — it seeks its name.[33] The proclamation of the gospel, therefore, aims to turn the anonymous Christian into someone who knows about his Christian belief in the depths of his grace-endowed being by objective reflection and profession of the faith in a given social form, the Church.[34]

Christians, therefore, go out to the world with serenity and patience, with the knowledge that non-Christians do not know what they really are, and with the aim of bringing them to their real selves by making their faith explicit.[35] Awareness of implicit Christianity does not diminish the significance of missions, but, on the contrary, it banishes panic and releases energies which can work toward making the redeeming love of God known as such.[36] The Church, therefore, is not to be regarded as the exclusive community of those who have a claim to salvation, but rather as the visible, tangible vanguard and the historically and socially constituted expression of what Christians hope is present as a hidden reality outside the visible Church.[37]

Non-Christian Religious Traditions and Salvation

By and large, the approach of Catholic theology with regard to the salvation of non-Christians has been from the standpoint of individual salvation. Theories centered upon implicit faith and the *votum ecclesiae* are concerned with the relation of the indi-

---

Religions," *Zeitschrift für Missionswissenschaft und Religionswissenschaft,* 54 (1970), 253-78; 55 (1971), 81-97.

[33] Rahner, "Christianity and the Non-Christian Religions," *Theological Investigations,* V, 131; "Salvation of the Non-Evangelized," *Sacramentum Mundi,* eds. Rahner et al., IV, 80.

[34] Rahner, "Christianity and the Non-Christian Religions," *Theological Investigations,* V, 132.

[35] Rahner, *The Christian of the Future,* p. 85.

[36] Rahner, "Salvation of the Non-Evangelized," *Sacramentum Mundi,* eds. Rahner et al., IV, 81.

[37] Rahner, "Christianity and the Non-Christian Religions," *Theological Investigations,* V, 133.

vidual vis-à-vis his personal salvation. Less mention is made of the role of non-Christian religious traditions in salvation. Rahner's theory attempts to come to terms with this problem too. Men are not only personally religious but they receive and express their religion in a social form. The nature of religion itself must include a social constitution, and a social form is necessary for salvation. Therefore, Rahner concludes, until the moment when the gospel really enters into the historical situation of an individual, a non-Christian religion does not merely contain elements of a natural knowledge of God, but supernatural elements which arise from grace. Non-Christian religious traditions, therefore, are not simply illegitimate but have a positive and lawful role as means of bringing men to salvation.[38]

Heinz Robert Schlette has developed Rahner's notions in this area in his presentation of a theology of religions. Schlette distinguishes between general and special sacred history. In the former, which involves God's relation with all men, the non-Christian religions are sanctified by God and are viewed as the ordinary means for salvation. Special sacred history includes the Old and New Covenants according to which the Church becomes the extraordinary way towards salvation, the eschatological community whose function is to be representative of what God is doing through all the religions, and the community charged with the role of bearing witness to that towards which the religions, the ordinary ways of salvation, are leading. The importance of special sacred history and the Church does not rest in the fact that salvation is more secure and advantageous, but in God's freedom to reveal his glory before the world in an explicit fashion. Non-Christian religions, therefore, are legitimate and normal ways of salvation for their members; yet, because of God's special dispensation in Christianity, they are imperfect. The meaning of Christian mission consists in God's offering his incomparable way to all who will accept it.[39]

It must be admitted, however, that theories such as those of Rahner and Schlette are definitely intramural positions developed by, and presented to, Christians. They sound sensible to the Christian, especially to one who has had little contact with members of other religious traditions; they ease his conscience and

---

[38] Rahner, *ibid.*, pp. 120-31.

[39] Schlette, *Towards a Theology of Religions*, pp. 63-107.

restrain him from panic and excessive worry about the salvation of non-Christians; they may hold him back from blind and inconsiderate zeal in approaching men of other religious traditions; but they are hardly complimentary to, or meaningful for, committed members of other religions. There is a hint of triumphalism and condescension in a theological framework of this sort which urges Christians to approach non-Christians with the attitude that those who do not accept Christ really do not know their true identity because they are anonymously Christian. Would a Christian accept the same in reverse if he were told that he does not know his true religious identity because he is an anonymous Buddhist or an anonymous Hindu? Rahner himself admits that his theory is not directed to those who do not believe.[40]

In the final analysis, perhaps the best that comes from the theory of anonymous Christianity or the religions as the ordinary ways of salvation is an operational stance which enables Christians to be open to the religions and to what Paul Tillich calls the quasi-religions of mankind, and attentive to the sources of grace and revelation which can be found there. Since these theories are so one-sidedly Catholic and Christian they can offer less towards helping to understand the true significance of the religious content and experience of non-Christian religious traditions.

And yet openness to the goodness and truth on the part of Christians vis-à-vis the religions of mankind is of no small value. It seems to have been present, in some degree, in the early centuries of the Church, in the approach of the Fathers to the ancient philosophers; it reached occasional high points in history, for example, in the work of some Jesuits in the sixteenth and seventeenth centuries in China and India; but, by and large, it has not been a predominating value in the missionary work of the Church. In the Catholic tradition, Vatican II, without fully endorsing theories such as those of Rahner, adopted a position of openness to non-Christian religious traditions. The Church went on record as rejecting nothing which is true and holy in the religions of mankind and it looked with respect upon those ways of conduct and life, rules and teachings, which reflect rays of that Truth which enlightens all men. Catholics are urged to dialogue and collaborate to preserve and promote the spiritual and moral

---

[40] Rahner, "Anonymous Christians," *Theological Investigations,* VI, 395.

goods found among non-Christians as well as the values expressed in their societies and cultures.[41]

In the Catholic tradition at the present time, therefore, three theological factors combine to make it impossible to take a stance of absolute truth versus absolute falsehood with regard to the religions of the world. Religious forms other than Christianity cannot be considered at best as merely natural religions or at worst devil worship as they have at times in the past. These three considerations are, first, the clear affirmation, because of God's universal salvific will, that salvation is possible and already operative outside the Church; second, the stance of openness and dialogue which the Church desires to take with regard to truth, goodness, and grace which makes salvation possible outside itself; third, the fact that, because of the truth and goodness they possess, the Church is related to and linked with other religions and men of good will in whatever form and context these values are embodied and expressed.

The framework of this approach stands independent of further elaborations given to it by the theory of anonymous Christianity or theories which see the non-Christian religions as ordinary means of salvation. Because of this approach, the Catholic tradition cannot feel at ease with the positions taken in recent years by Conservative Evangelicals in the Protestant world who, while strongly and correctly stressing the primacy of Christ and faith in Christ for salvation, reject the stance of openness taken

---

41 "The Catholic Church rejects nothing which is true and holy in these religions. She looks with sincere respect upon those ways of conduct and of life, those rules and teachings which, though differing in many particulars from what she holds and sets forth, nevertheless often reflect a ray of that Truth which enlightens all men. Indeed, she proclaims and must ever proclaim Christ, 'the way, the truth, and the life' (John 14:6), in whom men find the fullness of religious life, and in whom God has reconciled all things to Himself (cf. 2 Cor. 5:18-19).

"The Church therefore has this exhortation for her sons: prudently and lovingly, through dialogue and collaboration with the followers of other religions, and in witness of Christian faith and life, acknowledge, preserve, and promote the spiritual and moral goods found among these men, as well as the values in their society and culture." ("Declaration on the Relationship of the Church to Non-Christian Religions," Section 2).

Paul VI's recent apostolic exhortation on evangelization, *Evangelii Nuntiandi*, reaffirms this openness but it is interesting to note that it also sounds a negative note uncharacteristic of Vatican II when it says "our religion effectively establishes with God an authentic and living relationship which the other religions do not succeed in doing, even though they have, as it were, their arms stretched out towards heaven." (See Paul VI, *Evangelization in the Modern World,* Section 53.)

by the Catholic tradition and the World Council of Churches and the possibility of salvation for non-Christians.[42]

If from within the Catholic tradition the relationship between Christianity and the other religious traditions of the world cannot be stated simply and boldly as one of total truth on the one side and complete falsehood on the other, neither can it be expressed in terms of radical discontinuity, the position developed by the Neo-orthodox school within Protestantism. This position was given its most forceful expression for the missionary world by Hendrik Kraemer with the publication of his *Christian Message in a Non-Christian World* in 1938.[43] It is impossible to do justice to the depth and complexity of Dr. Kraemer's position here, but the negative assessment it gives to the religions of mankind and the radical difference which it ascribes to Christian faith, which stands under the continuous and direct influence and judgement of the gospel and revelation, as opposed to the religions of mankind, which can only be seen in radical antithesis to the gospel, make it difficult to reconcile Dr. Kraemer's position with the current stance of Catholicism or, for that matter, of the World Council of Churches. The relationship of Christianity and the religions is more one of continuity than Dr. Kraemer would allow it to be.

However, the position taken by Dr. Kraemer and the present-day Conservative Evangelicals place emphasis on one central truth which no Christian would be willing to surrender — the unique place of the gospel and the grace of Christ for the salvation of mankind. Their weakness lies in the excessively negative estimation they give to the religious traditions of the world. The truth they highlight, however, is of no small importance. It is the central role of the grace of Christ and the gospel which offers check to any tendencies to religious relativism (such as those which developed in the nineteenth century within Liberal Protestantism), to overly optimistic and abstract speculations about a common essence to be found among all the religious aspirations of mankind, and, finally, to simplistic attempts towards re-

---

[42] See "The Frankfurt Declaration," in Peter Beyerhaus, *Missions: Which Way? — Humanization or Redemption,* trans. Margaret Clarkson (Grand Rapids, Mich.: Zondervan Publishing House, 1971), pp. 107-20; "The Wheaton Declaration," *The Church's Worldwide Mission: An Analysis of the Current State of Evangelical Missions, and a Strategy for Future Activity,* ed. Harold Lindsell (Waco, Texas: Word Books, 1966), pp. 217-37.

[43] Hendrik Kraemer, *The Christian Message in a Non-Christian World* (Grand Rapids, Mich.: Kregal Publications, 1958).

ligious syncretism. This is not to deny that phenomenological analysis of similarities at the heart of all human religious experience is not of vital importance. On the contrary, it will be the fruit of, and at the heart of, any openness, sharing, and *rapprochement* between Christianity and the religions. In the final analysis, however, both Christian and non-Christian have to face the unique, *sui generis* position of Jesus Christ in God's plan for all mankind. This is what M. M. Thomas has referred to as the "scandal of objective happenedness" which is at the core of Christianity.[44]

Christianity as Fulfillment

In addition to openness to the goodness and truth present in the religions of mankind, and the continuity which exists between Christianity and the religions because of the relationship and link which this goodness and truth have to the gospel, there is another long-standing theological principle which is part of Schlette's theory and must be mentioned with regard to the position of Christianity and the other religious traditions of the world — the notion of fulfillment. When the Second Vatican Council speaks of the goodness and truth found in the religions of mankind, it speaks of these in relation to the fullness present in Christianity. The truth which is found among those who seek God is seen as a preparation for the gospel, and the goodness of the religious practices and cultures of mankind is healed, ennobled, and perfected through the work of the Church.[45] The theme of fulfillment has a long-honored tradition within Chris-

---

[44] M.M. Thomas in Paul Loffler (ed.), *Secular Man and Christian Mission*, CWME Study Pamphlet 3 (New York: Friendship Press, 1968), p. 22.

[45] "Nor does divine Providence deny the help necessary for salvation to those who, without blame on their part, have not yet arrived at an explicit knowledge of God, but who strive to live a good life, thanks to His grace. Whatever goodness or truth is found among them is looked upon by the Church as a preparation for the gospel. She regards such qualities as given by Him who enlightens all men so that they may finally have life . . . .

"Through her [the Church's] work, whatever good is in the minds and hearts of men, whatever good lies latent in the religious practices and cultures of diverse peoples, is not only saved from destruction but is also healed, ennobled, and perfected unto the glory of God, the confusion of the devil, and the happiness of man." ("Dogmatic Constitution on the Church," Sections 16-17); see also "Declaration on the Relationship of the Church to Non-Christian Religions," Section 2.

tianity going back to the earliest centuries of the Church. Because of the increased knowledge of, openness towards, and positive evaluation given to, non-Christian religions today, it is an important operative principle in any attempt to reconcile the role of Christ and Christian revelation on the one hand and the values found in other religious traditions on the other.

However, there is a certain drawback in considering Christianity as possessing the fullness of the truth. As W. C. Smith has observed, it may be validly argued that outside the Christian tradition men may know God in part and cannot know him fully. But the implications of this position are precarious, for is it possible for the Christian to know God fully?[46] It is certainly right that the only reason for being a Christian is because Christianity is true.[47] However, acknowledgement that truth and goodness, grace and revelation are present within other religious traditions of the world puts the Christian's concept of the truth of man's meaning and destiny vis-à-vis God into a much broader perspective.

Perhaps a more suitable approach would be to say that Christianity possesses an adequate knowledge of God's plan for man and the world, but that a certain fullness must also be recognized as possible outside the Christian tradition but definitely within the broader ambit of God's Mission. Those concerned about mission work will have to be cautious concerning theories of Christianity as possessing the fullness of truth. If this were the framework of the approach adopted in the past, perhaps for the future the emphasis and balance will have to be shifted slightly towards sensitivity to God's fullness, presence, revelation, truth, and grace operative beyond the Christian tradition.

Therefore, when the *sui generis* role of Christ and Christian revelation is presented as the fulfillment of all the religious aspirations of man, in no way can the richness of other religious traditions be devalued. Since God's plan for mankind has been worked out concretely and historically in the person of Jesus Christ, it suffers by necessity from cultural, historical, and temporal limitations. While upholding this, the men of our times are

---

[46] Wilfred Cantwell Smith, *The Faith of Other Men* (New York: New American Library, 1963), p. 137.

[47] Stephen Neill, *Call to Mission* (Philadelphia: Fortress, 1970), p. 10; Elton Trueblood, *The Validity of the Christian Mission* (New York: Harper and Row, 1972), p. 56.

confronted with the problem of relating the other fullness of God's presence in the non-Christian religious traditions of mankind to Christianity's place in salvation history. An elaboration of the ways and modes, the symbol and content of grace and revelation present beyond Christian revelation will have to be one of the focal points in all future theological reflection concerning Christianity and the religions of the world. Revelation will have to be approached as a universal phenomenon located in the inner depths of the experience of the Sacred common to all religious traditions.[48]

Finally, it is important to note that the ongoing relationship between Christianity and the religious traditions of mankind must be viewed not abstractly but historically, and ultimately in the light of eschatology. Fulfillment in Christ may not be historically attainable. It implies theological development and human interaction, and these demand time and history. Indeed, perhaps only in recent generations have Christianity and the other religious traditions been in a situation to begin mutually to understand and appreciate each other. It seems, therefore, that in the future conversions from other major religions to Christianity will be difficult and rare. It does not seem too presumptuous to suggest that perhaps only at the end of time, when the kingdom will be revealed in its fullness, will the plenitude and relatedness of all religious faith be made manifest and brought to fruition in Christ.[49]

A Spirituality of Dialogue and Openness

The relationship between Christianity and the other religions ot the world is not only the key theological problem confronting the mission of the Church today, but it is also a crucial area with important implications for missionary spirituality and the missionary life style. As mentioned in Chapter VI, the frontier between belief and non-belief is the area where the missionary intention becomes most explicit and self-conscious. From what

---

[48] See Robert Edward Whitson, *The Coming Convergence of World Religions* (New York: Newman, 1971), pp. 154-55.

[49] Congar, *The Wide World My Parish,* pp. 135-36; Charles Davis, *Christ and the World Religions* (London: Hodder and Stoughton, 1970), p. 130; Adrian Hastings, *Mission and Ministry* (London: Sheed and Ward, 1971), pp. 31-32.

has been presented so far in this chapter, the main quality demanded for the missionary vis-à-vis the other religions of the world is a stance of openness and dialogue. This is the case because the questions whether or not men outside the Church are saved, or whether or not truth, goodness, grace, and revelation are possible within the non-Christian religious traditions must be answered affirmatively. This positive evaluation of the religions of man will affect the missionary's approach to non-Christians independently of the theories which seek to answer the question how men are saved outside the Church. The following pages will relate them to themes already developed in the previous chapters.

The first thing that must be said with regard to the openness and dialogue required on the part of Christians when meeting men of other faiths is that it must be fostered in a climate of *humility*. The tension will have to be maintained and balanced between acknowledgement of the possibility of grace, revelation, and salvation in other religious traditions, and confession of the unique role of Christ, the Church, and Christian revelation in God's plan and Mission. It will neither be solved nor alleviated by pronouncing negative judgements upon the religions of mankind, nor by a stance of triumphalism or condescension on the part of Christians, nor by overly facile attempts at syncretism or religious relativism. It must be admitted in this regard that theological language can be disadvantageous. Terms such as anonymous Christianity, or implicit or latent Christianity, and analogies of fullness and less full, act and potency, fruit and seed, real presence and forerunner, reality and symbol can be questioned as to whether or not they are helpful towards openness, dialogue, and understanding.[50] Christians from the West are at a decided disadvantage in this area, and one of the reasons why Christianity has not succeeded in the East is because of its Westernness. The chances are that the role of revelation and presence of Christ in the non-Christian religious traditions will not be fully grasped and developed by Westerners or non-Westerners trained in the West but by the Christians of the East and Africa who will work towards a solution of the tension using the religious experience, symbols, philosophy, and theology of the cultures in which Christianity has not been indigenous. If it took the Church several

[50] For this last series of comparisons, see R. Panikkar, *The Unknown Christ of Hinduism* (London: Darton, Longman, and Todd, 1964), pp. 35 ff.

hundred years to express its doctrines through the medium of Greek philosophy, one cannot be too impatient with the present situation since only in recent times have openness, understanding, and dialogue been possible between Christianity and the other religious traditions of the world.

The theology of the *missio Dei,* coupled with an acknowledgment of the universal presence of grace and revelation in the non-Christian religious traditions, make the stance of humble openness and dialogue possible. As mentioned in Chapter V, a spirituality based upon this theological foundation cannot fail to be mindful of the truth that the Church is not greater than God and that the mission of the Church, although it is the historical community of explicit participation in the Mission of God, is not coextensive with God's Mission.[51] In this regard, the theory of anonymous Christianity could have another drawback. Although its intention is to reconcile the universal concern of God's Mission with the centrality of Christ and the Church in salvation history, it places heavy emphasis upon the latter mystery to the detriment of God's freedom in the economy of salvation. It seems, therefore, that one who would approach the non-Christian with the theological framework of anonymous Christianity, unbalanced by the equally important theological truth of the *missio Dei,* would be hindered from the start with regard to openness and dialogue.

When the two themes of the Mission of God and the extra-ecclesial possibility of grace and revelation are merged, the Christian engaged in mission is in a position to assume a stance in his life style and spirituality which is definitely in accord with post-Vatican II trends in the Catholic Church. At the Council, and in the documents of the Council, stress was given to a positive approach to the world and to the beliefs and religious traditions of different men. The concern was to look at those elements and values which unite men rather than those which cause men to differ. Since there can be religious faith and prophetic revelation outside the Christian tradition, Christians can in no way say that they have nothing to learn or gain from other traditions.[52] If in the past it was possible for Christian missionaries to consider themselves as bearers of Christ to the world of non-believers,

---

[51] See Küng, "The World Religions in God's Plan of Salvation," *Christian Revelation and World Religions,* ed. Neuner, p. 59.

[52] Davis, *Christ and the World Religions,* pp. 127-30.

this position is no longer tenable without the following qualification: the Christian engaged in mission speaks of Christ to other men, but, what is equally important for the times in which we live, he is also one who must seek to encounter Christ in the world of other religions.[53] Or, as proclaimed by the Catholic Church in India, in dialogue Christians seek both to share their experience of salvation in Christ with adherents of other religious traditions and to be open to the experience of God which other traditions have to offer Christianity.[54]

Arnold Toynbee had a point in maintaining that the challenge of Symmachus (c. 345-410) has never been adequately answered by Christianity. In a controversy with St. Ambrose, Symmachus entered this plea concerning the mystery of man's encounter with God: "It is impossible that so great a mystery should be approached by one road only."[55] The only way for Christians to answer the challenge of Symmachus is by an approach of humble openness and dialogue with men of other religions, openness and dialogue which will only be fulfilled if a double conversion is accepted as a possibility.

The Service of Spirituality

It was mentioned in Chapter V, that one of the most creative images currently used within the Catholic tradition to explicitate the mystery of the Church is the image of sign and sacrament. The Church is the sign and sacrament of God's plan and Mission for salvation. As sign, the Church points to what God is doing in the world; as sacramental sign, the Church realizes God's plan of reconciliation, forgiveness, and peace between men and between man and God. Hence, the Church has a prophetic function, a vanguard role — to point to and partially realize God's kingdom and salvific plan for creation.

---

[53] See Pedro Arrupe, S.J., "Our Apostolate in Africa and Madagascar Today," *Studies in the International Apostolate of Jesuits*, 1 (September, 1972), 72-73.

[54] Organizing Committee of All India Seminar on the Church in India Today, *All India Seminar: Church in India Today, Bengalore, 1969* (New Delhi: C.B.C.I. Center, 1969), p. 257.

[55] Arnold Toynbee, *Christianity Among the Religions of the World* (New York: Charles Schribner's Sons, 1957), pp. 111-12.

However, since the Mission of God is more far-reaching than the Church's participation in that Mission, and inasmuch as grace, revelation, and salvation are possible beyond the Church, it can be said that, although the Church enjoys a historical primacy and centrality in the Mission of God, the Church is not the only bearer of God's Mission. Therefore, in exercising its prophetic, representative, and vanguard function, the Church is obliged in truth and with humility to point to all sources wherein God's goodness, grace, truth, and reconciliation are possible both in its own tradition, and, more important for the present question, in other religious traditions of mankind.

The image of sign is basically a serving image. The role of the missionary as a man of service has deep roots in the history of missionary spirituality. In Chapter V, service was seen as the prime mode of mission today. It was pointed out, furthermore, that this service has a double orientation — towards God and towards men and the world. When all of these theological themes are reviewed with a concern for developing a spirituality for mission, they give one who intends to engage in mission a distinctive orientation which perhaps is one of the most important elements for the spirituality of mission in our times. Christianity as a faith does not simply co-exist with the other religions and quasi-religions of the world; rather, the only possible position it can assume is one of humble pro-existence for the other religious traditions of the world.[56] The missionary is a man of pro-existence, pointing to God's presence in his own tradition and in the other religious traditions of the world as well.

In this context, the spirituality of the missionary has a crucial role to play. In exercising his sacramental function of proclaiming and realizing the plan of God's Mission for men, in being a serving person of humble pro-existence, in looking towards, and working for, the eschatological realization of the unity of men with each other and with God and the recapitulation of all goodness in Christ, the role of shared religious experience is crucial. This is the locus of spirituality. The religious experience of the Sacred is the basic and most creative element in all religious traditions. Theology is the attempt systematically to analyze, conceptualize, and present to others the religious experience which

[56] See Küng, "The World Religions in God's Plan of Salvation," *Christian Revelation and World Religions,* ed. Neuner, p. 61.

is at the heart of each tradition. However, there will always be a gap between the conceptualization of religious experience in theology, which aims at grasping something which is ineffable, and the experience itself which is at the heart of a particular tradition.

Continuity, convergence, development towards Christ and in Christ will not ultimately be worked out on the level of doctrinal comparisons between religious traditions, although this will be important; much less will it be reached by merely sharing common social, economic, and political concerns, although this, too, will be a natural and necessary meeting ground between men of different traditions. Rather, the primary and basic point of contact will be in that area where the religious faith and experience of the Christian meet the richness and goodness of the faith and religious experience of the person from another tradition in humble openness and with a desire to serve. In other words, the point of contact will be where spirituality meets spirituality not conceptually but existentially and experientially.[57]

Furthermore, a link can be made at this point with the pilgrim spirituality of mission. The pilgrimage demanded for the Christian engaged in mission will not necessarily be a physical or geographical journey. Rather, in light of the present theme, it may well be a pilgrimage of the spirit, a radical and self-negating pilgrimage which seeks not only to live from the depths of the religious experience of the Christian tradition, but also to engage oneself in the depths of the religious experience of another tradition. In this regard, although terms such as accommodation and adaptation are important, they might not go far enough. Conversion is the more radical concept. Exercising the role of pro-existence and dedicated to humble service in what relates to the presence of the Sacred around him, the missionary, in his spirituality and life style, will by necessity and definition have to be open to double conversion.

The implications of this approach for the missionary's life style are vast and can only be sketched. The Christian engaged in mission will not only have to know the philosophical and theological positions of the people whom he serves, but also have to live these in his own religious experience and encounter them

---

[57] For these remarks I am indebted somewhat to Whitson, *The Coming Convergence of World Religions*, pp. 10-11, 56, 75, 108, 112, 128; see also D.S. Amalorpavadass, "The Apostolate to Non-Christians," *Foundations of Mission Theology*, ed. SEDOS, p. 86.

in his own spirituality. It was mentioned in Chapter II that the Bible is one of the primary factors in the formation of Christian spirituality. It can now be added that the sacred writings of other traditions will also be important for the spirituality of one who desires to engage in mission, not merely an abstract knowledge of them, but also an experiential living of them in contact with men who live by them.

By way of example, it can be noted that this approach on the level of spirituality and religious experience seems to be a direction being followed by segments of the Church in India today. Bede Griffiths, a monk from the West living in India, writes that a genuine meeting of East and West can only take place where the deepest levels of religious experience are shared. In his estimation, this would be by a merger of the monastic tradition of the West and the tradition of the ashrams in India.[58] This does not mean to say that the ideal missionary will once more be the monk; but rather that the attitude implied by this judgment will have to be operative in the life style of any Christian engaged in mission.

On a broader level, the Catholic Church in India affirms in a recent statement that, in view of the richness of the contemplative traditions indigenous to India, the local Church in that nation must make a special effort to fulfill her mission in the universal Church by reflecting the contemplative aspects of the mystery of Christ in conjunction with the deep strivings towards interiority and contemplation which have long existed in India.[59] At the same seminar, the working group concerned with dialogue with other religions reflected the same openness. Inter-religious dialogue is seen as far more than merely seeking an understanding of doctrines; at its highest levels it is described as an act of spiritual and religious communion in which the religious reality is experienced in common, and in which both partners undergo profound change.

In the concrete, the working group recommends that ashrams be established in which authentic Christian spirituality is lived and in which non-Christians may experience Christian fellowship.[60] Once again, it is to be noted that it is not the concrete

---

[58] Bede Griffiths, *Christ in India: Essays Towards a Hindu-Christian Dialogue* (New York: Charles Schribner's Sons, 1966), pp. 17-18.

[59] See *All India Seminar,* pp. 249-50.

[60] *Ibid.*, pp. 340-43.

details of these approaches being recommended in India which are the central point here, but rather the attitude and life style which they imply. It is this which one interested in mission must make his own. This, of course, ties in with the importance of local churches in the catholic communion of churches, for ultimately it will be the local Church which must decide those aspects of God's Mission, goodness, and grace to be accepted and explored in any one area.

Finally, a suggestion made by William Ernest Hocking thirty years ago has relevance today. The life style and spirituality suggested here will demand not only different attitudes from the past but also different institutional forms which embody these attitudes. Hocking saw this and suggested a new institution to complement the traditional institutions which were engaged in mission. The institutions for mission were set for teaching, the new ones must be set for learning as well; they were set for the announcement of doctrine, the new ones must be set as well for conversation and conference; they were set for activity, the new ones must be set for leisure, contemplation, and study; the institutions for mission were set for address to its own region, the new ones must be set for give and take with the thought and feeling of a nation and a world.[61]

In summary, a theology and spirituality for mission which claims that the Christian knows the real state of the world religions and has full and adequate knowledge of God's plan for man, and which sees the Church as the vanguard of God's Mission with links to, and obligations towards, the religious traditions of mankind, must be supplemented by another less sure orientation. According to this, and in the context of the *missio Dei,* there is much that the Christian does not yet know about God's dealings with man and the ways his grace and revelation are present to mankind. This theology and spirituality can only accept the stance of humble openness to the fullness beyond Christianity and to the fullness of God's time which is still working itself out within other religious traditions. The former stance is a present-day option being followed by many within the Church; the latter stance might well be the hallmark of mission theology and spirituality for the future.

---

[61] William Ernest Hocking, *Living Religions and a World Faith* (New York: Macmillan, 1940), p. 205.

VIII

CONTEMPORARY CULTURAL INFLUENCES

The theory of Christian spirituality presented here views the Christian life style as formed in a situation of interlocking influences which come from the Christian world view found in Scripture, the theological reflection of the Christian community, the traditions which Christians inherit and according to which they live, and the cultural situation of the times. This chapter is concerned with the last source of influence.

In Chapter II, culture was described as a complex reality—the sum and total of the ideological and structural elements which compose the human environment. Vatican II has described culture more dynamically from the viewpoint of human creativity as "all those factors by which man refines and unfolds his manifold spiritual and bodily qualities."[1] It is difficult to overestimate the influence of culture upon theology and spirituality, for these both form and are formed by culture. Reference was made to the developing discipline of the sociology of knowledge which works on the premise that man's understanding and appreciation of reality and his way of acting are greatly determined by the style of life followed by the society in which he lives. Therefore, a consideration of the present-day cultural and historical situation in which the Christian message must come alive is essential to mission spirituality for our times.

The theological foundation for this approach is rooted in the position developed in Chapter V that history is the context of the Mission of God. The stance taken here is based on the belief that Church and culture can be understood as mutually interpenetrating dimensions of God's activity in the world for men.[2] Therefore, those who reflect upon mission today are led to affirm that only by being aware of what modern men are saying in suffering and in success can theology and the mission of the

---

[1] "Pastoral Constitution on the Church in the Modern World," Section 53.
[2] Norman K. Gottwald, *The Church Unbound* (Philadelphia: J.B. Lippincott, 1967), pp. 169-70.

Church have any meaning.[3] Therefore, again, as expressed by the Fathers of Vatican II, in order for the Church to carry out the Mission of Christ it has the duty of scrutinizing the signs of the times and of interpreting them in the light of the gospel.[4]

The practical foundation for this approach comes from what has been said about the need for discernment and the possibility of many ways of participating in God's Mission. If the goal for the mission of the Church can be expressed as an answer to the question, How do the people of God participate in the Mission of God at this time and in this place?, only by knowing the context, environment and the problems of the particular time and place can the Church take up its missionary role with effectiveness.

At the heart of this approach and crucial to the meaning and intention of this chapter is the question of *theological method*. In Chapter V, the method of correlation was mentioned as an approach whereby theology attempts to make an analysis of the human situation out of which existential questions arise, and to demonstrate that the symbols used in the Christian message are the answers to these questions. An approach of this type is employed in Vatican II's consideration of the Church in the modern world. The Council intends to scrutinize the signs of the times and interpret them in the light of the gospel so that the Church can serve as a leaven for human society, and contribute toward making the family of man and its history more human.[5] This method seeks to develop theological positions and practical modes of action by reflection upon the tension which arises between two poles — the Word of revelation on the one hand, and the theoretical and practical problems of the present moment on the other. It makes assertions such as this: Where humanity has such needs and opportunities, the mystery of Christ and the mission of the Church demand a certain interpretation

[3] Walter J. Hollenweger (ed.), *The Church for Others and the Church for the World: A Quest for Structures for Missionary Congregations* (Geneva: World Council of Churches, 1968), p. 7.

[4] "Pastoral Constitution on the Church in the Modern World," Section 4; Juan Landazuri Ricketts, "Inaugural Address," Latin American Episcopal Council, *The Church in the Present-Day Transformation of Latin America in the Light of the Council*, ed. Louis Michael Colonnese, I (Bogotá: General Secretariat of CELAM, 1970), 53.

[5] "Pastoral Constitution on the Church in the Modern World," Sections 4, 40.

and definite individual and collective behavior in response to these needs and opportunities.[6]

The present chapter is concerned with the method of correlation as it applies to the spirituality of mission. The project is a bold venture, for it implies that it is possible in a few pages to come to terms with the characteristics of the modern world. Although I feel that certain general characteristics of the world culture of our period can be determined and related to spirituality, I am aware that this chapter is open to the charge of dealing in facile generalities. I recognize the necessity for the conclusions of many disciplines such as sociology, anthropology, psychology, economics, political science, and philosophy for a comprehensive understanding of the situation of our world both globally and locally. For this reason, it is necessary to underline the importance of the method proposed. The characteristics of the modern world presented here and the implications they have for mission spirituality will be offered as illustrative rather than definitive.

Another problem which must be faced in any description of modern culture is the tension and even contradiction which exists oftentimes between the general and the particular, between the oneness and the world and the diversity of different areas of the world. I am aware of the danger of taking any one characteristic or chain of characteristics and saying that they apply universally to the present-day situation. Exceptions must be allowed and accounted for. If the observations and conclusions developed here do not fit in a particular situation, the analysis might be defective; but the method followed will still be relevant.

Partial descriptions of the modern world and the context of present-day mission work have already appeared in the preceding chapters. In Chapter I, for example, Lesslie Newbigin's analysis of the causes for the present crisis in missions included the following elements: the breakdown of colonialism, the rise of nationalism, and the spread of democratic ideals in the world; the growing sense of global interdependence towards one world; the secularization of service which has been under way in recent

[6] For this method as applied to the theology of liberation see Zoltan Alszeghy, S.J. and Maurizio Flick, S.J., "Theology of Development: A Question of Method," *Theology Meets Progress: Human Implications of Development*, ed. Philip Land, Studia Socialia 10 (Rome: Gregorian University, 1971), pp. 112-19.

centuries; and the crisis of faith in the West. Other elements which form the context of the mission of the Church appeared in Chapters V, VI, and VII: the notion of the Church in diaspora, the new approach which Christianity must take to the non-Christian religious traditions, the identification of the missionary vocation and the vocation of all Christians, and the development of a theology of the local Church which takes into account the necessary pluralism which exists in the world today.

The present chapter will develop and give a stronger foundation to these characteristics and it will sketch other elements which form the context of the mission of the Church today. The chapter is divided into five sections, each containing a set of characteristics which are signs of our times. None of these five sections is independent of the others; rather, they are interlocking constellations of elements which form the present-day context of God's Mission and the mission of the Church.

One World

The first constellation of characteristics can be summarized under the heading of the developing one-world civilization. This condition can be expressed in a variety of ways. Some speak in terms of a global village: the mutual interaction of village life exists now on a world-wide scale. In Chapter I, it was described as global interdependence, a climate in which the human race recognizes more and more that it is bound together with common strivings and goals, and common dangers and problems. Vatican II speaks of the interdependence of men one upon the other and of a single world community.[7] It can be described as a cosmopolitanization and world-wide mingling of particular cultures. Peoples of the West can enjoy and make their own Japanese art and philosophy, Chinese and Korean cooking, Indian theology and mysticism, and African dance, music, and folk lore.[8] Those not in the West are influenced, perhaps to a greater extent, by the technological, industrial, and consumer culture and values of the Western nations.

[7] "Pastoral Constitution on the Church in the Modern World," Sections 23, 33.

[8] See David M. Stowe, "Strategy: The Church's Response to What God is Doing," *Protestant Crosscurrents in Mission*, ed. Normal A. Horner (Nashville: Abingdon, 1968), pp. 148-49.

The causes of the growing oneness of mankind are many, but they have their roots in the technological achievements of the past centuries: the electronic communications media, which through transistor radio and television can put men of every part of the globe into instant contact with all other areas; the development of rapid world-wide transportation; the interlocking network of trade and economic dependencies and needs; the fact that, by and large, the world is becoming less rural and more urbanized due to industrialization and population pressures; the development of world-wide governmental and international organizations which influence the lives of people in all parts of the world. Blocks of nations are coming together for purposes of trade and mutual support.

Signs seem to point to the possibility, although not in the near future, of a single form of world government growing from existing institutions such as the United Nations. Visionaries, such as Pierre Teilhard de Chardin, make much of these phenomena and envision a future in which the human race, like a gigantic biological organism, will cross another evolutionary threshold and reach a point of common reflection and consciousness.[9] What is to be noted from this brief description of the global village is not so much that the world and all men enjoy a basic unity, but the fact that men are aware of, and influenced by, their oneness and interdependence.

In view of the broadening and deepening process of world unification, it does not seem by chance or fortune that Vatican II describes the Church as the sign and sacrament of the intimate union of men with God and with each other,[10] or that the Uppsala meeting of the World Council of Churches describes Christ's Mission as that of bringing peoples of all times, of all races, and of all places and conditions into an organic and living unity in the Holy Spirit under the universal fatherhood of God.[11] The mission of the Church and the mission of Christians are missions of unification. If there are men of the world who are dedicated totally to secular pursuits and who have dedicated

---

[9] Pierre Teilhard de Chardin, *The Phenomenon of Man,* trans. Bernard Wall (New York: Harper and Row, 1959), Book IV.

[10] "Dogmatic Constitution on the Church," Section 1.

[11] Norman Goodall (ed.), *The Uppsala Report: Official Report of the Fourth Assembly of the World Council of Churches, Uppsala, July 4-20, 1968* (Geneva: World Council of Churches, 1968), p. 13.

themselves to world unification and reconciliation, the Christian — one who is intimately engaged in the Mission of God — cannot take second place to any and must be a man of reconciliation and unification between all men and peoples. However, the unity he seeks must be set within the total context of God's Mission and the integral view of humanity which forms the comprehensive meaning of salvation. He is concerned with unity and communion in the world; with the unity and community of the Christian community, a community dedicated to serving God and the world; and the union and reconciliation of all men with God.[12]

Dedicated to the task and mission of achieving this triple communion and unity in the world, the Christian engaged in mission can fittingly be called a bridge person — one who bridges cultures, one who bridges differences between men, one who bridges nations and races. He lives as a sign and sacrament of the universality and catholicity of God's Mission and plan for all men.[13] Ivan Illich, a truly intercultural figure in our times, can still describe the missionary as one who has left his own milieu to bring the gospel of reconciliation to an area not his own from birth.[14] Recalling what was said in Chapter VI, we can say that perhaps the journey will not be geographical, but it will be into a new milieu as witness to the universality of God's plan for man and as effective sign of the unification of peoples with each other and with God. R. Pierce Beaver has described this bridging function of the missionary as the role of a man who stands between the times: between the separated histories of peoples and universal world history, between the West and the East, between agrarian societies and the industrial age, between the partial realization of the kingdom of God here and its fullness which is to come.[15]

---

[12] See, for example, Eduardo F. Pironio, "Christian Interpretation of the Signs of the Time in Latin America Today," Latin American Episcopal Council, *The Church in the Present-Day Transformation of Latin America,* I, 123-26.

[13] See Joseph A. Grassi, M.M., "Blueprint for a Missionary Church — Scriptural Reflections on the Church as the People of God," ed. William J. Richardson, M.M. (Maryknoll, N.Y.: Maryknoll Publications, 1968), p. 31; J. Rossell, *Mission in a Dynamic Society,* trans. J. G. Davies (London, SCM Press, 1968), p. 113.

[14] Ivan Illich, *The Church, Change, and Development* (Chicago: Urban Training Press, 1970), p. 112.

[15] R. Pierce Beaver, *The Missionary Between the Times* (Garden City, N.Y.: Doubleday, 1968), p. 159.

In the context of the global village and the unification and interdependence of the world, the missionary is a man of two or, one might even say, three cultures — his own, that to which he is called and sent, and the growing one-world culture. His role is to bridge his own milieu with that into which he is received, and to work towards that oneness which is growing in the world today and which, under the gospel of reconciliation, is the direction and plan of God's Mission.

The work of reconciliation, unification, and peace between men, and between all men and God will be a dominant factor in missionary motivation and the missionary life style. It forms the backdrop to whatever secular endeavor a Christian might devote himself — works of development, of liberation, works towards justice and peace, works countering racism, unbounded nationalism, and regionalism. In the context of the global village, the religions of the world will develop together, not apart from one another.[16] In approaching men of other religious traditions, the missionary will have to be concerned with reconciliation not with displacement. Men of all faiths will explore together and in unity their approaches to, and experiences of, the Sacred. The context of world unification and human solidarity and reconciliation will also have to be a value in the area of personal prayer, and a theme influencing liturgical and public prayer. Finally, the context of one world offers new grounds for the practice of Christian asceticism — the denial and holding in check of one's regional preferences and particular values, the reaching out to the others in understanding, the office of forgiveness and reconciliation, the availability of service for all.

Historicity and Change

The second constellation of characteristics which make up the world culture of our times can be gathered under the heading of historicity and change. An awareness of history and the acknowledgement of the developing nature of human affairs, institutions, values, and ideas have been hallmarks of recent centuries. An evolutionary outlook upon man and upon all of reality

---

16 See Robert Edward Whitson, *The Coming Convergence of World Religions* (New York: Newman, 1971), p. 52.

has been generally accepted in the last hundred years. Evolution is no longer viewed as a system or hypothesis, but, in the words of Pierre Teilhard de Chardin, "it is a general condition to which all theories, all hypotheses, all systems must bow and which they must manifest henceforward if they are to be thinkable and true. Evolution is a light illuminating all facts, a curve that all lines must follow."[17] Vatican II was careful to avoid direct Teilhardian references, but it acknowledged that the world is passing through a new stage of history characterized by profound and rapid change so that "the human race has passed from a rather static concept of reality to a more dynamic, evolutionary one."[18] Moreover, it is not simply the fact of change which is pressing the men of our times, but the fact that change is occurring in an increasingly accelerated manner.[19] Furthermore, the awareness which man has of change is an important element in this constellation. Again, in the words of Teilhard de Chardin, "man is nothing else than evolution become conscious of itself."[20]

Because man views himself and his world in the light of accelerating change, process, evolution, and development, his knowledge, judgements, and conclusions concerning the world, and his commitments in life are marked by a quality of tentativeness and relativity. Modern men tend to be pragmatic and functional — that which works to explain and handle the immediate situation is that which is true and to be lived by. More than this is difficult to affirm because the situation is changing and in process. At the roots of this approach to reality is the scientific method which has made possible the advances in technology in recent centuries. The application of reason to the world tends to lead man to a positivistic stance before all things.

Some of the elements of this approach have been sketched by Emil Brunner: everything is relative; what cannot be proved cannot be believed; scientific knowledge is certain and the standard of truth; matters of faith are uncertain; beyond death nobody knows; real means seen and handled.[21] The application of

---

[17] Teilhard de Chardin, *The Phenomenon of Man*, p. 219.

[18] "Pastoral Constitution on the Church in the Modern World," Sections 4-5.

[19] See, for example, Alvin Toffler, *Future Shock* (New York: Bantam Books, 1971), especially pp. 19-32.

[20] Teilhard de Chardin, *The Phenomenon of Man*, p. 221.

[21] Quoted from Hans J. Margull, *Hope in Action: The Church's Task in the World*, trans. Eugene Peters (Philadelphia: Muhlenberg, 1962), p. 157.

reason to know and control the changing world has led to a corresponding skepticism concerning areas of knowledge and realities which cannot be handled adequately by the scientific method; that is, areas of faith, the spirit, and revelation. In short, human reason and the world have come to their own and are considered to be autonomous and independent of any other source of control. This is the phenomenon of secularization.

Secularization

The modern world as it becomes more industrial and urban is the world of the secular city and secular man. Secularization has been one of the dominant interests in theological writing in recent years. The reality and interpretation of this phenomenon is complex. For the present purpose, two aspects of secularization can be stressed: first, it means a shift of responsibility from ecclesiastical authority and control to worldly authority and control in all areas of society; secondly, it represents a process of social differentiation, an increasing specialization of groups, institutions, and interests in society.[22] It is the liberation of culture, scholarly and scientific investigation, development of technology, etc. from control by religious structures into the control of purely worldly, secular structures.[23] In Chapter I, the secularization of service, that is, its removal from ecclesiastical to worldly control, was accounted as one of the reasons for the present crisis in missions. If in the past Christian missions could make significant contributions towards the development in many areas of the world, at the present time their resources and potentials are becoming increasingly marginal in comparison with the gargantuan development operations of governments, international organizations, and business.[24] This is but one example of how the traditional mission work of the Church has been affected by the shift from ecclesiastical to worldly control and the process of social differentiation.

---

[22] See J. G. Davies, *Worship and Mission* (New York: Association Press, 1967), pp. 64-65; Hollenweger (ed.), *The Church for Others,* p. 9.

[23] See Goodall (ed.), *The Uppsala Report,* p. 79.

[24] See Stowe, "Strategy: The Church's Response," *Protestant Crosscurrents in Mission,* ed. N.A. Horner, p. 151.

Friedrich Gogarten has pointed to the heart of the process of secularization when he describes it as involving a transformed relation between man and the world. Man is no longer under the subservience of cosmic forces but has entered into a relationship of responsibility for the world. He has come of age, sees himself as the driving power of historical movements, and feels responsible for his own destiny. Man, therefore, is no longer responsible *before* the world or *to* the world, but he is responsible *for* the world.[25] Positively, the process of secularization means that man bears responsibility for history and building the world for weal or woe; negatively, the process can be described according to Harvey Cox's famous trilogy — the disenchantment of nature, the desacralization of politics, and the deconsecration of values.[26]

In speaking of secularization, it is important to distinguish the social-cultural and historical aspects of the process, that is, social differentiation and the shift from ecclesiastical control to secular control, from philosophical and theological interpretations given to the process.[27] With this in mind, I do not wish to enter into a discussion of the theories of those such as Friedrich Gogarten, Harvey Cox, and Arend Theodoor van Leeuwen who attempt to show, with some validity I believe, the compatibility and causal relationships between the biblical tradition and the process of secularization.[28] Nor do I wish to enter here into a discussion of the meaning and possibility of religionless Christianity as the mode of being a Christian in the secular society, the question raised so well by Dietrich Bonhoeffer. In this regard, much depends upon the meaning and interpretation one chooses to give to religion. If religion is seen as a longing to escape from the world, or if it is identified with individualism and personal salvation, with concern only for the beyond, and

[25] See Friedrich Gogarten, *The Reality of Faith: The Problem of Subjectivism in Theology*, trans. Carl Michalson et al. (Philadelphia: Westminster Press, 1969), pp. 168, 172; Larry Shiner, *The Secularization of History: An Introduction to the Theology of Friedrich Gogarten* (Nashville: Abingdon, 1966), p. 26.

[26] See Harvey Cox, *The Secular City: Secularization and Urbanization in Theological Perspective* (New York: Macmillan, 1965), Chapter I.

[27] See Edward Schillebeeckx, O.P., *God the Future of Man*, trans. N.D. Smith (New York: Sheed and Ward, 1968), pp. 67-69.

[28] See Cox, *The Secular City;* Gogarten, *The Reality of Faith;* Arend Theodoor van Leeuwen, *Christianity in World History: The Meeting of the Faiths of East and West*, trans. H.H. Hoskins (New York: Charles Scribner's Sons, 1964).

with God only as a stop-gap for our human embarrassments,[29] then, obviously, it will be dysfunctional in the secular society. This is not the meaning of Christianity or being religious which is advocated here.

God's Mission is conjoined to the world, and therefore God does not stand apart from historical process. Salvation is a complex reality which has both worldly and otherworldly qualities. Service in and for the world is essential to the Mission of God and to our participation in God's Mission. Man's meaning and destiny are only understood through an approach of integral or transcendent humanism which views man as incomplete without reference to, and direction towards, the kingdom of God which ultimately remains beyond his power. Secularization, the process of differentiation and worldly autonomy, is compatible with Christianity as long as these qualifications are kept in mind. What would be incompatible is secularism, a closed ideology which gives absolute value to the historical with no possible reference to, and no need for, God and no place for spiritual transcendence.[30]

Development and Liberation

Speaking of historicity, change, and man's responsibility for the world leads naturally to the topic of development. This theme has already been mentioned in connection with evangelization and the continuity which exists between worldly progress and the kingdom of God. However, the condition of the underdeveloped world and the project of developing that world must be listed as prime factors which influence the missionary life style today. If it is a fact that between two-thirds and three-fourths of mankind live in poverty and deprivation, then the Christian cannot but agree with what Dr. W. A. Visser't Hooft is reported to have said at the Uppsala meeting of the World Council of Churches — a Church not committed to the poor would be a Church in heresy. In view of the sign value essential to

---

[29] See Dietrich Bonhoeffer, *Letters and Papers from Prison,* trans. Reginald H. Fuller (New York: Macmillan Co., 1966), pp. 162-68, 236; Robert L. Richard, *Secularization Theology* (New York: Herder and Herder, 1967), p. 96.

[30] For secularism see Hollenweger (ed.), *The Church for Others,* p. 9; E.L. Mascall, *The Secularization of Christianity: An Analysis and a Critique* (London: Darton, Longman & Todd, 1965), p. 191; Ronald Gregor Smith, *Secular Christianity* (New York: Harper & Row, 1966), pp. 142-47.

the Church and the stance of service which incarnates this sign, the mission of the Church today would be a countersign if it were not concerned with the development of peoples and the alleviation of poverty, hunger, and social injustice.

The term development is open to possible misunderstanding. Because it implies a profound socio-cultural transformation of the poor areas of the world, by necessity it has economic aspects. However, the development spoken of here is more than quantitative economic progress and growth. It implies economic progress but includes a qualitative enhancement of the whole man and every man. Basically it is the transition from what is less human to what is more human, that complete and integral humanism spoken of by Paul VI in *Populorum Progressio:*

> Less human conditions: the lack of material necessities for those who are without the minimum essential for life, the moral deficiencies of those who are mutilated by selfishness. Less human conditions: oppressive social structures, whether due to the abuses of ownership or to the abuses of power, to the exploitation of workers or to unjust transactions. Conditions that are more human: the passage from misery towards the possession of necessities, victory over social scourges, the growth of knowledge, the acquisition of culture. Additional conditions that are more human: increased esteem for the dignity of others, the turning toward the spirit of poverty, cooperation for the common good, the will and desire for peace. Conditions that are still more human: the acknowledgement by man of supreme values, and of God their source and their finality. Conditions that, finally and above all, are more human: faith, a gift of God accepted by the good will of man, and unity in the charity of Christ, Who calls us all to share as sons in the life of the living God, the Father of all men.[31]

In essence, therefore, development has to do with freeing man from physical and spiritual bondage caused by a lack of basic

---

[31] Paul VI, *On the Development of Peoples [Populorum Progressio]* (Paterson, N.J.: Association for International Development, 1967), Section 21, also sections 14, 42; see also René Coste, "The Fostering of Peace and the Promotion of a Community of Nations," *Commentary on the Documents of Vatican II*, ed. Herbert Vorgrimler, I (New York: Herder and Herder, 1969), 364; Latin American Episcopal Council, "Presence of the Church in the Present-Day Transformation of Latin America," *The Church in the Present-Day Transformation of Latin America*, II, 49-50; Paul VI, "Evangelization in the Modern World," Sections 29-36.

human needs to the end that he might make use of his God-given creative powers to take charge of his destiny in the world.[32] Because it is a matter of freedom, the term *liberation* is preferred by many, especially those from the Latin American churches. The theology of liberation which has been elaborated in Latin America is the unique contribution of the local churches there to the universal Church's understanding of salvation. Christian revelation and God's Mission as it is working itself out through the peoples of Latin America today is a call to liberation. It is the great sign of the times in the experience of the Latin Americans.[33] Because of the unique situation which exists there, men of that continent are coming to see that there can be no proclamation of salvation history without the practice of salvation in history. Yet, because salvation is understood as liberation and liberation as salvation, the interaction between the two saves Christian life from two dangers: liberation as a merely immanent process, and salvation as a merely transcendent process.[34] Hence the theology of liberation seems to preserve the balance of all of the dimensions of God's Mission and the total meaning of salvation.

Finally, a connection may be drawn between development and liberation and the meaning of redemption for men today. It might be shown that the interpretation of redemption as it applies to men of different ages offers a good example of the principle of correlation mentioned above. Irenaeus, in reaction to dualistic tendencies of his time, interpreted the redemption in terms of the unity of the human race in Christ and the recapitulation of all things in Christ through the incarnation. In the Middle Ages, Anselm viewed God much in terms of a feudal lord and saw redemption as the satisfaction required for one who had gone against his lord. Hence it was a matter of justice—the

---

[32] Exploratory Committee on Society, Development, and Peace, *World Development: The Challenge to the Churches,* Conference on World Cooperation for Development, Beirut, Lebanon, April 21-27, 1968 (Geneva: Exploratory Committee on Society, Development, and Peace, 1968), p. 22; Gustavo Gutiérrez Merino, "Notes for a Theology of Liberation," *Theology Digest,* 19 (Summer, 1971), 142.

[33] See César Jerez, S.J., "On the Theology of Liberation," (paper delivered at the Institute on the International Dimensions of the U.S. Jesuit Apostolate, LeMoyne College, Syracuse, N.Y., August 20-25, 1972), pp. 2-3; Marcos McGrath, "The Signs of the Time in Latin America Today," Latin American Episcopal Council, *The Church in the Present-Day Transformation of Latin America,* I, 102.

[34] Jerez, "On the Theology of Liberation," pp. 15, 21.

infinite satisfaction made by Christ, the God-man, for all men.[35] In the present-day world, which is a world in process, which affirms the autonomy of the secular and man's responsibility for the world, and which witnesses vast differences between rich and poor, redemption can well be understood in terms of the liberation of man from the bondage of material want and the spiritual deprivation which follows it, liberation into freedom for the purposes of building an integrally human world in preparation for the coming of God's kingdom.

Spirituality in a Changing, Secular World

Reflection upon the modern world as a world of change, secularity, development, and liberation offers an almost unlimited area for speculation concerning a Christian spirituality attuned to that world. Because the Mission of God is historical, the Church in her mission can readily accept the modern world of change. Because secularization need not be secularism, the Church can accept the autonomy of the secular and engage in a new relation with the world together with all men.

The Christian engaged in mission can readily welcome the world of change, for missionaries have always been agents of change — most fundamentally, of the radical change required by *metanoia* and faith in Christ; but equally pervasive, of the changes caused by the introduction of a religious tradition and the ensuing life style which is foreign to those who accept the gospel. In the context of the changing world, the Church will have to face the same prospects faced by other institutions in the world — the necessity of institutionalizing change. Diversity and development will inevitably have to be accepted on many levels where they were thought impossible in the past — on the levels of idea and symbol as well as in the areas of structure and institution.

In a changing world, one function of the Christian engaged in mission would seem to be that of a conservative initiator of change, one who can innovate and accept change and at the same time maintain contact with the values of the Christian tradition. One thing is clear: in a rapidly changing world, it will no longer

[35] See Boniface Willems, *The Reality of Redemption* (New York: Herder and Herder, 1970), pp. 45-53.

be possible for structures, forms, and practices to remain absolute and frozen for centuries as, for example, the Latin liturgy in the Roman Catholic Church. Historical development will have the effect of relativizing to some extent all forms of worship, expressions of ideas, and structures. A frame of mind which is open to this will have to be operative in the missionary life style of the future. The question of what changes are to be accepted and inaugurated and how the values of Christianity are to be preserved in change will be a matter for particular discernment and decision. Therefore, the spirituality of the pilgrim finds a grounding not only in the theology of mission developed in Chapter V but also in the cultural context of the present world.

As a help to discernment, another characteristic of the modern world can be employed — the functional approach. Stated most simply, this approach evaluates what is good and true according to what functions successfully. Forms and structures, ways of worshiping, praying, and serving will have to stand up to a kind of pragmatic test. The semiological function of the Church will offer one norm for such a test. What works towards making the Church an effective sign for the unification of men and the union of men with God, and what works towards being the sign and sacrament of God's salvation and *shalom* in history will have to be used. Ideas, symbols, and structures which do not realize and make the sign visible can be questioned to determine whether or not they are countersigns and therefore dysfunctional. This will be an area for continual conversion and *metanoia* on the part of local churches and those engaged in mission. The point is not that the Church and Christians subject everything to the world's quest for relevance and "what works" — there will always be ways in which the gospel will be a sign of contradiction to the world — but it is important that Christians engaged in mission examine their life styles, their methods, and their work to be sure that the signs of God's kingdom and Mission of salvation are not clouded.

Just as the Christian engaged in mission has nothing to fear from the world of accelerating change, so too he can be at home in the secular world. He can welcome man's responsibility for the world and for building the world in participation with God, for such an approach gives further ground to missionary works of service towards humanization and liberation. In a world of technological and social change where most problems are seen as accessible to human reason, Christianity can offer an extraordinary source of dynamic power and change to see that reason's answers are applied.[36]

However, the process of social differentiation and the passing of control from ecclesiastical to secular power will make demands upon the life style of one interested in mission. First of all, there is the question of professional qualifications. In service-oriented projects, projects which will often be directed by, and under the control of, secular agencies, the Christian interested in participating in the Mission of God in this manner will have to be a professional among professionals.

Secondly, in a world of secularization, the Christian engaged in mission will have to discern whether the task he sets himself to can best be achieved within ecclesiastical structures or beyond them. With much of the traditional service work of the Church now being done by governmental and international agencies, the decision to serve for humanization and development outside of ecclesiastical structures is a real possibility.

Thirdly, since geographic location, that is, going to a foreign land, can no longer be a norm for discernment as to where the mission of the Church can best be furthered, it is possible for a Christian to engage in God's worldly work more effectively at home than by going to another land. Bartolomé de las Casas worked in Spain in the sixteenth century to plead the cause of justice and humanity on behalf of the peoples of Latin America. It might be the case that Christians wishing to engage in the work of development, peace, justice, and humanization will remain at home to work upon the policies and practices of one of the developed nations insofar as these influence underdeveloped countries.[37]

Fourthly, the role of the laity is increasingly important for mission in the secular world. In Chapters V and VI, it was said that the vocation of the Christian and that of the missionary

---

[36] Barbara Ward, "Am I My Brother's Keeper?" *Christianity Amid Rising Men and Nations,* ed. Creighton Lacy (New York: Association Press, 1965), p. 17.

[37] See Joseph A. Alemán, S.J., "The Role of the North American Jesuit in the Latin American Apostolate," *Studies in the International Apostolate of Jesuits,* 1 (January, 1972), 11.

are coterminous so that every Christian bears a responsibility for participating in the Mission of God and all Christian spirituality has a missionary dimension. The secular world is the world of the laity — theirs is the vocation to seek the kingdom of God by engaging in temporal affairs and by ordering them according to the plan of God; they are called to make the Church operative in those places and circumstances into which only they can enter and thus become instruments of the mission of the Church.[38] Therefore, in the secular world God's Mission will be furthered by those to whom this world belongs by vocation — the laity.

There seems to be no doubt that at the present time, in view of the process of secularization and the diaspora situation of the Church, the context of mission work is not too dissimilar from that of the early centuries of the Church. The burden for spreading the good news and witnessing by service to God's kingdom will fall upon the laity and not upon the traditional type of missionary. In this context the role of the ordained minister becomes the role of an enabler — one of service to the laity to equip them in their participation in God's Mission.[39]

From what has been said in this chapter and in previous chapters concerning the importance of service and pro-existence, concerning the Church as the effective sign and sacrament of God's Mission, concerning the multidimensional nature of salvation, and concerning the importance of establishing God's *shalom* in the world, the motivation for works dedicated to development and liberation is clear. In view of the tremendous disparity between rich nations and poor nations, with the greater part of the human family living in the latter, this must be one of the foremost concerns of the present-day mission of the Church. It might be suggested, furthermore, that in certain places human development and liberation are of such importance that for the time being Christians must devote themselves to these tasks even to the possible exclusion of direct evangelization and attempts to plant the Church. When one-third of the human family lives in an inhuman manner, the verses of the twenty-fifth chapter of Matthew's gospel cannot but echo loudly in Christian consciences.

---

[38] "Dogmatic Constitution on the Church," Sections 31, 33.

[39] See J.C. Hoekendijk, *The Church Inside Out*, trans. Isaac Rottenberg (Philadelphia: Westminster, 1966), p. 86.

In the context of human development and liberation, the asceticism demanded for Christians engaged in mission is a world-affirming asceticism rather than a world-denying asceticism. The premise of secularization is that man exists in a new relationship with the world, a relationship of responsibility for building the world. The world is not a threat to the Christian but a challenge. His asceticism, therefore, centers not upon flight, abdication of responsibility, or negation of the world, but upon commitment to the world, and work for the betterment and development of the world. If a sense of history, a sense of change, and a sense of responsibility for the world are at the heart of modern man's experience of human existence, the Christian engaged in mission will give of himself to make certain that the world is changed so that the signs of God's *shalom* are realized and made present. The situation demands a new life style and a new type of "saint" modelled upon one who gives himself in the service of neighbor through dedication to reforming the world.[40]

In Chapter VI the importance of intention for the Christian engaged in mission was stressed — the missionary is a man or woman dedicated to the kingdom with the intention of bringing other men to belief in Christ. There are many ways of working toward this goal, but no matter what the Christian engaged in mission does, he must be sustained by deep personal faith and holiness. This is necessary lest he be co-opted by the secular world and fall either in belief or in practice into living only by the closed ideology of secularism with no reference in what he says and does to God's wider Mission. The sources which will sustain his spirituality are Scripture, prayer, the Eucharistic fellowship with other believers, and the community of God's people.

However, the life of prayer and the Eucharistic and sacramental life cannot be lived in an ahistorical fashion; they must be experienced within the historical context. Thus, for example, in a situation of development, theological symbol and language must be made historically relevant. Grace cannot remain an abstraction but must be transformed into a living experience of justice, of love in service and action, of reconciliation, and of

---

[40] See M. Richard Shaull, "Christian Participation in the Latin American Revolution," *Christianity Amid Rising Men and Nations,* ed. C. Lacy, p. 100, also Michael C. Reilly, S.J., "Holiness and Development," *America* 133 (Oct. 11, 1975), 205-207.

peace. The powers, principalities, and demons of the New Testament, the meaning of salvation and sin must be translated to fit the realities of injustice, dehumanization, crippling structures, and self-seeking interests which are active in keeping men in a less than human situation and from which he must be freed.[41] The call of the missionary to holiness — that is, to profound, personal encounter with God in prayer and in others — is as valid today as it ever was for mission spirituality. In the secular world, with its tendencies towards self-sufficiency and autonomy, it is perhaps of more importance than ever if the Christian engaged in mission is to balance commitment to the world with the fuller dimensions of God's plan and Mission for the world.

Finally, in the secular situation where the Church is required to work for development and liberation together with secular institutions and structures, the role of the Church as social critic is important. This is the prophetic function of the Christian community. The role of prophet is necessary lest the Church be co-opted by the secular, and in order that the weakness and ambiguity of all social and political structures can be revealed.

In this regard, something can be said concerning what has been termed "political theology." As presented by Johannes Metz, political theology stands in opposition to individualizing tendencies within Christianity and focuses in hope upon the social and eschatological nature of salvation. The eschatological promises of the biblical tradition — freedom, peace, justice, reconciliation — are not private matters but social and political realities. The Church and Christians engaged in God's Mission can join forces with secular political structures and powers in order to work for these blessings, but the Church must always safeguard its role as prophet, a role of social criticism of all human institutions. She is an institution of free criticism by faith. Her relation to human creativity and human works must be a relationship of involved detachment and critical responsibility.[42] By virtue of the gospel the Church proclaims the rights of man and she esteems the dy-

---

[41] Juan Luis Segundo, S.J., "Liberación: Fe e Ideologia," *Mensaje*, 21 (1972), 250-52.

[42] See R.K. Orchard, *Missions in a Time of Testing: Thought and Practice in Contemporary Missions* (London: Lutterworth, 1964), p. 68; for "political theology," see Johannes B. Metz, "The Church's Social Function in the Light of a 'Political Theology,'" *Faith and the World of Politics*, ed. Johannes B. Metz, Concilium 36 (New York: Paulist Press, 1968), pp. 2-18.

namic movements of today by which these rights are everywhere fostered, yet all movements must be penetrated by the spirit of the gospel and protected against any kind of false autonomy.[43]

The New Man of Rising Expectations

Pope John XXIII in *Mater et Magistra* and Vatican II in its "Pastoral Constitution on the Church in the Modern World" have used the term *socialization* to describe the reciprocal relationships which have given rise to the variety of associations and organizations, both public and private in nature, and for economic, cultural, social, recreational, professional, and political ends in the modern world.[44] Modern man finds himself living and working under a variety of bureaucratic structures and organizations. At times the fear can arise that the individual is being lost in the group or that the person is being made to serve the institution. Although these fears exist and although structures can and have worked to the detriment of the individual, their basic necessity cannot be denied, for they serve to enable people to attain aims and objectives which are beyond the means and capabilities of individuals.[45] What must be realized, therefore, is that the subject and goal of all social institutions is the human person.[46] All social, political, and economic structures have for their purpose the enrichment of human life.

The individual person in the world today, therefore, who lives in the interlocking network of social, political, and economic structures, and who, through modern communications, knows the goods and services possible from the scientific and technological advances of the present century, is an individual with rising expectations of human progress and betterment. In short, persons and societies thirst for a full and free life worthy of man, a life in which they can subject to their own welfare all that the modern world can offer them so abundantly.[47] Humanization has

---

[43] "Pastoral Constitution on the Church in the Modern World," Section 41.

[44] John XXIII, "*Mater et Magistra,*" *The Encyclicals and Other Messages of John XXIII*, ed. Staff of *The Pope Speaks* Magazine (Washington: TPS Press, 1964), Sections 59-60; "Pastoral Constitution on the Church in the Modern World," Section 25.

[45] John XXIII, "*Mater et Magistra,*" Section 59.

[46] "Pastoral Constitution on the Church in the Modern World," Section 25.

[47] *Ibid.,* Section 9.

been seen as the one common major concern of the peoples of Latin America in their struggle for development and liberation,[48] but it seems that this characteristic cannot be limited to that continent alone. Rising expectations for human betterment are present in all nations, especially among the underprivileged classes and groups.

Perhaps representative of the aspirations towards which people around the world are longing is the "Universal Declaration of Human Rights" proclaimed by the General Assembly of the United Nations in 1948. It affirms that all human beings are born free and equal and entitled to the following basic rights without distinction of race, color, sex, language, religion, politics, national or social origin, property, birth, or other status: the right to life, liberty, and security of person, freedom from slavery, equality before the law, freedom of movement and residence, the right to nationality, the right to marry and raise a family, the right to own property, freedom of thought, conscience, and religion, freedom of opinion and public expression, freedom of assembly, the right to participate in government, the right to social security, the right to work and a just remuneration from work, the right to form trade unions, the right to rest and leisure and a standard of living adequate for health and well-being, the right to education and freely to participate in the cultural life of the community and share in the benefits of scientific advancement.[49] It should be noted that these rights were proclaimed as a "common standard of achievement" for all peoples and nations. It must be admitted that they are not realized in many places in the world. They clearly indicate, however, the direction of the rising aspirations of men in the modern world.

From its earliest sources faith in Christ has been associated with the creation of a new man. It might be said that the "Universal Declaration of Human Rights" symbolizes the expectations of men of our times to be new men in the modern world. The position taken here has consistently been that divinization and humanization are intimately unified in the plan of God for salvation. The aspirations of men from all nations concerning the quality of human life might be described as a sign of God's Mission in

---

[48] See Shaull, "Christian Participation in the Latin American Revolution," *Christianity Amid Rising Men and Nations*, ed. C. Lacy, pp. 91-94.

[49] See "The Universal Declaration of Human Rights," Maurice Cranston, *What Are Human Rights?* (New York: Basic Books, 1962), pp. 93-102.

the world today which calls for a response on the part of those who participate in that Mission. In reading the signs of the times, the Christian cannot fail to be attentive to these strivings for humanization.

Much has already been said concerning service towards humanization as one of the marks of the life style of Christians engaged in mission in the modern world. The rising expectations of mankind offer the context for missionary service directed to humanization. Their implication for spirituality comes down to one important principle: Christian spirituality and a spirituality for mission today must be a *human spirituality*. The Christian life style must be a fully human life style. This is in accord with the continuity which exists between humanization and divinization, between the fruits and signs of God's kingdom here and its final realization. Holiness remains a *sine qua non* requirement for the Christian engaged in mission, but the holiness required must have a human face. Forms of asceticism which reject and despise the world might be dysfunctional in the present context. Debasing poverty, seen to be a curse for mankind, cannot be the ideal. This does not mean, however, that individual Christians might not be called to witness in an extraordinary manner by means of radical asceticism and poverty, the ideal, for example, of Charles de Foucauld. By and large, however, asceticism and poverty will call for a detached and generous use of the blessings of modern culture for the betterment of others.

A human spirituality for mission in the present-day world will also require that the setting and rhythm of the modern world be respected. Forms and ways of praying, the occasions for, and structures of, liturgical celebrations, the feasts kept in the Christian community, hymns and songs used, the churches and places of worship employed will have to correlate with the style and rhythm of modern living. For example, feasts suited to pastoral cycles or prayers and hymns evoking agricultural images might be ill-suited to urbanized living. In order to offset the dehumanizing and demoralizing effects of urban life, or the commonness of suburban living, forms of prayer and worship will have to correlate not by evoking and continuing ways used for rural peoples in an agrarian age, but by developing new ways which can sustain and strengthen faith by accepting and celebrating the achievements of modern civilization.

Another characteristic for a human spirituality in the modern world will be personalism. If the pressures and structures of the world have the effect of depersonalizing people, the mission of the Church can only be forwarded by Christians whose life style never loses concern for the personal dimension. God's Mission is not only cosmic but is also concerned with each and every individual. Indeed, stress upon the individual person and his salvation has been a strong point of focus in the missionary work of the Church. A personal approach can be manifested in many ways. I shall mention two possibilities.

The first concerns the sacramental and liturgical life of the Church. In the Roman Catholic Church at the present time, stress has shifted from an almost magical and impersonal view of the sacraments, which sees them as efficacious, grace-giving signs, to a view of the sacraments which defines them as personal encounters with the Lord.[50] If the sacraments are personal encounters with Chirst, they must be celebrated in a personal manner. This would indicate, for example, that the large and rather anonymous Eucharistic celebration which crowds hundreds or thousands into a church might not fit the needs of modern man. This does not mean that there is no longer a place for such celebrations. There will always be need and occasion for whole communities and localities or classes to join together in worship. It does indicate, however, that in a world where personalism is so necessary, the small group type of prayer and worship might be more functional in bringing men into contact with each other and with Christ. The second implication which can be drawn from a concern for personalism concerns the openness of the Christian community. All men must feel wanted and accepted into Christian fellowship. It can be said that in the present context an attitude of graciousness and welcoming will be one of the cardinal missionary virtues.[51] The Christian with God's concern for all men in mind must be open to all and all should feel welcome into the Christian fellowship.

Finally, respect for the freedom of others must be a part of the stance of welcoming openness. Because of the freedom of

[50] See Edward Schillebeeckx, O.P., *Christ the Sacrament of the Encounter with God* (New York: Sheed and Ward, 1963).

[51] See Abbé G. Michonneau, *The Missionary Spirit in Parish Life* (Westminster, Md.: Newman , 1952), p. 155.

conscience which is the right of all men, the modern world is a pluralistic world. Christians live as a minority in diaspora in the secular world. The Christian accepts this and remains open to the goodness of God working through all men. Pluralism and freedom of thought, however, have to be accepted not only between Christians and men who do not profess Christ, but also within the Christian community itself. Much stress has been given to the secular and urban style of the present world; however, it must be acknowledged that there are Christians in places where these qualities do not dominate. For these men and women perhaps the traditional pastoral images of the Psalms and hymns of the Church speak meaningfully. In respect for freedom and the local situation, therefore, the Christian in mission must remain cautious lest he overrun that very freedom which other Christians and peoples possess in their expression of the faith.

Local Diversity

In the introduction to this chapter mention was made of the tension that exists between the characteristics which are used to describe the growing one-world culture and conditions which exist in different areas of the world. Hence a certain caution is in order when the qualities of the one-world culture are applied to different areas of the globe. The technological society, an acceptance and appreciation of change, the meaning of man's control over his destiny in history, secularity, and a pragmatic approach to reality might well describe the culture of the West in Europe and North America. However, these characteristics might not adequately correlate with the experience of peoples in more traditional societies, although it could be argued that Western influence is so strong that they soon will pervade all societies. Arend van Leeuwen has a point in proposing the thesis that one of the most urgent lines of Christian mission service is to make tribal and village societies ready, materially and spiritually, for the arrival of modern civilization.[52] Christians of the West must exercise caution, however, lest they read every situation too readily through glasses tinted with the secular values which dominate technological culture.

---

[52] Van Leeuwen, *Christianity in World History*, p. 424.

Therefore, it is important to include a place for particular and regional characteristics in a consideration of the context of mission today. This is necessary for several reasons. First of all, the West has lost considerable respect among the peoples of the third world in recent years because of its past involvement in colonialism, its recent history of devastating wars, and its present economic relationships with underdeveloped countries. Hence Western values will not be accepted uncritically. Secondly, a sense of local pride seems to be present in all nations today. This has resulted in a deep concern for nationalism and nation-building, and it helps to explain other factors important to the mission of the Church such as the renaissance of the great religious traditions of the world. Thirdly, in the next thirty years it is possible that the center of gravity of Christianity will shift from the West to the countries of the third world. It has been projected that there will be 350 million Christians in Africa by the turn of the century. It has likewise been suggested that by the year 2000 the third world will dominate in creative Christian theology, action, and outreach.[53] If these projections are correct, it seems that the Christian life style and the missionary life style will be affected greatly by non-Western values and contributions in the years to come.

The purpose of this section is merely to highlight this situation of tension between the one-world culture and local diversity, for the unity of the one-world culture will be a unity amid local diversity. It is impossible to develop adequately all the regional characteristics which form this constellation of particularism within the one-world culture. The intention here is merely to suggest the direction.

The Uppsala meeting of the World Council of Churches in 1968 suggested some of the needs of local areas within the worldwide Christian community in the Appendix to its report "Towards New Styles of Living." Regional specifications of the Christian life style were seen as responses to key questions concerning different parts of the world. In Asia the challenge facing the Chris-

---

[53] David Barrett, "AD 2000: 350 Million Christians in Africa," *International Review of Mission,* 59 (1970), 50-52; W. Richey Hogg, "*The Oikoumene,*" *The Future of the Christian World Mission: Studies in Honor of R. Pierce Beaver,* ed. William J. Danker and Wi Jo Kang (Grand Rapids, Mich.: Eerdmans, 1971), p. 21.

tian life style centers around how Christians can be creative minorities in a non-Christian culture, how solidarity with men of other faiths can be expressed, and how Christians can share in and encourage national development. In Africa the key problems are how to contribute in the struggle for nation-building, how to fight for racial justice and harmony, how to bridge the gulf between the educated elite and the masses, and how to relate Christian teaching on the family to the traditional African values. In South America Christians must be committed to effective means of changing economic, political, and social structures to ensure justice and progress, and to unify within the churches widely differing Christian responses to the needs of society. In Eastern Europe the problems focus upon being a Christian in an officially secularized society and developing ways of cooperation and dialogue with Marxists. In Western Europe the questions are how to identify and deal with the problems posed by modern technology, new patterns of work, leisure, family life and the relationships between men and women and the generations; how to make use of the present absence of war in Europe; and how to be responsible citizens of rich nations in a predominantly poor world. Finally, in North America the following are the key areas: how to relate to Latin America, how to be responsible citizens of nations which control much of the power and resources of the world, and how to participate responsibly in the struggle for racial justice.[54]

Other examples of particularism could be added. For example, the culture of Japan might offer the following contributions to the Christian life style: deep respect for community values, attention to self-discipline and interiority as paths to spiritual enlightenment and growth, and an optimistic acceptance of the world.[55] In India the challenge consists in the construction of a theology and ensuing life style which takes into consideration the rich philosophical and theological tradition of the sacred writings of Hinduism.[56] A similar project will have to be undertaken on

---

[54] See Goodall (ed.), *The Uppsala Report,* pp. 94-95.

[55] Joseph J. Spae, C.I.C.M., "Religions of Asia — Aid or Obstacle?" *The Church is Mission,* ed. Enda McDonagh et al. (London: Geoffrey Chapman, 1969), p. 145.

[56] Bede Griffiths, *Christ in India: Essays Towards a Hindu-Christian Dialogue* (New York: Charles Scribner's Sons, 1966), p. 168.

the continent of Africa where it will be necessary to correlate traditional religions with the gospel.[57]

From this constellation of local diversity it can be concluded that the spirituality and life style of Christians engaged in mission today and in the future will be tinted by a variety of values and local needs within the developing world culture which will be the technological culture from the West. The role of the missionary as a bridge person is once more highlighted. The stance of openness seen as necessary in Chapter VII is given a wider foundation. The importance of giving freedom and responsibility to local churches to develop their own theology and spiritual styles within the catholic communion of local churches is rendered more important.

Finally, in view of the six-continent theory of mission developed in Chapter VI, it can be said that if the role of the non-Western churches predominates in the decades to come, and if missionary sending becomes more than a one-way movement from the West to the non-West, then the Christian life styles of the peoples of the West will be formed and influenced by the insights and values of non-Western Christians. Accordingly, they must be open and ready for this development.

Disvalues in the Present Situation

The tone of this chapter and the previous chapters has been optimistic. I have looked positively at the world, have taken the position that Christians in our times can accept the world for what it is, and work in it and with it to further the Mission of God. However, there is a danger in such an optimistic approach that it might too easily blind itself to those aspects of the world which are not good. That is, it might overlook the world in the Johannine sense of creation which, although loved by God, is in the darkness of sin and under the judgement of God. With the last constellation of characteristics describing the

[57] For the theology and philosophy of African religious traditions see the following works by John S. Mbiti: *African Religions and Philosophy* (Garden City, N.Y.: Doubleday Anchor Books, 1970); *Concepts of God in Africa* (New York: Praeger Publishers, 1970); *New Testament Eschatology in an African Background: A Study of the Encounter between New Testament Theology and Traditional Concepts* (London: Oxford University, 1971).

present context of mission, we must now focus upon some of the disvalues of the modern world. It is important to do this because the Mission of God and the mission of the Church must always confront the reality of sin and evil. The Roman Catholic Church in Latin America has been criticized for overlooking the dehumanizing factors in society and being overly optimistic regarding the nature of man and the possibilities regarding the establishment of a just and harmonious social order.[58] Therefore, to maintain a balance and to offset false optimism, we must consider the disvalues in the present world situation.

The problem here, then, is the problem of sin and evil. Sinfulness, however, is understood in a broader context than that of personal sin. Although it is rooted in individual decisions and attitudes, it refers here to those evils which have been institutionalized in the modern world, to the sinful structures and conditions which plague mankind. In a speech given in England in 1969, Dom Helder Camara summarized the seven capital sins which can no longer be tolerated in the modern world — racialism, colonialism, war, paternalism, Pharisaism, alienation, and fear.[59] These are evils which either have been or are present in the structures of the world today, or evils which flow from the structures of the present-day world.

The disvalues present in the structures of the modern world produce the situations of conflict which are present today. At the root of the challenges of development and liberation lies the great disparity which exists among men. There is a wide gap between the developed nations and the less developed countries, between the rich and the poor. It is due to the unequal distribution of the goods and services of the world and it exists not only between rich and poor nations but also within the rich nations themselves. The United States can be offered as an example of this disparity, for it has been estimated that this country, with about 6 percent of the world's population, consumes about 40 percent of the goods of the earth.[60] The challenge facing men

[58] See Shaull, "Christian Participation in the Latin American Revolution," *Christianity Amid Rising Men and Nations*, ed. C. Lacy, pp. 105-106.

[59] Dom Helder Camara, *Spiral of Violence*, trans. Della Couling (Denville, N.J.: Dimension Books, 1971), p. 77.

[60] Louis-J. Lebret, *The Last Revolution: The Destiny of Over- and Underdeveloped Nations*, trans. John Horgan (New York: Sheed and Ward, 1965), p. 96.

today is that of creating a new civilization where this disparity cannot exist.[61]

Another situation of conflict arises from racism and discrimination due to color, creed, and nationality both within nations and among nations. When these conflicts are related to the rising expectations of mankind and the force of national pride which is growing among nations and peoples, revolution becomes almost unavoidable.[62]

Finally, there is the very real and tragic conflict which ensues from decisions to use war as a means for achieving goals. National policies of war and of stockpiling armaments can only be seen as an evil in the present-day world. With so many people living a marginal and less than marginal form of existence, Christians cannot consider it "normal" that the nations of the world spend $150,000 millions on weaponry and only $10,000 millions upon economic and social development.[63]

Another series of disvalues can be sketched from the effects which the modern technological culture produces upon individuals: the deracination of peoples and disruption of family structures because of the demands of life in an industrialized society; the empty materialism which cloys many, especially of the younger generation; the sense of hopelessness which can oppress individuals who have to live and work in seemingly impersonal and meaningless structures; the dissatisfaction and fears which result from living in a world which at times seems to stand on the verge of total war, ecological disaster, or uncontrolled population explosion; the alienation which can exist between different generations because of the rapidity of change, or between the individual and the society which he feels powerless to change. These problems and the situations which produce them are representative of the negative forces and powers at work in the world, the disvalues and sinfulness of modern civilization.

Finally, it can be acknowledged that the Church itself is not free from participation in the sinfulness of the world. It remains the Church of sinners. Until recent times, those branches of Christianity which have expanded most widely have been from the

---

[61] Lebret, *ibid.*, p. 4.

[62] See Melvin Gingerich, *The Christian and Revolution* (Scottdale, Pa.: Herald Press, 1968), Chapter I.

[63] See Exploratory Committee on Society, Development, and Peace, *World Development*, p. 9.

nations of the West and have participated, willingly or unwillingly, in the attitudes, policies, and structures used by the West to dominate the world. The Church, accordingly, shares in the loss of face and weakening of moral leadership which has been suffered by the Western, white nations due to this, and due to the materialism, economic domination, and warring tendencies of the West. The Church has never been a pure sign but has at times been guilty of Pharisaism, of an unhistorical approach to men, of intolerance, and often of a commitment to the *status quo* and the oppressing elements in different places. The Church has not always furthered God's *shalom* and reconciliation; it has not always been a sign of God's kingdom; it has not always worked for the redemptive liberation of men. To the extent that it has been guilty of this, it has participated in evil and been a countersign to the world.

The constellation of disvalues present in the world today demand the following attitudes for the spirituality and life style of Christians concerned about God's Mission at the present time. First of all, the humility to admit sinfulness when one is implicated in it, and a striving for continual conversion and change of heart. Secondly, the boldness and courage to speak and act concerning the evils of the time. The Church must relate the Word to the times; it must name the demons of the modern world before attempting to exorcise them. In its ministry of the Word and sacraments, the unhistorical approach which speaks of grace and sin abstractly without relating these notions concretely to the grace-filled situations and sin-filled structures of the local situation must be rejected. Christians, therefore, have the obligation of being awake to the ambiguities of all human institutions and of correcting them in relation to the eschatological promises of the gospel and God's kingdom.

The espousal of violence as a means towards a solution of situations of conflict is an area of special importance for Christians engaged in mission today. In recent years quite a bit has been written concerning the theology of revolution. The term *revolution* is an ambivalent word which can apply to both violent and less violent changes in the political and social structures of a society. When it is interpreted as the use of violence to effect changes, however, it seems that caution is necessary for Christians. Depending upon the local situation, Christians might seriously consider the methods of non-violence as advocated and developed by Mahatma Gandhi and Dr. Martin Luther King, an approach which places great stress upon a positive attitude towards suffering and sacrifice for good. The use of violence to effect change can be a strong temptation in today's world. It is sustained by a passion for justice and a desire for a better situation through an almost catastrophic demolition of an existing order. At the same time, however, it contains within itself great potentials for destruction and the possibility of producing new injustices.[64] If involved in situations of violent revolution, Christians cannot forget the primary thrust of God's Mission in the world — the need to reconcile men with each other and with God. Forgiveness and reconciliation, therefore, are essential in any life style which engages in revolutionary activity to achieve justice and a more human society.

Finally, in a world situation which manifests great promise as well as great threat for the human race, it is not surprising that the virtue of hope is given such prominence in theological writing and reflection today. Hope is the virtue which maintains the tension between reality and promise, between the double aspects of God's kingdom as present and future.[65] It is based upon the firm belief that God's concern is not removed from the world but that his Mission is in history and he goes before men in their strivings toward the kingdom. Thus Christianity is understood as the community of those who on the basis of the resurrection of Christ wait in hope for the kingdom of God and whose life is determined by this expectation. Hope makes the Church a constant disturbance in human society, the source of continual new impulses towards the realization of righteousness, freedom, and humanity in the light of the promised future that is to come.[66] Hope is grounded in the tensions which exist in the present-day world and remains one of the primary virtues for the pilgrimaging people of God who participate in the *missio Dei* in our times.

---

[64] See Paul VI, *On the Development of Peoples,* Sections 30-31; Harvey Cox (ed.), *The Church Amid Revolution* (New York: Association Press, 1967), pp. 29-30.

[65] Rolland F. Smith, "A Theology of Rebellion," *Theology Today,* 25 (April, 1968), 20.

[66] Jürgen Moltmann, *Theology of Hope: On the Ground and Implications of a Christian Eschatology,* trans. James W. Leitch (New York: Harper and Row, 1967), pp. 22, 236.

IX

RETROSPECT AND SUMMARY: THE FOUNDATIONS OF MISSION SPIRITUALITY

The present-day crisis in missions has been caused by a number of complex historical, theological, and cultural factors. In approaching mission theology in this situation and in attempting to outline a spirituality for mission, the models of missionary work from the past must be viewed critically. Therefore, in this book a wide-angle approach has been employed in the description of the missionary. He was defined most fundamentally in terms of who he is rather than in terms of what he does, in terms of being rather than in terms of action. Since the Church is by nature for mission, the vocations of the missionary and the Christian are identical. All Christians have the privilege to respond to God's love and thereby to glorify God by offering themselves in gratitude, love, and joy to participate in the *missio Dei*. All Christian spirituality must, in one way or another, be for mission.[1]

Because God's plan and Mission are multidimensional, and because salvation is multifaceted, one who participates in God's Mission can exercise a variety of roles in the Church and in the world. Some are devoted full-time to the ministry of the Word and to preaching the gospel; others are tent-making missionaries, engaged in a non-ecclesiastical profession and dedicated to the ministry of Word and sacrament on a part-time basis; others, still, are totally given to God's worldly work of humanization, development, and liberation with little chance and perhaps no opportunity to name the Name and speak the Word.

Although it cannot easily be defined in terms of its role in the Church and the world, the missionary vocation can be distinguished from other vocations and charisms within the Christian community by its intention. The missionary is one whose interior life is oriented to non-believers, to those who do not profess

[1] For Paul VI's views on mission spirituality, see "Evangelization in the Modern World," Sections 74-80.

faith in Jesus Christ. It is this orientation which determines his life style and spirituality. Its intensity is the clearest way to distinguish missionary spirituality from other spiritualities within the Christian community. The missionary is one who intends to bring others to faith in Christ, one who intends to bring all men to explicit awareness of God's loving plan for men, and one who works to establish the goals of God's Mission of *shalom* so that men may both enjoy them and praise their source.

The intensity of this orientation will determine the need for the qualities of mission spirituality developed in the preceding chapters. The greater the intensity, the greater the need. It may be argued that in the present situation the terms *missions* and *missionary* be dropped from the universe of theological discourse. This does not seem necessary if it is remembered that these terms are to be understood in an analogous fashion when describing the role which Christians exercise. No longer can they be understood in a univocal fashion based upon sixteenth- or nineteenth-century models. The missionary, therefore, is not only one who evangelizes or establishes churches; rather, he can exercise many roles in the Church, always, however, with a basic orientation to non-believers, and with the intention of inviting others to come from non-belief to belief in Christ.

Christian spirituality is based upon a sevenfold scriptural foundation: faith and a change of heart, eschatology and an interpretation of the world and history, participation in the life of the Trinity, hope in the context of the paschal mystery of Christ, charity and service directed to God and man, prayer and the sacramental life, and some form of self-discipline and asceticism. However, these elements are historicized in the lives of men of different ages and places. They assume different forms and expressions according to different traditions, different theological insights, and different historical and cultural situations. A present-day spirituality for mission will be determined by the historical-cultural situation of today's world, by theology, especially the theology of the Church and mission, and by the tradition of mission spirituality in the Church.

The study made in Chapters III and IV of some key figures in the missionary tradition of the Western Church revealed that four constants have been present in missionary spirituality over the ages: (1) the love of God and love of Christ, an awareness of the need men have for Christ and the gospel, and a desire to share with others God's loving plan, and to invite all men to faith in Christ; (2) holiness of life; (3) profound trust and confidence in God's will and guidance, and the strength, boldness, and joy which follow from this; (4) loving, humble service. All these characteristics of missionary spirituality can be given a foundation in the present theological and cultural situation of the Church in mission.

The love of God and the desire to tell others of this love in order to lead them to give glory and praise to God is the heart of missionary spirituality and the driving force in the orientation of the missionary's interior life to the non-believer. It is the primary motive for mission. Since faith is something which is personally conveyed, holiness of life is the primary means for mission. From Columban and Boniface down through the centuries to J. Hudson Taylor and Charles de Foucauld, the witness of Christian living has been a constant and essential foundation of mission spirituality and the missionary life style and apostolate. The essence of holiness consists in a life in imitation of, and identification with, Christ. Holiness is a Christ-informed life, St. Paul's "no longer I who live, but Christ who lives in me" (Gal. 2:20). Hence, one who participates in the Mission of God must put on the mind of Christ through contact with Christ in the Scriptures, in the community, in the sacraments, in prayer, and in the world and one's neighbor.

The forms which Christian holiness take today will correlate with the needs and situation of the present-day world. In a secular age which sees men as responsible for the destiny of the world, it will be world-affirming rather than world-denying, although it will always stand in judgement upon the sinful tendencies and structures of the world. It will wear a human face, be attuned to the rhythms of the modern world, and be concerned with the humanization and liberation of mankind. In imitation of Christ (see Phil. 2:5-7), holiness will be reached through a life of service and pro-existence: service of God and his presence and grace in the gospel, service of, and openness to, God's grace and presence in the religious traditions of mankind, and service of the world in response to the needs of humanity and the rising expectations of men in the global village. Finally, it will be a form of holiness less given to withdrawn contemplation, although there will always be a place and need for this charism, and more to following the insight of Dag Hammarskjold: "In our era, the road to holiness necessarily passes through the world of action."[2]

All Christian spirituality is trinitarian. The theology of the *missio Dei* is at the heart of mission theology and spirituality. Mission spirituality is directly formed by the awareness it has of the Mission of the Trinity and the privilege which Christians have of participating in that Mission. Mission, therefore, is not a human project or a Church-centered enterprise but a God-directed activity. God's Mission is concerned with all men and, in a mysterious fashion, it is operative among all men. Christians, however, have the privilege of participating in the visible, historical community of the Church whose role is to explicitate God's plan. Because their role is one of participation in a work which is of God, Christians engaged in mission go out with trust and confidence, and with boldness, strength, and joy. Their orientation to non-believers is based upon the gratitude and joy they have of participating with their lives of witness in God's plan and Mission for all men.

Chapters V, VI, and VII outlined a present-day theology of mission which must inform mission spirituality. Through a number of images, the mystery of the Church was elaborated in open rather than in closed terms. Based upon the ecclesiology of Vatican II, this approach viewed the Catholic Church as linked and related to the presence of God's Mission and his goodness and truth in all Christian churches, in the other religious traditions of mankind, and in the aspirations and strivings of all men of good will. Mission spirituality in this context will possess a strong ecumenical thrust, and be marked by humble openness to the presence of God's goodness, truth, grace, and revelation beyond the visible boundaries of the Church. Part of its role of pro-existence will be service to God's presence wherever it is found.

The Church was presented more in terms of community than in terms of institution. In view of the diaspora situation in which the Church exists in the world today, in view of the necessary pluralism of values, ideas, and institutions in the present-day world, and in view of the heightened respect for human freedom, missionary spirituality will have to be strongly communitarian and

---

[2] Dag Hammarskjöld, *Markings,* trans. Leif Sjöberg and W.H. Auden (New York: Alfred A. Knopf, 1964), p. 122.

personal. The community of faith will be that which sustains Christians in the diaspora. Those engaged in mission will live as Abrahamic minorities,[3] small communities of witness to God's plan and Mission for all men, groups who remain open to transcendence and God's full plan of salvation for all men, communities of mutual support which avoid secularism and loss of belief in the transcendent dimensions of God's total Mission.

When the Church is viewed as the community of God's pilgrim people, the ancient, Celtic theme of mission as pilgrimage is given new force for missionary spirituality. In view of the demise of Christendom and the six-continent theory of mission, there are no longer clear geographical boundaries delimiting the Church's mission territories. Every country of the globe is missionary territory, and in every country Christians are confronted with non-belief and the necessity of witnessing to God's Mission and inviting others to faith. In a world which has come of age, but which nonetheless has staggering problems and needs amid a situation of accelerating change and development, the missionary's pilgrimage may not involve travel to far-off places. It will, however, be a pilgrimage of the Spirit and for the Spirit, a pilgrimage of going out to non-belief and non-believers wherever they are found. Finally, this pilgrimage will be to the world and not from the world, a going out in partnership with the God of Mission whose concern is for the world and for the humanization and liberation of men.

Since participation in the Mission of God determines the nature of the Church and since the Church can be described as a function of God's Mission, the most fertile images which can be used to describe the mystery of the Church are sacramental images. The Church is the sign, sacrament, and instrument of God's work of reconciling and unifying men with himself and with each other. In a world which is more than ever aware of global interdependence, the mission of unification and reconciliation will be essential to the missionary life style. The missionary is a bridge person, bridging the differences among men, and bridging the differences between men and God.

Essential to the sacramental character of the Church is the fact that it must be an efficacious instrument for these purposes,

---

[3] Dom Helder Camara, *Spiral of Violence,* trans. Della Couling (Denville, N.J.: Dimension Books, 1971), pp. 69-71.

an efficacious sign pointing to, working for, and partially realizing, the *shalom* of God's kingdom — peace, justice, love, and reconciliation. Discernment towards fidelity to this mission is an important aspect of the ongoing *metanoia* required for missionary spirituality. In working for the goals of God's total Mission of salvation, the missionary can avail himself of the functional, pragmatic approach characteristic of the modern world, employing those forms, patterns, structures, and methods which make the Church an effective sign of *shalom* among men; rejecting those means which do not work towards this end.

Finally, the theology of the local Church has an important effect upon the missionary life style. The Church universal can be viewed as a catholic communion of local churches, each with its own legitimate customs, theological expressions, and institutions. Mission-sending is primarily a project from local Church to local Church. The missionary is one who forms a bridge between local churches within the Church universal, one who is invited by the local Church, if one exists in the territory to which he comes, and one who is at the service of the local Church which invites him.

The local Church, too, is the place of discernment concerning which aspects of God's total Mission must be emphasized in a particular time and place, always, of course, in dialogue with other local churches within the catholic communion of churches. The final object of mission is the glorification of God by participation in his loving Mission for all men and the world. Specific aims of missionary work as they have appeared in the tradition of the Church — evangelization and conversion, the planting of the Church, Christian presence among non-believers, and works for humanization, liberation, and development — can all be valid goals for mission depending upon the local situation.

In general, Christians cannot but name the Name of Jesus and, by preaching the gospel of the kingdom, invite others to confess Christ and enter the community of God's pilgrim people. However, concrete needs and situations may demand that emphasis be given to one or another aspect of God's Mission at a particular time and place. The situation is variable. Therefore, the life style of the Christian missionary in the local situation may have a variety of expressions. The only caution necessary for one engaged in God's worldly work of liberation and humanization is that the total plan of God be not forgotten and that work towards these goals be inspired by that total, integral humanism which sees men as incomplete without reference to God. No matter what his role, the missionary's intention and orientation is always to the non-belief of other men, and his desire is to invite others to confess Christ as the Lord of history.

A more positive approach to the religious traditions of mankind and a more positive estimation of the possibility of salvation for men and women who do not accept Christ has been the reason for confusion and lack of purpose in some missionary circles in recent years. One of the long-standing assumptions of missionary motivation, that there is no salvation without explicit faith in Christ and membership in the Church, has been neutralized. Working in this context, Christians must remember that salvation is a multifaceted gift and reality with material and spiritual dimensions and with present and future implications. The Mission of God and the mission of the Church are concerned with all these dimensions.

Concerning the future or eternal dimensions of salvation, it must be acknowledged that this is available to all men because of the mysterious presence of God's revelation and the grace of Christ in many different ways in the world. The Christian, therefore, goes forth to non-believers with peace, hope, and confidence that God's presence and grace have gone before him. He goes forth with the gospel as the explicit plan of God for all men and with the gracious invitation that men accept Christ as the source of all goodness and truth.

Essential to mission spirituality in this situation will be the humble openness and dialogue necessary to enter into the goodness and truth of other traditions and beliefs, to be of service to God's grace and presence there, and to correlate this with the explicitness of God's plan as it is presented in the gospel and preserved in the community of the Church. In this regard, accommodation and indigenization will take the radical form of "double conversion." The Christian enters into the religious experiences and traditions of other men and, in turn, invites other men to participate in the religious experiences of the Christian tradition.

During the early centuries of the Church when Christians were a minority in a hostile and indifferent world, the faith spread in a spontaneous fashion by means of informal missionaries. The ordinary Christian was the principal agent of missionary outreach. At the present time, when the Church exists in diaspora in the midst of an indifferent, if not hostile, world, the world of post-Christendom and secularization, the situation for missionary outreach has become similar to that of the early Church. This historical-cultural situation gives further grounds for the identification of the missionary vocation and the vocations of all Christians. The laity will have a predominant role to play in spreading faith in Christ and witnessing to the kingdom. In the context of social differentiation which is part of the process of secularization, Christians engaged in service-oriented tasks once dominated by the churches have to face the prospects of working for these goals in structures disconnected from the churches.

The situations of injustice and want suffered by a large part of the human family offer a challenge for Christians to devote themselves to the material and temporal values of salvation, and to work for humanization, development, and liberation. In this situation amid the rising aspirations of men to enjoy the results of modern science and technology, liberation might be suggested as an apt present-day term to express the meaning of redemption. God's Mission of redemption is concerned with liberating men from sinful situations of deprivation, hunger, oppression, and violence, for freedom to participate in the goods possible from modern technology and culture, and for freedom to be open to the fuller dimensions of transcendent humanism which sees man fulfilled only by his relationship and orientation to God. In no matter what role it is exercised, the missionary's life style must be open to God's complete plan and Mission in order that the Christian and those for whom he works may not be co-opted by secularism and a totally this-worldly approach to the meaning of life.

In conclusion, it can be reaffirmed that there is but one motive for the missionary endeavor of the Church. It is the theocentric motive of the glory of God. Towards God's glory, the missionary lives a life of profound faith in God's plan and Mission for each man and for the world. He goes out in love and with hope, bearing the privilege of witnessing to, speaking of, and rendering partially present, the plan of God to unify all men in his kingdom. Christians dedicated to the Mission of God in the present world cannot be certain whether our times mark a period of advance or a period of recession in the ebb and flow of the expansion of Christianity. Concern for this, however, is no cause for discouragement. It does not seem by chance that there has been a renewal of interest in Christian hope in recent years. Hope and confidence remain foundational to mission spirituality. Mission in the last decades of the present century and in the twenty-first century can be faced with confidence and boldness because it is the Mission of God. In the words of Adoniram Judson, the great Baptist missionary of Burma, "The future is as bright as the promises of God."

SELECTED BIBLIOGRAPHY

Allen, Roland. *Missionary Methods, St. Paul's or Ours?* 1912. London: Lutterworth, 1968.

Anderson, Gerald H. (ed. and intro.). *The Theology of the Christian Mission.* Nashville: Abingdon, 1961.

Berg, Johannes van den. *Constrained by Jesus' Love: An Inquiry into the Motives of the Missionary Awakening in Great Britain in the Period between 1698 and 1815.* Kampen: J. H. Kok, 1956.

Berger, Peter L. *The Sacred Canopy: Elements of a Sociological Theory of Religion.* Garden City, N.Y.: Anchor Books, 1969.

Beyerhaus, Peter. *Missions: Which Way? — Humanization or Redemption,* trans. Margaret Clarkson. Grand Rapids, Mich.: Zondervan Publishing House, 1971.

Blauw, Johannes. *The Missionary Nature of the Church: A Survey of the Biblical Theology of Mission.* New York: McGraw-Hill, 1962.

Boberg, John T., S.V.D. and James A. Scherer (eds.). *Mission in the '70s — What Direction?* Chicago, Ill.: Chicago Cluster of Theological Schools, 1972.

Bouyer, Louis *et al. A History of Christian Spirituality.* Vol. I, Louis Bouyer, *The Spirituality of the New Testament and the Fathers,* trans. Mary Perkins Ryan. Vol. II, Jean Leclercq, Francois Vandenbroucke, and Louis Bouyer, *The Spirituality of the Middle Ages,* trans. The Benedictines of Holme Eden Abbey. Vol. III, Louis Bouyer, *Orthodox Spirituality and Protestant and Anglican Spirituality,* trans. Barbara Wall. New York: Desclee, 1963, 1968, 1969.

Camara, Dom Helder. *Spiral of Violence,* trans. Della Couling. Denville, N.J.: Dimension Books, 1971.

Carey, William. *An Enquiry into the Obligations of Christians to Use Means for the Conversion of the Heathens.* New facsimile edition with an introduction by Ernest A. Payne. London: Carey Kingsgate, 1961.

Congar, Yves. *The Wide World My Parish: Salvation and Its Problems,* trans. Donald Attwater. Baltimore: Helicon, 1961.

Cox, Harvey (ed.). *The Secular City: Secularization and Urbanization in Theological Perspective.* New York: Macmillan, 1965.

Danker, William J., and Wi Jo Kang (eds.). *The Future of the Christian World Mission: Studies in Honor of R. Pierce Beaver.* Grand Rapids, Mich.: Eerdmans, 1971.

Davies, J. G. *Worship and Mission.* New York: Association Press, 1967.

Davis, Charles. *Christ and the World Religions.* London: Hodder and Stoughton, 1970.

Delacroix, S. (ed.). *Histoire universelle des missions catholiques.* 4 vols. Paris: Librairie Grund, 1956-59.

Douglass, James W. *The Non-Violent Cross: A Theology of Revolution and Peace.* New York: Macmillan, 1968.

Dulles, Avery, S.J. "Current Trends in Mission Theology," *Studies in the International Apostolate of Jesuits,* 1 (January, 1972), 21-37.

Emerton, Ephraim (trans. and intro.). *The Letters of Saint Boniface.* New York: Columbia University, 1940.

Eminyan, Maurice, S.J. *The Theology of Salvation.* Boston: St. Paul Editions, 1960.

Fey, Harold E. *The Ecumenical Advance, A History of the Ecumenical Movement, Vol. II; 1948-68.* Philadelphia: Westminster, 1970.

Gannon, Thomas M., S.J. and George W. Traub, S.J. *The Desert and the City: An Interpretation of the History of Christian Spirituality.* London: Macmillan, 1968.

Gheddo, Piero. *Why is the Third World Poor?* trans. Kathryn Sullivan. Maryknoll: Orbis Books, 1973.

Gorrée, George. *Memories of Charles de Foucauld Explorer and Hermit Seen in His Letters,* trans. Donald Attwater. London: Burns, Oates & Washbourne, 1938.

Green, Michael. *Evangelism in the Early Church.* Grand Rapids, Mich.: Eerdmans, 1970.

Griffiths, Bede. *Christ in India: Essays Towards a Hindu-Christian Dialogue.* New York: Charles Scribner's Sons, 1966.

Gutierrez Merino, Gustavo. *A Theology of Liberation: History, Politics, and Salvation,* trans. and eds. Caridad Inda and John Eagleson. Maryknoll, N.Y.: Orbis Books, 1973.

Hahn, Ferdinand. *Mission in the New Testament,* trans. Frank Clarke. Studies in Biblical Theology, No. 47. Naperville, Ill.: Alec R. Allenson, 1965.

Harnack, Adolf von. *The Expansion of Christianity in the First Three Centuries,* trans. James Moffatt. Theological Translation Library, Vols. 19-20. New York: G.P. Putnam's Sons, 1905.

Heilbroner, Robert L. *The Great Ascent: The Struggle for Economic Development in Our Time.* New York: Harper & Row, 1963.

Hillman, Eugene, C.S.Sp. *The Church as Mission.* New York: Herder and Herder, 1965.

———. *The Wider Ecumenism: Anonymous Christianity and the Church.* London: Burns and Oates, Compass Books, 1968.

Hocking, William Ernest. *Living Religions and a World Faith.* New York: Macmillan, 1940.

Hogg, William Richey. *Ecumenical Foundations: A History of the International Missionary Council And Its Nineteenth-Century Background.* New York: Harper & Brothers, 1952.

Jeremias, Joachim. *Jesus' Promise to the Nations,* trans. S. H. Hooke. Studies in Biblical Theology, No. 24. Naperville, Ill.: Alec R. Allenson, 1958.

Jonas. *The Life of St. Columban,* ed. Dana Carlton Munro. *Translations and Reprints from the Original Sources of European History,* Vol. II, No. 7. Philadelphia: University of Pennsylvania, (c. 1902).

Kelly, Bernard J. *Missionary Spirituality.* Dublin: M. H. Gill and Son, 1960.

Kraemer, Hendrik. *The Christian Message in a Non-Christian World.* 3rd ed. Grand Rapids, Mich.: Kregel Publications, 1956.

———. *World Cultures and World Religions: The Coming Dialogue.* Philadelphia: Westminster, 1960.

Land, Philip (ed.). *Theology Meets Progress: Human Implications of Development.* Studia Socialia 10. Rome: Gregorian University, 1971.

Latourette, Kenneth Scott. *A History of the Expansion of Christianity.* 7 vols. New York: Harper & Brothers, 1937-45.

Laurentin, René. *Liberation, Development, and Salvation,* trans. Charles Underhill Quinn. Maryknoll, N.Y.: Orbis Books, 1972.

Leeuwen, Arend Theodoor van. *Christianity in World History: The Meeting of the Faiths of East and West,* trans. H. H. Hoskins. New York: Charles Scribner's Sons, 1964.

Lewis, A. J. *Zinzendorf the Ecumenical Pioneer: A Study in the Moravian Contribution to Christian Mission and Unity.* Philadelphia: Westminster, 1962.

Lubac, Henri de, S.J. *Catholicism: A Study of Dogma in Relation to the Corporate Destiny of Mankind,* trans. Lancelot C. Sheppard. New York: Longmans, Green and Co., 1950.

Luckmann, Thomas. *The Invisible Religion: The Problem of Religion in Modern Society*. New York: Macmillan, 1967.

McDonagh, Enda *et al. The Church is Mission*. London: Geoffrey Chapman, 1969.

McGavran, Donald Anderson. *Understanding Church Growth*. Grand Rapids, Mich.: Eerdmans, 1970.

Mannheim, Karl. *Ideology and Utopia: An Introduction to the Sociology of Knowledge*, trans. Louis Wirth and Edward Shils. 1929. New York: Harcourt, Brace & World, Harvest Book, n.d.

Marshman, John Clark. *The Life and Times of Carey, Marshman, and Ward: Embracing the History of the Serampore Mission*. 2 vols. London: Longman, Brown, Green, Longmans, & Roberts, 1859.

Moltmann, Jürgen. *Theology of Hope: On the Ground and the Implications of a Christian Eschatology*, trans. James W. Leitch. New York: Harper and Row, 1967.

Neill, Stephen. *Call to Mission*. Philadelphia: Fortress, 1970.

———. *Christian Faith and Other Faiths: The Christian Dialogue with Other Religions*. 2d ed. London: Oxford University, 1970.

———. *A History of Christian Missions*. The Pelican History of the Church, Vol. VI. Baltimore: Penguin Books, 1966.

Neuner, Joseph, S.J. (ed. and intro.). *Christian Revelation and the World Religions*. London: Burns and Oates, Compass Books, 1967.

Newbigin, J. E. Lesslie. *A Faith for This One World*. New York: Harper & Brothers, 1961.

Panikkar, R. *The Unknown Christ of Hinduism*. London: Darton, Longman & Todd, 1964.

Pathrapankal, Joseph, C.M.I. (ed.). *Service and Salvation*. Report on the Nagpur Theological Conference on Mission Theology and Dialogue, October, 1971. Bangalore: Theological Publications in India, 1973.

Peers, E. Allison. *Ramon Lull*. London: Society for Promoting Christian Knowledge, 1929.

Pourrat, Pierre. *Christian Spirituality*, trans. W. H. Mitchell, S. P. Jacques, and Donald Attwater. 4 vols. Westminster, Md.: Newman, 1953-55.

Power, John, S.M.A. *Mission Theology Today*. Maryknoll, N.Y.: Orbis Books, 1971.

Raguin, Yves. "Y a-t-il une spiritualité missionnaire?" *Spiritus*, 11 (August-September, 1970), 243-53.

———. *I am Sending You: Spirituality of the Missioner*, trans. Sr. Kathleen England, O. S. U. Manila: East Asian Pastoral Institute, 1973.

Rahner, Karl (ed.). *Re-Thinking the Church's Mission*. Concilium 13. New York: Paulist, 1966.

———. *The Christian of the Future*, trans. W.J. O'Hara. Quaestiones Disputatae 18. New York: Herder and Herder, 1967.

Ramsey, Michael, and Leon-Joseph Cardinal Suenens. *The Future of the Christian Church*. New York: Morehouse-Barlow, 1970.

Rayan, Samuel, S.J. "Mission After Vatican II: Problems and Positions," *International Review of Mission*, 59 (October, 1970), 414-26.

Richardson, William J., M.M. (ed.). *The Church as Sign*. Maryknoll, N.Y.: Maryknoll Publications, 1968.

Röper, Anita, *The Anonymous Christian*, trans. Joseph Donceel, S.J. New York: Sheed and Ward, 1966.

Schillebeeckx, Edward, O.P. *Christ the Sacrament of the Encounter with God*. New York: Sheed and Ward, 1963.

———. *God the Future of Man*, trans. N. D. Smith, New York: Sheed and Ward, 1968.

Schlette, Heinz Robert. *Toward a Theology of Religions*, trans. W. J. O'Hara. Quaestiones Disputatae 14. New York: Herder and Herder, 1966.

Schnackenburg, Rudolf. *God's Rule and Kingdom,* trans. John Murray. New York: Herder and Herder, 1963.

Schurhammer, George, S.J. and Joseph Wicki, S.J. (eds.). *Epistolae S. Francisci Xaverii aliaque eius scripta.* Monumenta Historica Societatis Jesu, Vols. 67-68. Rome: Monumenta Historica Societatis Jesu, 1944-45.

SEDOS (ed.). *Foundations of Mission Theology,* trans. John Drury. Maryknoll, N.Y.: Orbis Books, 1972.

Segundo, Juan Luis, S.J. "Liberacion: fe e ideologia," *Mensaje,* 21 (May, 1972), 248-54.

Six, Jean-Francois (ed.). *Spiritual Autobiography of Charles de Foucauld,* trans. J. Holland Smith. New York: P. J. Kenedy & Sons, 1964.

Smith, Wilfred Cantwell. *The Meaning and End of Religion: A New Approach to the Religious Traditions of Mankind.* New York: New American Library, 1964.

Taylor, Dr. and Mrs. Howard. *Hudson Taylor and the China Inland Mission: The Growth of a Work of God.* London: Morgan & Scott, 1918.

———. *Hudson Taylor in Early Years: The Growth of a Soul.* London: Morgan & Scott, 1912.

Taylor, J. Hudson. *China's Spiritual Needs and Claims.* 6th ed. London: Morgan & Scott, 1884.

———. *A Retrospect.* Toronto: China Inland Mission, 1898.

Thils, Gustave. *Christian Holiness: A Précis of Ascetical Theology,* trans. John L. Farrand, S.J. Tielt, Belgium: Lannoo, 1961.

———. *A "Non-Religious" Christianity?* trans. John A. Otto, New York: Alba House, 1970.

Tillich, Paul. *Christianity and the Encounter of the World Religions.* Bampton Lectures, Columbia University, 1961. New York: Columbia University, 1963.

Underwood, Joel (ed.). *In Search of Mission: An Interconfessional and Intercultural Quest.* Proceedings and readings of the "Future of the Missionary Enterprise" Seminar/Workshop, Ventnor, N.J., May, 1974. IDOC Future of the Missionary Enterprise Dossier No. 9. Rome: IDOC, 1974.

Vicedom, George F. *The Mission of God: An Introduction to a Theology of Mission,* trans. Gilbert A. Thiele and Dennis Hilgendorf. St. Louis: Concordia Publishing House, 1965.

Walker, G. S. M. (ed.). *Sancti Columbani opera.* Scriptores Latini Hiberniae, Vol. II. Dublin: Dublin Institute for Advanced Studies, 1957.

Ward, Maisie. *France Pagan? The Mission of Abbé Godin.* New York: Sheed and Ward, 1949.

Whitson, Robert Edward. *The Coming Convergence of World Religions.* New York: Newman, 1971.

Young, Robert D. *Encounter with World Religions.* Philadelphia: Westminster, 1970.

INDEX OF AUTHORS

INDEX OF SUBJECTS